THE WORKS OF SHAKESPEARE

EDITED FOR THE SYNDICS OF THE
CAMBRIDGE UNIVERSITY PRESS
BY
JOHN DOVER WILSON

TROILUS AND CRESSIDA

EDITED BY
ALICE WALKER

TROILUS AND CRESSIDA

CAMBRIDGE

AT THE UNIVERSITY PRESS

1957

Published by the Syndics of the Cambridge University Press
Bentley House, 200 Euston Road, London, NW1 2DB
American Branch: 32 East 57th Street, New York, N.Y.10022

© Cambridge University Press 1957

ISBNS:
0 521 07560 2 hard covers
0 521 09503 4 paperback

First published 1957
Reprinted 1963
First paperback edition 1969
Reprinted 1972

First printed in Great Britain at the University Press, Cambridge
Reprinted in Great Britain by Hazell Watson & Viney Ltd,
Aylesbury, Bucks

CONTENTS

PREFATORY NOTE

As regards both text and commentary *Troilus and Cressida* sets an editor one of the most difficult tasks in the canon. Dr Alice Walker therefore earns my special gratitude by accepting full responsibility for everything in the present volume except the Stage History, which belongs as usual to Mr C. B. Young.

J.D.W.

My thanks are due to Professor Dover Wilson, who made arrangements for the frontispiece and other fac-similes, and to Mr C. B. Young for ready help with proof-reading. I owe a very special debt to Miss J. R. Bacon and Professor G. D. Willcock for the time they have so generously given to friendly discussion of this edition in all its stages and to reading all in typescript.

A.W.

INTRODUCTION

We first hear of what is probably Shakespeare's *Troilus and Cressida* in a Stationers' Register entry of 7 February 1603, when James Roberts was conditionally licensed to print a play of this title belonging to the Chamberlain's men.[1] We hear of what is certainly this play in a second entry of 28 January 1609, when 'a booke called the history of Troylus and Cressida' was licensed to Richard Bonian and Henry Walley[2] for, in accordance with this entry, a quarto appeared the same year, attributing the play to Shakespeare.[3] But before the quarto was published the original title-page was cancelled in order to withdraw the statement that the play had been acted 'by the Kings Maiesties seruants at the Globe'.[4] At the same time a preface was added, describing it as 'a new play, neuer stal'd with the Stage' and as the wittiest of Shakespeare's comedies. We are led to infer that it was published against the wishes of the players and the preface closes with a prayer 'for the states of their wits healths that will not praise it'.

This early eulogy seems to have been wide of the

[1] 'in full Court, to print when he hath gotten sufficient aucthority: the booke of Troilus and Cressida, as yt is acted by my Lord Chamberlens men' (Greg, *Bibliography of the English Printed Drama to the Restoration*, I (1939), item 279).

[2] 'lic. Segar deputy to G. Bucke: a booke called the history of Troylus and Cressida' (Greg, as above).

[3] See facsimile title-pages (frontispiece and p. lvii).

[4] On the two states of the preliminaries (formerly taken as two issues of the quarto) see Philip Williams, 'The "Second Issue" of Shakespeare's *Troilus and Cressida*, 1609' (in *Studies in Bibliography*, University of Virginia, II (1949), pp. 25–33).

mark in the estimate of most later critics, who have
found the play less a birth of Shakespeare's brain than
an abortion—lacking in dramatic effectiveness, in unity
of style and purpose, and in respect for what Homer
and Chaucer had treated with such generosity of spirit.
Hence it has been doubted whether the play was wholly
Shakespeare's: some would exclude the Prologue,
others the Epilogue, and others most of Act 5. Many
have thought that it was begun about the time of *The
Merchant of Venice* and completed *c.* 1602 or even later
(*c.* 1606–8). It has been interpreted as a contribution
to the War of the Theatres (directed against Ben
Jonson), as a political allegory (a mirror for the Earl of
Essex), and as the bitter expression of some personal
experience.[1] There is even no agreement on the kind
of play intended, for the quarto praised it as a comedy
and Jaggard classified it as a tragedy; in 1938 O. J.
Campbell[2] labelled it a 'comical satire', but in 1940
E. K. Chambers[3] preferred to call it 'a tragedy of
disillusionment'.

I. *Comedy or Tragedy?*

This is the first question to be asked, and it seems to
me that to see Troilus as a tragic figure is to ignore the
many precautions Shakespeare took to preclude a

[1] What the diversity of opinion has been, and still is, can
be seen from the New Variorum edition, edited by Hillebrand and Baldwin (1953). Since this gives so recent a
survey, it has seemed to me unnecessary to give more than
my own interpretation of Shakespeare's aims and I have
simply developed some of the views expressed in my review
of the New Variorum edition (in *Review of English Studies*,
N.S. v (1954), pp. 288–91).

[2] *Comicall Satyre and Shakespeare's 'Troilus and Cressida'*
(1938).

[3] 'Shakespeare: An Epilogue' (in *Review of English
Studies*, XVI (1940), p. 400).

sentimental interest in the love story. Troilus' infatuation is never allowed to engage our sympathies. There
is anticlimax in his first entry, for the heroic temper of
the 'Prologue armed' is at once abated by the fretful
Troilus, preparing to unarm and apathetic about the
quarrel:

> Call here my varlet; I'll unarm again:
> Why should I war without the walls of Troy
> That find such cruel battle here within?
> Each Trojan that is master of his heart,
> Let him to field; Troilus, alas, hath none!
>   *Pandarus.* Will this gear ne'er be mended?

Throughout the first scene, the juxtaposition of cliché-
packed verse and colloquial prose prepares the audience
for Pandarus' role as a comic bias in the love story, and
his fatuous and farcical ubiquity keeps it for most of its
course on the highroad of broad comedy:

> *Pandarus.* Have you seen my cousin?
> *Troilus.* No, Pandarus; I stalk about her door,
> Like a strange soul upon the Stygian banks
> Staying for waftage. O, be thou my Charon,
> And give me swift transportance to those fields
> Where I may wallow in the lily beds
> Proposed for the deserver! O gentle Pandar,
> From Cupid's shoulder pluck his painted wings,
> And fly with me to Cressid!
>
>   (3. 2. 7–15)

That such transports were intentionally ridiculous is
deftly conveyed by the simplicity of Pandarus' reply:

> Walk here i'th'orchard; I'll bring her straight.

Shakespeare's manipulation of Pandarus throughout
this scene—encouraging and expostulating, admiring
and instructing, and finally shepherding the lovers to
bed—keeps the comic design to the fore with an

adroitness which is all the more effective because
Pandarus is unconscious of his own buffoonery. To see
him as fooling with the deliberate aim of relieving the
tension[1] is to make him less an object of ridicule in
himself than he is.

In conformity with this comic intention, Cressida is
immediately shown as anything but the pearl or Daphne
of Troilus' fancy. Her trite avowal in the couplets
which conclude 1. 2 clinches what Shakespeare has
demonstrated throughout this scene—that Cressida is
cheap stuff not only in what she says but in the way she
says it.[2] Since there went but a pair of shears between
uncle and niece in so far as both speak colloquial prose,
Alexander, her servant, is used as a foil to Cressida's
uncouthness. His elaborate conceit of the husbandman
(1. 2. 7–11) and the copiousness of his character of
Ajax (1. 2. 19–30) contrast conspicuously with
Cressida's bald questions and blunt answers, and when
Alexander has served this dramatic purpose he dis-
appears from the Trojan scene. When Troilus later

---

[1] G. Wilson Knight (*The Wheel of Fire* (1930), pp. 65–7)
found Pandarus akin to the Fool in *Lear* and the symptoms
of venereal disease (5. 3. 104–5) pathetic. The old Vice is
a buffoon in his noisy, hurly-burly manners (Cressida
twice rebukes him in 1. 2 for speaking too loudly—ll. 185,
231), and it is not to be supposed that the legacy of diseases
he promised in the Epilogue was intended as a recommendation.

[2] Cressida is—as one would expect—something of a
chameleon, whose manners and speech take colour from
her environment, but it needs the stimulus of flirtation to
oil her tongue. She is noticeably unresponsive to Alexander's
wit and it is significant that, face to face with Cressida for
the first time (3. 2), Troilus for the first time speaks prose.
Alexander has to make the same concession in his reply to
Cressida's captious and inelegant 'So do all men, unless
they are drunk, sick, or have no legs' (1. 2. 17–18).

asks concerning Helen 'What's aught, but as 'tis valued?' (2. 2. 52), the audience already knows what the answer is in respect of Cressida. She has, in fact, said it:

Men prize the thing ungained more than it is.

(1. 2. 290)

It is in Hector's reply to Troilus' question that Shakespeare clarifies the dramatic significance of Troilus' infatuation, which, despite its mainly farcical course, springs from a deeper and more far-reaching comic purpose than mere burlesque. In this scene of giddy eloquence (2. 2), the Trojan ship of state proves a bauble boat, driven by every wind but that of reason. Hector is, indeed, more culpable than Troilus, for he abandons what he knows to be prudent and right to satisfy his own obsession—love of honour. The debate (if anything so volatile can be dignified by that name) is a family matter and provides scope for a free exchange of home truths between the Trojan brothers. In this respect, Shakespeare followed tradition.[1] What he adds of significance for the love story is Hector's warning to Troilus of the dangers of self-will and 'mad idolatry':

> *Troilus.* What's aught, but as 'tis valued?
> *Hector.* But value dwells not in particular will:
> It holds his estimate and dignity
> As well wherein 'tis precious of itself
> As in the prizer. 'Tis mad idolatry
> To make the service greater than the god;
> And the will dotes that is attributive
> To what infectiously itself affects,
> Without some image of th'affected merit.

(2. 2. 52–60)

[1] See note to 2. 2 for an account of the source material for this scene.

The outcome of Troilus' infatuation is thus fore-
shadowed not only in Cressida's character but in his
own lack of judgement, and however painful his disillusionment may be when he has to reassess Cressida's
imagined worth with what it proves to be (5. 2),
Shakespeare takes the precaution of deflecting the
audience's sympathies by the blunt comment of
Thersites—

> Will 'a swagger himself out on's own eyes?
>
> (5. 2. 136)

and by the astringent judgement of Ulysses, who is
shocked by his wild generalizations ('What hath she
done, prince, that can soil our mothers?', 5. 2. 134)
and by his hysterical blindness to reason:

> May worthy Troilus be but half attached
> With that which here his passion doth express?
>   *Troilus.* Ay, Greek; and that shall be divulgéd well
> In characters as red as Mars his heart
> Inflamed with Venus. Never did young man fancy
> With so eternal and so fixed a soul.
> Hark, Greek: as much as I do Cressid love,
> So much by weight hate I her Diomed.
> That sleeve is mine that he'll bear on his helm.
> Were it a casque composed by Vulcan's skill,
> My sword should bite it. Not the dreadful spout
> Which shipmen do the hurricano call,
> Constringed in mass by the almighty sun,
> Shall dizzy with more clamour Neptune's ear
> In his descent, than shall my prompted sword
> Falling on Diomed.   (5. 2. 161–176)

Though one may feel sorry for Troilus, revenge on
Diomedes (seeing red instead of seeing reason) will no
more restore his shattered illusion than threats of
vengeance on Achilles will later bring Hector back to
life.

Through the means of shrewder commentators than the silly Pandarus, Shakespeare makes his satiric purpose clear in this scene, and it is the more pointed because what Ulysses says here expresses his own judgement. The eulogy of Troilus put into his mouth at 4. 5. 96 ff. simply records the opinion of Æneas, and the sum total of Troilus is no more here than the sum total of Hector is contained in Æneas' praise of his valour and modesty a little earlier (4. 5. 78–82).

It is a mistake to think that Shakespeare's anatomy of folly spares the Trojans. They wear the motley with better grace but they are as much the victims of ruling passions as the Greeks. When we first hear of Hector (1. 2. 4 ff.), the shame of having been worsted by Ajax has fouled his temper:

> He chid Andromache and struck his armourer;
> (1. 2. 6)

and when he leaves Troy to meet his death at the hands of Achilles (5. 3), he is deaf to every claim but that of 'honour'. There is unconscious irony in his warning to Troilus of the dangers of 'mad idolatry' and again in the condescension of his rebuke to Troilus and Paris a little later (2. 2. 163 ff.) for, after arguing in favour of the law of nature and of nations, which require the return of Helen, what he finally proposes is to keep her,

> For 'tis a cause that hath no mean dependence
> Upon our joint and several dignities.   (2. 2. 192–3)

Here again, Shakespeare gives an ironic twist to his source by inventing a *volte-face* which makes Hector as vulnerable to satire as the thoughtless Troilus. That most of the Greeks are satirically represented seems not to be in question.

If a comprehensive comic purpose is kept in mind, what have seemed to many critics inconsistencies in style and temper fall into focus. What superficially resembles the manner of the mid-nineties in the love story proves merely a caricature of devices which had become fair game for ridicule by the turn of the century. In 1. 1, which has often been regarded as early work, Troilus' constant recourse to classical allusion, hyperbole, apostrophe and aposiopesis, his trite similes and ingenuous metaphors, are as intentionally ridiculous as his call to Pandar to pluck Cupid's wings in 3. 2:

> Tell me, Apollo, for thy Daphne's love,
> What Cressid is, what Pandar, and what we?
> Her bed is India; there she lies, a pearl;
> Between our Ilium and where she resides
> Let it be called the wild and wandering flood;
> Ourself the merchant, and this sailing Pandar,
> Our doubtful hope, our convoy and our bark.
>
> (1. 1. 100–6)

This is affected and strained calculation, and it was meant to be, for it sterilizes the love story by substituting artifice for ardour. This is why it is both like and unlike the genuinely lyrical vein of the romantic comedies.

In the same way, if we keep a satiric purpose in mind, the closing scenes round off the design as a whole. Dryden was in error when he saw them as 'nothing but a confusion of drums and trumpets, excursions and alarms',[1] for the frenzied Troilus, the honour-seeking Hector, the mean Achilles and the foaming Ajax are not part of the old-fashioned chronicle play symbolism, in which a crooked figure might attest a million, but

[1] 'Preface to *Troilus and Cressida*', 1679 (*Essays of John Dryden*, ed. W. P. Ker, 1, p. 203).

individuals madly intent on personal ends—an ironic commentary on the chivalric manifesto of the Trojans in 2. 2—

> She is a theme of honour and renown   (l. 199)

—and the dignified proposition of the Prologue:

> Sixty and nine, that wore
> Their crownets regal, from th'Athenian bay
> Put forth toward Phrygia, and their vow is made
> To ransack Troy, within whose strong immures
> The ravished Helen, Menelaus' queen,
> With wanton Paris sleeps—and that's the quarrel.

In the closing scenes the quarrel is remembered only in so far as 'the cuckold and the cuckold-maker are at it', tarred on by the cynical Thersites, who recognizes the scene for the bear-garden it is:

Now, bull! now, dog! 'Loo, Paris, 'loo; now, my double-horned Spartan! 'loo, Paris, 'loo! The bull has the game. Ware horns, ho!   (5. 7. 10–12)

But this is the only reminder of Helen. Hector is afield 'i'th'vein of chivalry' (5. 3. 32):

> *Hector.* What art thou, Greek? Art thou for Hector's match?
> Art thou of blood and honour?
> *Thersites.* No, no; I am a rascal; a scurvy railing knave; a very filthy rogue.
> *Hector.* I do believe thee. Live.   (5. 4. 25–9)

Troilus and Diomedes are battling for the sleeve; Achilles is savagely bent on revenge for the death of Patroclus, 'weeping, cursing, vowing vengeance' (5. 5. 31); Ajax 'hath lost a friend, And foams at mouth...Roaring for Troilus' (5. 5. 35–7). The Greeks indeed draw together (5. 5. 44), though not

from policy or in the common interest but to settle
personal scores. Such folly could not end better than
it does, nor does Shakespeare ever lead us to suppose
that it would. To Ulysses 'the death-tokens' of
Achilles' plaguey pride cry 'no recovery' (2. 3. 175–6)
and there is nothing to suggest that there was more
hope for Troilus, who beats the air as wildly and as
vainly for Hector as for Cressida.

Campbell was, I think, right when he labelled the
play a 'comical satire', aiming, like Ben Jonson's *Every
Man Out of His Humour*, at the correction of manners
through the ridicule of folly. No major character
except Ulysses is distinguished for wisdom. Agamemnon
has dignity and magnanimity, but no judgement. He is
in error when he takes comfort from History and
attributes the Greek failure to the protractive trials of
great Jove (1. 3. 1–30); for, as Ulysses argues, it is not
the will of the gods but the self-will of man that
thwarts their undertaking—the mischief comes from
within and not from without. Nestor's courtesy is
unfailing, but his silver tongue is garrulous, tuned first
to Agamemnon's argument (1. 3. 31–54) and then to
Ulysses' (1. 3. 185–96). Achilles' better parts are
eaten up by his pride, and Ajax' vanity is only
occasionally alleviated by flashes of generosity. Thersites, though as critically alert as Ulysses, gets more
pleasure from vice and folly than wisdom. The Trojans,
though superficially more agreeable than most of the
Greeks, are just as unserviceable. Priam is ineffective
and Troilus is giddy-headed. Paris is kindly but a
carpet-knight, dancing attendance on Helen:

I would fain have armed today, but my Nell would not
have it so.
                                                    (3. 1. 137–8)

And the honey-tongued Helen cultivates her reputation
    ...rm as sedulously as Hector pursues honour:

'Twill make us proud to be his servant, Paris;
Yea, what he shall receive of us in duty
Gives us more palm in beauty than we have,
Yea, overshines ourself.   (3. 1. 156–9)

It is perhaps not an accident that Antenor, 'one o'th'
soundest judgements in Troy whosoever' (1. 2. 191–2),
appears in three scenes but is always mute.

The soundest judgement of the Greeks has, by
contrast, a great deal to say that is not only memorable
but very much to the purpose of 'comical satire'.
Into Ulysses' role as commentator, Shakespeare freely
poured more ample propositions than the mere purge
of individual humours could have accommodated—
thereby avoiding as well the rigours of Jonsonian
plotting. The play ends with seeming casualness by the
simple expedient of giving the antic Pandarus the last
word and leaving the correction of folly to the audience's
own good sense.

II. *Troilus*

In stressing the precautions Shakespeare took to
preclude a sentimental interest in the love story, I am
not suggesting that Troilus is insincere (for his proverbial 'truth' is not in question) or without attractive
qualities. Face to face with the paltering Cressida, he
grows in stature because he is as simple as he professes,
and the dignity with which he accepts the news that
she must be returned to her father is enhanced by the
dramatic irony of her clamorous protests. But even in
the lines of moving sincerity with which he accepts
their parting (4. 4. 33–48), the imagination is carried
away from Troilus by the vivid personifications of
Misfortune, roughly jostling the lovers out of the
picture, and Time the Robber, hastily fumbling up 'as
many farewells as be stars in heaven' into 'a loose adieu'.
Nor even here is Pandarus any more ceremonious in his

rich thievery, for he rushes from the scene with a call
for tears to lay his sighs before his heart is blown up by
the roots. When Lafeu boasted that he was 'Cressid's
uncle, That dare leave two together' (*All's Well*,
2. 1. 97–8), he did what Pandarus was never allowed
to do for long in this play—and never without anticlimax.

We should therefore allow for a far greater variety
of comic emphasis than Campbell did. Troilus' trepida-
tions while awaiting his first meeting with Cressida
(3. 2), from which Campbell drew a picture of 'the
educated sensuality of an Italianate English roué'
(p. 212), seem to me simply amusing hyperbole—
a reminder, like Pandarus' excited interruptions, that
the scales are weighted against sentimentality. The
scene closes in the same merry vein with Pandarus
impatiently clapping up their vows with 'Go to, a
bargain made' and hustling them away. Thersites'
verdict on Troilus is in this connexion important. To
Thersites, Troilus is a 'doting foolish young knave'
and a 'young Trojan ass' (5. 4. 3–5). The latter seems
to me to put Troilus in a nutshell, and it would be
strangely lenient from Thersites if it did not contain
the kernel of the truth. To Thersites, there is a difference between Troilus on the one hand and the
'whore-masterly' Diomedes (the son of the game)
with the 'luxurious drab' Cressida (the daughter of the
game) on the other. The head of the Trojan ass is
meant, I think, to be of more serious concern than his
heart, and for this reason the Trojan council (2. 2) is
more important for the understanding of Troilus than
the love scenes.

I have already mentioned two of the significant
changes Shakespeare made in dramatizing this scene
(Hector's warning to Troilus about 'mad idolatry' and
the *volte-face* which makes Hector too a legitimate

object for satire). Another significant departure from tradition occurs at the beginning of 2. 2 when Troilus darts in, after Hector's first pause, with the fantastic notion that so great a king as Priam is not to be controlled 'With spans and inches so diminutive As fears and reasons' (2. 2. 31–2). This provokes Helenus to the spiteful retort that Troilus snaps at reasons because he is 'so empty of them', and how right Helenus is appears throughout the scene as Troilus slithers from one untenable position to another. In 1. 1. 91–5, Helen was not worth fighting for:

> Peace, you ungracious clamours! peace, rude sounds!
> Fools on both sides! Helen must needs be fair
> When with your blood you daily paint her thus.
> I cannot fight upon this argument;
> It is too starved a subject for my sword.

In 2. 2. 81–3,

>   she is a pearl
> Whose price hath launched above a thousand ships
> And turned crowned kings to merchants.

But as soon as Hector has cast his vote for keeping Helen because their 'joint and several dignities' require it, her value slumps again:

> Why, there you touched the life of our design:
> Were it not glory that we more affected
> Than the performance of our heaving spleens,
> I would not wish a drop of Trojan blood
> Spent more in her defence. But, worthy Hector,
> She is a theme of honour and renown,
> A spur to valiant and magnanimous deeds,
> .   .   .   .
> For I presume brave Hector would not lose
> So rich advantage of a promised glory
> As smiles upon the forehead of this action
> For the wide world's revenue.   (2. 2. 194–206)

Helen is of no account in herself, but merely a carrot to be dangled before the nose of the honour-loving Hector. There is no intentional guile in this, but there is a great lack of responsible argument and much confused thinking.

III. *Shakespeare and the Troy story*

Whether the love story had ever exercised an attraction for Shakespeare seems very doubtful. Before the end of the sixteenth century, Cressida was not merely proverbial for her faithlessness but the wretched warning into which Henryson's *Testament of Cresseid* had transformed her[1]—a slut to be mentioned in the same breath as Doll Tearsheet (*Henry V*, 2. 1. 74–7). Pandar was a common noun (=a bawd) and an epithet of abuse for any disreputable go-between; and Pandarus' fall carried Troilus with it. It needed moonlight to work the spell of Troilus on the Trojan walls, sighing for Cressida (*Merchant of Venice*, 5. 1. 1–6). Elsewhere his fidelity is recalled in the name of Petruchio's spaniel (*The Shrew*, 4. 1. 140); but, so long as Pandarus was remembered, Troilus was no more likely to lose his dubious distinction as 'the first employer of pandars' (*Much Ado*, 5. 2. 31) than Leander his association with the Hellespont. All this Shakespeare turns to rich ironic advantage whenever Cressida[2] and Pandarus put their reputations to the hazard of 'that old common arbitrator, Time', and there is nothing to suggest that he had any quarrel with Time's verdict; for what had

[1] According to Henryson's *Testament*, printed first in Thynne's 1532 Chaucer and regarded in Shakespeare's day as Chaucer's, Cressida was cast off by Diomedes, became a prostitute, and died miserably as a leper in the spital, repentant of her wantonness and a warning to women.

[2] This is why the most memorable lines of 3. 2 (ll. 183 ff). come (at first sight so unexpectedly) from Cressida.

always fired his imagination was Troy, not Troilus—
Vergil's account of the terror of its destruction rather
than Chaucer's tragi-comedians. In *Lucrece*, 1366 ff.,
2 *Henry IV*, 1. 1. 70 ff., and the Player's speech in
Hamlet, as well as in many passing allusions, Vergil's
picture of the fall of Troy was for Shakespeare the
symbol of tragic loss and horror. Troilus' associations
were with comedy, but Troy's with tragedy, and
Vergil may have supplied the hint for Trojan wrong-
headedness which Shakespeare developed in his play.
It occurs in *Aeneid*, II. 40–56, when Laocoon, having
accused his fellow Trojans of madness for thinking that
the Greeks would so lightly have abandoned the siege
('quae tanta insania, cives?'), flung his spear at the
wooden horse, confident that it meant treachery:

> et si fata deum, *si mens non laeva fuisset,*
> impulerat ferro Argolicas foedare latebras,
> *Troiaque nunc staret,* Priamique arx alta maneres.

Had Shakespeare carried his story further, Laocoon
could have stepped into his picture of Trojan folly
straight from Vergil, even sharing with Hector and
Troilus the misfortune of seeing the madness of others
rather than his own.

IV. *The Audience*

If Shakespeare had ever contemplated a tragedy on
the siege of Troy, the signs are that his attention would
have been focused on its fall, and on Priam and Hecuba,
instead of on the medieval love story, which had become
by his day a thoroughly disreputable business and a
theme for scald rhymers.[1] To the instructed, Troilus'
associations with the archetype of all pandars must have

[1] Cf. p. xliv, n. 3. It is tempting to speculate that the
source of the unidentified verses quoted by Pandarus, 4. 4.
16–20, was one of these ballads.

seemed fair game for ribaldry—and on account of the play's scurrility and the quarto publishers' retraction of the statement that their play had been acted at the Globe, Peter Alexander[1] suggested that it was written for some festivity at one of the Inns of Court. In spite of the lack of supporting external evidence, the suggestion has been generally accepted as it accords with what is known of Inns of Court tastes. Further, the play requires neither inner stage nor balcony—the latter surprisingly if it was meant for the Globe, since the walls of Troy would seem an inevitable accessory in the Trojan scene, as they are indeed in two contemporary plays dealing with the same material—the Admiral's Company plot of a Troilus and Cressida play[2] and Heywood's *Iron Age*.[3]

What Inns of Court revels might amount to is shown by the one full record available—the Gray's Inn Revels of Christmas 1594.[4] With the consent of the Readers and Ancients, the Termers elected a Prince to govern their 'state' and they amused themselves for the twelve days of Christmas in the conduct of mock state business and entertainments appropriate to a court. The revels are (and were) remembered for the tumults and disorders which disgraced the night when *The Comedy of Errors*[5]

[1] See Peter Alexander, '*Troilus and Cressida*, 1609' (in *Library*, IX (1929), pp. 267–86).

[2] The plot, which is fragmentary, was printed by Greg, *Henslowe Papers* (1907), p. 142 and in *Dramatic Documents from the Elizabethan Playhouses* (1931). See also New Variorum, pp. 459–61.

[3] The New Variorum prints extracts, pp. 462–88.

[4] Printed as *Gesta Grayorum* in 1688 and edited by Greg (Malone Society Reprints, 1914). I cite from the latter.

[5] The play is described as 'a Comedy of Errors (like to *Plautus* his *Menechmus*)', p. 22, and is naturally identified with Shakespeare's.

was performed; but, apart from this one blot on their scutcheon, the Grayans managed their affairs so much to their pleasure that they would have resumed them after the vacation had not 'the Readers and Ancients of the House, by reason of the Term', removed the scaffolds from the Hall and forbidden them to be built up again.[1]

The 'state' of Gray's Inn in 1594 seems to have had attentive listeners with a keen appreciation of verbal ingenuity and good invention, and it needs no stretch of the imagination to see that a legal audience, trained in the debating of cases, would have found more interest and amusement than the general public in the mockery of the young Trojans in council over the return of Helen. The Gray's Inn revels of 1594 were perhaps more ambitious than the average, since they 'had been intermitted by the space of three or four Years, by reason of Sickness and Discontinuances',[2] and discontinuance for reasons other than the plague was ordered by the Benchers of Gray's Inn's close associate, the Inner Temple, in 1611 'For that great disorder and scurrility is brought into this House by lewd and lascivious plays'.[3] But whatever the level of the entertainment, the object of the traditional revels was amusement—a performance in which any tears shed were more likely to be those of laughter than of grief. A high-spirited audience of young men in the forefront of the revolt against sugared love poetry was not likely to waste an evening's fun in sighing over Troilus. On the other hand, a satire on Misrule (a new kind of comedy of errors) might be expected to appeal to the Ancients.

[1] p. 53.
[2] p. 1.
[3] Cited Greg, *The Shakespeare First Folio* (1955), p. 340 n. 8.

Pandarus makes an obvious bid for ticklish young ears in the legal allusions of 3. 2:

How now! a kiss in fee-farm!   (ll. 49–50)

Words pay no debts, give her deeds; but she'll bereave you o'th'deeds too, if she call your activity in question. What, billing again? Here's 'In witness whereof the parties inter-changeably'—   (ll. 54–7)

Go to, a bargain made. Seal it, seal it. I'll be the witness
                                                          (ll. 196–7)

and at the end of this scene he directly addresses all young Troiluses in the audience, hoping that they will be as fortunate in their pandars. This is why the rejected Pandarus speaks the Epilogue—a ludicrous appeal for the despised bawd, with promise of a testa-ment as undesirable as Cressida's on his return from the powdering-tub of infamy.

In dedicating *Every Man Out of His Humour* (1600) to the Inns of Court, Jonson addressed them as 'the noblest nurseries of humanity and liberty in the kingdom'. In the 1590's they had fostered the first formal satirists, and a mixture of satire and irony with farce and scurrility would presumably have catered for the tastes of both Benchers and Termers. But, what-ever the occasion for which *Troilus and Cressida* was written, it can never have appealed to anything but a limited audience, for burlesque and irony are sophisti-cated tastes—as Beaumont discovered from the failure of even so simple a piece as *The Knight of the Burning Pestle*.

V. *The Satire*

Though it is not surprising that *Troilus and Cressida* has never been popular in the theatre, it is curious that literary critics take no pleasure in it as a book. This is partly due, I suspect, to the mistake of approaching it through Homer and Chaucer. Such comparisons are totally irrelevant. If we accept as dramatically valid Shakespeare's Ulysses, maintaining the responsibility of the individual to 'the specialty of rule'—something no critic seems to have boggled at—then those who neglect this obligation lie open to censure. Hector's honour, consistent with the Homeric code, is personal indulgence, like Achilles' pride, in a society in which individualism was a menace. This was self-will or 'appetite' that could only end in barbarism, like Ajax' refusal to support the common cause when his self-importance made him as unserviceable as Achilles. In rejecting the anachronism of Hector's allusion to Aristotle and substituting 'whom graver sages think' for 'whom Aristotle thought' (2. 2. 166), Rowe struck at a mere twig, for Shakespeare's politically minded Ulysses is as unhomeric as his Achilles, and most unhomeric of all, of course, is that typically medieval accretion, the love story.

In *Troilus and Cressida* Shakespeare exercised, in fact, the same prerogative as medieval writers when they invented and elaborated a love story for Troilus—he interpreted the story of the Trojan war after his own fashion, though it was not entirely a new one. Horace's reflections on the matter were fundamentally much the same:[1]

> While you at Rome, dear Lollius, train your tongue,
> I at Praeneste read what Homer sung:

* * * * * * * * *

[1] *Epistles*, 1. 2. 1–2, 6–16. I quote Conington's translation. Erasmus endorses the opinion (*Adagia*, In Stupidos, 'aut regem aut fatuum nasci oportere'): 'Consentaneum est igitur, priscos illos reges, maxima ex parte insigni stultitia praeditos fuisse... Tota Ilias, quam est longa, nihil aliud quam quod eleganter scripsit Horatius: "Stultorum regum et populorum continet aestus".' The view was, of course, likely to have a special appeal at a time when the paradox was in fashion.

The tale that tells how Greece and Asia strove
In tedious battle all for Paris' love,
Talks of the passions that excite the brain
Of mad-cap kings and peoples not more sane.
Antenor moves to cut away the cause
Of all their sufferings: does he gain applause?
No; none shall force young Paris to enjoy
Life, power and riches in his own fair Troy.
Nestor takes pains the quarrel to compose
That makes Atrides and Achilles foes:
In vain; their passions are too strong to quell;
Both burn with wrath, and one with love as well.
Let kings go mad and blunder as they may,
The people in the end are sure to pay.
Strife, treachery, crime, lust, rage, 'tis error all,
One mass of faults within, without the wall.

The passions that excite hare-brained Trojans and beef-witted Greeks ('hot blood', 'distempered blood', 'too much blood and too little brain'—the disorders which afflict the besiegers and the besieged) are the mainspring of Shakespeare's satire to which the love story is sub-ordinated in spite of its importance for the plot. This is why the play does not end with the disillusionment of Troilus, for the more serious thinking belongs to the war theme. In revenge for the Greeks' refusal to free Hesione, the Trojans sent a marauding expedition to Greece to secure a hostage to exchange for her. The rape of Helen thus became the 'quarrel'. Was she worth the cost in lives? Had the Trojans sufficient reason for failing to return her to Menelaus?—or was the quarrel a ludicrous business, a bad cause persevered in from equally bad motives? When Andromache fruitlessly appealed to Hector to unarm and Hector at the same time failed to deter Troilus from tempting 'the brushes of the war', was Hector's engagement to many Greeks (5. 3. 68) any less 'heroi-comical' than Troilus' setting the loss of an arm against the recovery of the sleeve? Hector lost his life and Troilus lost his horse—and the latter, like Ajax' horse, may have been the more capable creature.

The juxtaposition of Hector and a horse may seem a crude one, but it is important to remember that there appeared in 1622 the first of a series of mock-heroic rapes—Tassoni's *La Secchia Rapita* ('The Rape of the Bucket'). Hector cuts a fantastic figure when pricking on the Trojan plain—first in encounter with the scurvy Thersites and then with a mute but mobile suit of armour; and although the massed attack on him by Achilles and his Myrmidons was not in accordance with the rules of the tilt-yard, like the rest of the battle scenes its aim was to amuse. Achilles' stratagem of making a massed attack on the unarmed Hector—first crying to his 'fellows' to strike and then to acclaim his victory—is intentionally ludicrous. The couplets show it, and why else should Shakespeare have transferred to Hector's death the circumstances in which (according to tradition) Troilus was slain except that the 'odds of multitude' against a quixotic figure of discredited fiction made the victor and the vanquished more mock-heroical?

'Wars, hitherto the only argument heroic deemed' had been under heavy fire from humanists throughout the sixteenth century. Two essays in the well-known *Adagia* of Erasmus ('dulce bellum inexpertis' and 'aut regem aut fatuum nasci oportere'), which had mustered classical and Christian condemnation of war as brutality and folly, had made a profound impression on responsible opinion at a time when the cost of war was painfully clear to most nations of western Europe; and chivalric conventions (with which the heroic had come to be linked) were challenged long before they finally fell from grace in the 1590s. Ascham's denunciation of the *Morte D'Arthur* as 'open manslaughter and bold

bawdry'[1] is an Elizabethan counterpart to Plato's
ethical criticism of Homer. Ascham's standpoint was
that of the moralist; so too was Horace's; and so too was
Shakespeare's when he took on the role of satirist. Nor
is the attitude unexpected in view of his English
historical plays. Burgundy's picture of war as 'disorder',
'wildness' and 'savagery' in *Henry V* (5. 2. 34 ff.)
simply expresses in terms of the countryside what is
expressed in the characterization of *Troilus and Cressida*
and insisted on in its pathological and animal imagery.

The approach to this play through Homer and
Chaucer is, in fact, the wrong one. The best guide to
the underlying significance of its theme and spirit is
Burton's study of brain-sickness in the *Anatomy of
Melancholy* and his satiric picture of a mad world bent
on self-destruction in his preface. In lighter vein the
play looks forward to the mock-heroic.

For burlesque and satire, a well-known tale manifestly provided a less cumbersome stalking horse than
an unfamiliar story. The tedious brief scene of Pyramus
and Thisbe or the motion of Hero and Leander in
Bartholomew Fair would not be funny to an unin-
structed audience. Shakespeare offered his apology for
his handling of the matter when he made 'envious and
calumniating Time' the villain of the piece—'a great-
sized monster of ingratitude', neglectful of the past,
rapacious in his rich thievery of the present, and eager
for change:

> For time is like a fashionable host
> That slightly shakes his parting guest by th'hand
> And, with his arms outstretched as he would fly,
> Grasps in the comer.   (3. 3. 165–8)

Because he could not turn back the pages of history,
we should not assume that this was due to distemper or

[1] *Schoolmaster*, ed. Arber, p. 80.

in a controversial spirit. Like Achilles, a dramatist had
to keep 'the instant way'; and although the way was
not, I think, the one that Shakespeare might have chosen
for himself, there is no evidence that he did not enjoy
the challenge—for what had distinguished his work
from that of his fellow dramatists from the start was its
variety and adaptability. *Troilus and Cressida*, though
serious in its satiric purpose, is both amusing and gay
for those who do not mistake the Trojan geese for swans,
and there is no spleen in its mockery. How nicely
calculated and controlled the effects were is nowhere
better seen than in the lively silliness of the Trojan
council or the covert ironies of the vignette of Helen in
3. 1—the most brilliant scene of pure comedy in the
canon.

VI. *The integrity of the play*

It will be evident that *Troilus and Cressida* seems to
me of a piece. The comic method is the same throughout. The dialogue of 3. 2 (the scene where Pandarus
first brings Troilus and Cressida together) makes use
of the same kind of juxtaposition as the two opening
scenes, and the device is repeated in 4. 4 (the scene of
their parting). The decorum of the Greek council
(1. 3) acts as a foil to the erratic course of the Trojan
council (2. 2); and the same kind of juxtaposition is
devastatingly used in the closing scene where Troilus'
belated recognition of what the death of Hector means
to Troy recalls Cassandra's warning which he had
earlier so thoughtlessly and so impatiently swept aside:

> O, farewell, dear Hector!
> Look how thou diest! look how thy eye turns pale!
> Look how thy wounds do bleed at many vents!
> Hark how Troy roars! how Hecuba cries out!
> How poor Andromache shrills her dolours forth!
> Behold, distraction, frenzy, and amazement,

> Like witless antics, one another meet,
> And all cry 'Hector! Hector's dead! O Hector!'
>   *Troilus.* Away! away!   [leave;
>   *Cassandra.* Farewell—yet soft! Hector, I take my
> Thou dost thyself and all our Troy deceive.
>
>   (5. 3. 80–90)

It was not, I think, an accident that the couplet with which Troilus makes his exit a few lines later echoes Cassandra's rhyme—

> They are at it, hark! Proud Diomed, believe,
> I come to lose my arm, or win my sleeve

—for 'hope of revenge' (5. 10. 31) is still Troilus' only cure for 'inward woe' after the death of Hector, and his wildness is no more intended to arouse sympathy than the aching bones of Pandarus, who, as usual, quickly swings the pendulum to the farcical.

A similar continuity of pattern is seen in the leading themes of the play's imagery. Much of this is concerned with values. What is Cressida? The question is put by Troilus in a passage already cited (1. 1. 100–6) and it is plainly answered by Cressida herself at the close of the next scene. The same image occurs again in Troilus' estimate of Helen as a pearl, with the 'sixty and nine that wore their crownets regal' (Prol. 5–6) as merchants. Is her value any higher than Cressida's? Hector, measuring her worth against the price paid in Trojan blood, finds her not worth the keeping:

> Since the first sword was drawn about this question,
> Every tithe-soul 'mongst many thousand dismes
> Hath been as dear as Helen—I mean, of ours.
> If we have lost so many tenths of ours
> To guard a thing not ours, nor worth to us—
> Had it our name—the value of one ten,
> What merit's in that reason which denies
> The yielding of her up?   (2. 2. 18–25)

The less chivalrous Diomedes calculates that she is a cruel loss to both Greeks and Trojans:

> She's bitter to her country. Hear me, Paris:
> For every false drop in her bawdy veins
> A Grecian's life hath sunk; for every scruple
> Of her contaminated carrion weight
> A Trojan hath been slain; since she could speak,
> She hath not given so many good words breath
> As for her Greeks and Trojans suffered death.
>
> (4. 1. 70–6)

Paris' reply in terms of the chaffering of merchants recalls Ulysses' simile of 1. 3. 358–61. Most of this imagery comes from the hot-headed Troilus (who will neither count the cost himself nor listen to the reckoning of others) and from the cool judgement of Ulysses, but its main purpose is to keep the mind alert to the traffic of the stage and to encourage the audience to balance the account for itself.

The pathological imagery is, as I have already suggested, closely connected with the satiric picture of a mad and blundering world ruled by the passions (or 'blood') instead of reason. Ulysses' indictment of Achilles and those who are infected by his example is that they

> esteem no act
> But that of hand; the still and mental parts
> That do contrive how many hands shall strike
> When fitness calls them on, and know by measure
> Of their observant toil the enemy's weight—
> Why, this hath not a finger's dignity.
>
> (1. 3. 199–204)

Excited by the loud applause of their physical prowess, they are more likely to overthrow the pales and forts of their own reason than to take Troy:

> imagined worth
> Holds in his blood such swollen and hot discourse

> That 'twixt his mental and his active parts
> Kingdomed Achilles in commotion rages
> And batters down himself. What should I say?
> He is so plaguey proud that the death-tokens of it
> Cry 'No recovery'.   (2. 3. 170–6)

Shakespeare's Ajax, all brawn and no brain, is, of course, Ovid's, from *Metamorphoses*, xiii, where Ulysses and Ajax dispute their claims to the arms of Achilles; and Achilles is also represented, by Shakespeare, as more remarkable for his size than for the capacity of his understanding. When Ulysses offers 'derision medicinable' in 3. 3, he accordingly appeals not to his sense of responsibility but to his pride.

Thersites is the character from whom we hear most about the maladies that afflict the Greeks. That he is 'lost in the labyrinth of his fury' (2. 3. 1–2), a disease in itself, precludes his having any medicinal function, but his invectives against the patients and their maladies serve to emphasize the dramatic significance of the diagnosis—for Thersites is as shrewd as Pandarus is fatuous, and as merciless as Pandarus is indulgent. As one of Shakespeare's bastards (5. 7. 16), he was born with his eyes open and without illusions. When he first appears his mind is festering in abuse of Agamemnon's stupidity:

Agamemnon—how if he had boils, full, all over, generally. ...And those boils did run?...Then would come some matter from him; I see none now.   (2. 1. 2–9)

Ajax, 'who wears his wit in his belly and his guts in his head' (2. 1. 72–3), Achilles and Patroclus, who 'with too much blood and too little brain...may run mad' (5. 1. 47–8), are scarified as brainless fools. Ajax and Achilles understand only violence—they are unable even to deliver a fly from a spider 'without drawing their massy irons' (2. 3. 14–17); and in foolishly warring for a placket they invite the curse of the Neapolitan bone-ache (2. 3. 18–20), whose plagues are rained on the 'masculine whore' by Thersites in 5. 1. 17–23 and more selectively described by Pandarus in 5. 3. 101–7.

The sick-list starts in 1. 1. 55 with the 'open ulcer' of Troilus' heart. Alexander has the idiom of the times in describing Ajax as a mass of conflicting humours which make his brutal strength quite useless—'a gouty Briareus, many hands and no use, or a purblind Argus, all eyes and no sight' (1. 2. 21–30). The Greek council scene opens with Agamemnon's metaphor of the jaundice—a line of thought developed in Ulysses' diagnosis of the Greek fever.

It is perhaps the lack of a 'medicinable eye' like that of Ulysses and an irritant like Thersites that makes the Trojan state appear healthier than it is, for Antenor is mute and Priam is merely testy with the doting Paris (2. 2. 142–5). Hector (very much the patronizing older brother) is well aware of Troilus' intemperate judgement:

> Now youthful Troilus, do not these high strains
> Of divination in our sister work
> Some touches of remorse, or is your blood
> So madly hot that no discourse of reason,
> Nor fear of bad success in a bad cause,
> Can qualify the same?   (2. 2. 113–18)

But the irresponsible Troilus dismisses what he calls Cassandra's 'brainsick raptures' as madness; and although Hector has one more fling at the 'hot passion of dis-tempered blood' (2. 2. 169), his own reason is finally infected when honour prevails over the moral laws of nature and of nations (2. 2. 184–6).

Thersites has similarly the lion's share of the animal imagery, which serves as a reminder of the antithesis between brain and brawn and of the long-established

connexion of animal imagery with the passions. Achilles
and Ajax are the draught-oxen, yoked to the task of
ploughing up the wars by the wily Ulysses and Nestor
(2. 1. 103–6), and for their stupidity they are often
associated with the heavier beasts of burden—the
elephant (2. 3. 2), the camel (2. 1. 52) and the horse—
or, for their quarrelsomeness, with the dog. Thersites'
most sustained contempt is for Menelaus who began
the stir:

the primitive statue and oblique memorial of cuckolds...to
what form but that he is, should wit larded with malice
and malice forced with wit turn him to? To an ass, were
nothing; he is both ass and ox; to an ox, were nothing: he
is both ox and ass. To be a dog, a mule, a cat, a fitchew,
a toad, a lizard, an owl, a puttock, or a herring without
a roe, I would not care; but to be Menelaus, I would
conspire against destiny! Ask me not what I would be,
if I were not Thersites; for I care not to be the louse of a
lazar, so I were not Menelaus.   (5. 1. 53–64)

This kind of metamorphosis appears as early as
1. 2. 19–21 in Alexander's description of Ajax—

This man, lady, hath robbed many beasts of their particular
additions: he is as valiant as the lion, churlish as the bear,
slow as the elephant—

and Pandarus adds his mite in labelling Achilles 'a very
camel' (1. 2. 250). Ulysses and Nestor confirm the
impression of churlishness and stupidity on the part of
Achilles and Ajax: if the prosecution of the war depends
on brute force 'Achilles' horse makes many Thetis' sons'
(1. 3. 211–2); 'the elephant hath joints, but none for
courtesy' (2. 3. 104–5) is Ulysses' verdict on Achilles'
manners.

Although 'the common curse of mankind, folly and
ignorance' (2. 3. 26–7) falls on Trojans and Greeks
alike, Trojan folly is spared the stick that belabours the

dull and factious Greeks. Trojan lightheadedness runs
to bird imagery, though I doubt whether this has
much significance, for Animal Grab is to some extent
a symbolic game for the idle Greeks until the dogs of
war are unleashed and can show their paces in Act 5.
Its significance for the integrity of the play is that it
begins, like the disease imagery, in the opening scenes,
which some would divorce from the war story, as early
work.

Finally, as a constant reminder of the 'hot digestion
of this cormorant war' (2. 2. 6) and 'raging appetites
that are most disobedient and refractory' (2. 2. 181–2),
there is the symbolism of food—being prepared, consumed, allowed to rot (like Achilles' reputation) or go
musty. Pandarus is anxious that it shall be enjoyed:
Troilus must wait until the cake (Cressida) is ready
(1. 1. 14ff.); and on the other hand he tries to whet
Cressida's appetite by enumerating the spices which
make up Troilus' attractions (1. 2. 252–6). Troilus
naturally finds 'crammed reason' noxious fare with
which to 'fat' the thoughts (2. 2. 46–50). His taste is
fastidious—for 'love's thrice repuréd nectar' and
'strained purity'; and although he recognizes that
'sweet love is food for fortune's tooth' (4. 5. 293), the
'greasy relics' and 'orts' of love do not enter into his
calculations until he has seen them (5. 2). Ulysses sees
'appetite' as an alarming thing—'an universal wolf'
(1. 3. 121) and a promoter of the kind of dangerous
heat that inflames the passions and destroys the judgement. Achilles, broiling in loud applause (1. 3. 378) or
basting his arrogance with his own seam (2. 3. 183), is
as repellent as the frying of lechery is exciting to Thersites (5. 2. 57–8).

VII. *The date*

The link between the play's theme and its imagery seems a particularly strong one and, for this reason, it is difficult to see how it could have been written incoherently—either at a time when Shakespeare had not made up his mind what he was doing or disjointedly over a period of anything between five or ten years. Nor do I think there is anything to suggest there was any authoritative revision of the text of the play after its first writing.[1] For this reason, Chambers's date, *c.* 1602, seems a likely one. The Prologue contains an allusion to Ben Jonson's *Poetaster* (1601) and it is too appropriate as the opening gambit to Shakespeare's variations on the heroic theme to have been written independently. Troilus' intention to unarm comes too pat upon the 'Prologue armed' for the juxtaposition to be accidental. For the terminal date, the Stationers' Register entry of 7 February 1603 seems satisfactory enough, for it is not very likely that the Chamberlain's men would have had two *Troilus and Cressida* plays at the same time.

VIII. *The Sources*

Shakespeare's main source was *The Recuyell of the Historyes of Troye*, a prose translation from the French of Raoul le Fèvre made by Caxton and a work in steady demand from its first printing *c.* 1475 down to the time of Pope. Homer had for centuries been discredited as an authority on the siege of Troy. He had mixed fiction with fact in making the gods take part in the fighting; as a Greek, he was biased; and he was not born until long after the siege and saw nothing of it— so ran the indictment of Homer in the forebears of le

---

[1] See note on the Copy, pp. 126–8.

Fèvre's book, itself a translation (so fa_ as the ground covered by Shakespeare's play is concerned) from the Latin *Historia Troiana* (1287) of Guido delle Colonne, which in turn was a translation of the *Roman de Troie* (*c.* 1160) of Benoît de Sainte-More, an anglo-norman trouvère of the court of Henry II. The *Ephemeris Belli Troiani* attributed to Dictys the Cretan (a follower of Idomeneus)[1] and the *Historia de Excidio Troiae* attributed to Dares the Phrygian (a Trojan priest)[2] were, on the face of it, more reliable witnesses to what actually happened. What traditional material is preserved in the works attributed to Dictys and Dares (the former said to have been an abridged translation of a manuscript in his tomb brought to light by an earthquake in the time of Nero, and the latter allegedly a translation of an Iliad older than Homer's) is fortunately of no relevance to the reputation they enjoyed as chroniclers. In the medieval period and for long after, they had pride of place as the authorities for the events they were thought to have witnessed, and for the nations of western Europe, tracing their pedigrees back to Aeneas,[3] the Trojan Dares redressed the Greek bias of Homer.

The substance of Dictys and Dares, as selected, elaborated, and adapted to medieval tastes by Benoît, was widely known in sixteenth-century England from Caxton's *Recuyell*, which had gone through at least five editions before 1600; Lydgate's verse translation of Guido had also been twice printed (in 1513 and 1555),

---

[1] Idomeneus (*Iliad*, II, 645) led the Cretans against Troy.
[2] A priest of Hephaestus (*Iliad*, V, 9).
[3] This was of long standing. In England, the legend that Brutus, the son of Ascanius, the son of Aeneas, had settled in Albion (then inhabited only by giants) and re-named it Britain is found as late as Holinshed's Chronicle, and it was not dismissed until the time of Camden.

and a new translation of Guido appeared in 1553. Whether in verse or in prose, these descendants of Benoît have the family likeness one would expect and, factually, differ very little one from another so far as the story of Helen and Troy is concerned.[1] They all describe how, after a fruitless effort of Antenor to negotiate the return of the captive Hesione, the Trojans sent a marauding expedition to Greece under Paris, encouraged by the promise made to him on Mount Ida of the fairest woman in Greece and with the intention of exchanging their prize for Hesione. After telling of the rape of Helen, they all describe the assembly of the Greeks at Athens, their arrival at Tenedos, and the ten years' siege, battle by battle and truce by truce.

How very different in detail these versions of the matter were from Homer's can be seen from the résumés of the relevant passages from Caxton in my notes.[2] The account of the Trojan council (2. 2), for instance, goes back to Dares; so too does the story of Andromache's dream and the efforts to restrain Hector (initially successful in all accounts known before Shakespeare). The case for Caxton's *Recuyell* as the particular authority consulted rests mainly on the evidence of the Prologue (see note on its sources); on Lydgate's omission of any reference to Cressida's

[1] How much elaborated the matter might be (and usually was) can be seen from the fact that the story of Mount Ida occupies 6 lines in Dares' prose and 60 lines in Caxton's. In Benoît's verse it occupies nearly 70 lines, in the alliterative Troy Book (an independent translation of Guido) just over 100, and in Lydgate close on 450.

[2] References in the notes are to H. Oskar Sommer's reprint (1894) of Caxton's first edition. This was sophisticated in the 1596 edition, 'newly corrected by W. Fiston' and printed by Creede, which the New Variorum edition (1953) suggests as the one Shakespeare used and from which it gives extracts.

welcome by the Greek princes, of Hector's embracing
Ajax, and of his reference to him as his 'cousin-german'
(all in 4. 5); and of Lydgate's use of the term 'archer'
instead of 'sagittary' (5. 5. 14).[1] Against this there are
a few coincidences between Shakespeare and Lydgate,
but they are none of them such as cannot be explained
as due to independent elaboration—for what one writer
invented by way of embellishment was in most cases
well within the compass of another. What significance
these coincidences have can be judged from the notes
where I have recorded them.[2]

What is of most importance is, of course, less the
particular source or edition Shakespeare used than his
manipulation of what is common to all of them, for
substantially they tell the same story. The most drastic
changes in chronology are that the death of Patroclus
(in Caxton's second battle) is delayed so as to provide
(as in Homer) the motive for Achilles' participation in
the *grand finale*; that Achilles' falling in love with
Polyxena (which occurred on the anniversary of
Hector's death according to Caxton) is anticipated so
as to provide Achilles' excuse for failing to keep the
engagement by which Hector, on the contrary, set
such store; and that the circumstances of the death of

[1] See also my note to 3. 3. 4, where the emendation in
accordance with Caxton's translation seems to be inevitable.

[2] My acquaintance with Guido is limited to Sommer's
extracts and what I have been able to deduce from the Middle
English alliterative Troy Book (E.E.T.S.) and Lydgate's
(E.E.T.S.). Since these were independent translations of
Guido, what is common to them was presumably in this
source. A few extracts from the 1555 edition of Lydgate
are given in the New Variorum edition. See also my notes
to 3. 3. 18–19, 193–4; 4. 2. 107; 4. 5. 196–7, 215–16; 5. 2.
Guido's Latin *Historia*, or a translation of it, would have
provided, it seems to me, both the Caxton and Lydgate
material.

Troilus at Achilles' hands (in Caxton's nineteenth battle) are transferred to the death of Hector (Caxton's sixth battle).

This manœuvring to motivate Achilles' actions (especially, of course, in representing Patroclus' death as what finally goaded him into action) naturally suggests an awareness of Homeric material, though whether Shakespeare had a first-hand acquaintance with any translation of Homer is questionable, since so much Homeric matter had filtered through Latin authors. Investigation is made the more difficult because so many plays of Shakespeare's day have been lost. The disappearance of the *Troilus and Cressida* written for Henslowe by Dekker and Chettle is particularly unfortunate since it may have stimulated Shakespeare to do something more novel with the same material. All that survives of it is probably the fragmentary 'plot' of the Admiral's Company[1] and this certainly suggests that the related play similarly represented Achilles' participation in the fighting as beginning after Patroclus' body had been carried to Achilles' tent, for (so far as the 'plot' evidence goes) Achilles does not figure in the alarums and excursions until the first scene of this kind after Patroclus' death.[2]

What seems to me quite certain is Shakespeare's knowledge of Ovid's account of the debate between Ajax and Ulysses for the arms of Achilles (*Metamorphoses*, XIII),[3] for here there is the blockish Ajax and the antithesis between brute force and mental reach

[1] Greg, very reasonably, thinks the 'plot' belonged to the Dekker and Chettle play, written in 1599.

[2] See the New Variorum edition, p. 460, scenes numbered 10 and 13. The writers of the play were clearly using either Caxton or some similar related account of the matter and not Homer.

[3] First pointed out by Steevens.

(see especially *Met*. XIII. 360–9), which Ulysses elaborates in his indictment of the malcontent warriors in I. 3. Ovid further alludes to Ajax' ability to hold his own against Hector (cf. I. 2. 33–4), to Hector's challenge and the lottery (*Met*. XIII. 85–90, 275–9), as well as to the impudent Thersites (*Met*. XIII. 231–5); and, although Shakespeare's Thersites is thought to have come from Chapman's 1598 translation of Homer, Thersites was proverbial for his deformity of body and his ill-conditioned mind—the features Shakespeare stresses.[1]

If I seem sceptical about Shakespeare's acquaintance with Homer it is because so much relating to the *Iliad* might have been picked up in the schoolroom or from plays now lost; and where there is nothing in the particularities of his play to tell us whether the matter suggesting an acquaintance with Homer came direct from a translation or from something long familiar picked up who knows where, it seems best to maintain an attitude of reserve. It would be strange if Shakespeare had not had the curiosity to look into one of the many translations in Latin or French of the *Iliad* or into Hall's ten books (I–X), published in 1581, or Chapman's seven books (I, II, VII–XI) of 1598, but neither the temper nor the reorganization of Caxton material suggests that he had the *Iliad* particularly in mind.

There seems similarly no certainty of a debt at

[1] See Erasmus, *Adagia*, 'Thersitae facies'—'De prodigiose deformi dici solitum, quod Homerus scripserit hunc omnium qui ad Trojam venissent, foedissimum fuisse. Ac totum hominem a capite, quod aiunt, usque ad pedes ita graphice depingit et corporis vitia et animi morbos, ut dicas pessimum ingenium in domicilio se digno habitasse.' Cooper in his Dictionary describes him as 'a prince that came with the Greeks to the siege of Troy, which in person and conditions was of all other most deformed'.

first-hand to Chaucer's tale. The story of Troilus[1] and
Briseida seems to have been the invention of Benoît,
which achieved independent fame when Boccaccio
elaborated, from Guido's translation of Benoît, his
Il Filostrato (Chaucer's source) in which the heroine's
name was changed to Griseida (and later by Chaucer
to Criseyde). Pandarus,[2] Griseida's cousin in Boccaccio
(uncle in Chaucer), never obtained a footing in the
chronicles of Troy. The Chaucer story and Henryson's
sequel to it had been balladed;[3] and it had been staged
as early as the beginning of the century[4] and as recently
as the Admiral's Company play[5]—thus making Shake-

[1] Troilus is merely mentioned by name as one of Priam's
dead sons in *Il.* XXIV. 257. His name suggests an eponymous
hero and many stories were told of his death, among them
Vergil's (*Aen.* I. 474–8).

[2] Pandarus in the *Iliad* was a Lycian supporter of Priam;
he was killed by Diomedes (*Il.* v. 173, 290 ff.; cf. Dictys,
Caps. XXV, XL–XLI). He is mentioned by Vergil (*Aen.* v.
495–7), but it was Boccaccio who first attached him to the
love story of Troilus and Cressida.

[3] 'a ballet intituled *the history of Troilus Whose throtes
hath Well bene tryed*' was entered to Purfoot between July
1565 and July 1566 (Arber, I, 134b), and '*A proper ballad
Dialoge wise betwene Troylus and Cressida*' was entered to
Edward White on 23 June 1581 (Arber, II, 180b).
Halliwell printed a ballad, seemingly not the latter, in his
edition of *The Marriage of Wit and Wisdom* (Sh. Soc. 1846).

[4] See Chambers, *William Shakespeare* (1930), I, p. 448.

[5] There is also a Welsh play of unknown authorship,
which was described by J. S. P. Tatlock (*Modern Language
Review*, X (1915), pp. 265–82). This was, he thought, an
imitation of some English play, though all we know about
its composition is that the terminal date was 1613. It
follows Chaucer and Henryson except that (rather oddly)
there is a kind of Trojan Council scene on the *return* of
Helen (as in Shakespeare), representing Antenor and Æneas
as taking part in it (as in Heywood's *Iron Age*). The latter,

speare's immediate debt to Chaucer just as difficult to assess as his indebtedness to Homer. Whether we need suppose that Shakespeare made any deliberate effort to supplement Caxton's material is, of course, the more doubtful because his entertainment depended on the audience's recognition that this was the Troy story with a difference; and their ability to see the difference depended on their starting with a general knowledge of the matter and their seeing that the play's originality lay in the manner in which he was handling familiar material.

The manner includes the poet as well as the dramatist. The lyrical pressure that is denied to Troilus' transports is concentrated in a stream of reflections on Time and Change. There can be little doubt that Shakespeare had here in mind the prelude to the last book of the *Metamorphoses* and that his imagery of conception, gestation, birth, and infancy springs not from the love story but from the Pythagorean exposition of Time and Nature, ceaselessly destroying and renewing old matter in new forms—an interpretation of matter which harmonizes the satiric and poetic themes. Shakespeare's emphasis, as a poet, is naturally on the end of the cycle—on envious Time, the Great Devourer ('tempus edax rerum...invidiosa vetustas'). 'Faith and troth', as Agamemnon recognises (4. 5. 168), belong to the 'extant moment'. There is more, therefore, than dramatic irony in Troilus' fears that Cressida's constancy may not withstand Time and Change (3. 2. 157 ff.) and in her confidence that the strong base and building of her love will endure (4. 2.

now dated 1611–13, contains many echoes of Shakespeare's play, but whether Shakespeare and Heywood were independently influenced by the play of which we have only the fragmentary plot is an unprofitable subject for speculation.

101–5). Mighty states serve to witness the vanity of such hopeful expectation.

It is this poetic aura that gives *Troilus and Cressida* its subtlety; but, however electric the moments when the poet and satirist can make common cause, what provides the poetic spark is not sentiment but realism. How little Shakespeare conceded to sentiment is evident from his rejection of the pathetic possibilities of 5. 3, where, in Caxton's account of the matter, Hecuba, Helen, and Hector's sisters and children reinforce Andromache's pleading with Hector. Shakespeare blots out the superfluous Trojan women and children and turns the spotlight on the antics of the Great Goose Hector and the Wild Goose Troilus, emphasizing, in Cassandra's warning, the frenzy and folly of their heedlessness.

THE STAGE HISTORY OF
TROILUS AND CRESSIDA

This play, with its difficult problems for both scholars and theatrical producers, has probably been less seen by the general public than most others in the canon. Hardly staged at all till the present century, revivals up to date have been largely either in universities, or by special groups and companies.

The earliest mention of Shakespeare's *Troilus and Cressida* occurs in the entry of a play with this title in the Stationers' Register, on 7 February 1603; another was made on 28 January 1609. The first entry was probably a 'blocking' one;[1] the second was followed the same year by the publication of a quarto, described as 'a new play' in the preface.[2] No records of performances have been found; but some possible allusions to the play occur in the earliest years. One, of 1603, seems fairly certain, as it combines its subject with those of *Richard III* and *Lucrece*:

> Of Helens rape and Troyes beseiged Towne,
> Of Troylus faith, and Cressids falsitie,
> Of Rychards stratagems for the English crowne,
> Of Tarquins lust, and Lucrece chastitie,
> Of these, of none of these my muse nowe treates.[3]

[1] See W. W. Greg, *Some Aspects and Problems of London Publishing between* 1550 *and* 1650 (1956), pp. 114 ff.

[2] For these S.R. entries and the quarto, see the fuller account and discussion, *supra*, Introduction, p. ix; cf. also p. xxiv, for the probable place of staging.

[3] From the lines in I.C., *Saint Marie Magdalen's Conversion*.

If these lines do refer to the play, it must have been
staged soon after its first entry in S.R.[1]

After the Restoration the play was never seen in the
English theatre till the present century—though John
Philip Kemble made, but never produced, an acting
version with a tentative cast which is now in the Folger
Library, Washington.[2] In its place Dryden's adaptation
Troilus and Cressida, or, Truth Found too Late (1679),
held the stage till 1734. It was first produced by the
Duke's company at the Dorset Garden Theatre in its
year of publication,[3] with Betterton as Troilus and also
the speaker of Dryden's new Prologue, 'representing
the ghost of Shakespeare', Mrs Mary Lee as Cressida,
and Mrs Betterton as Andromache (a more important
character than in Shakespeare). Harris, Underhill and
Smith were Ulysses, Thersites and Hector; Crosby
played Diomedes, Bowman Patroclus, Leigh Pandarus,
Gillow Agamemnon, and Norris Nestor. In the next
revival, at Drury Lane in 1709 (2 June), Betterton
took Thersites, and Wilks and Mrs Bradshaw took the
title parts; the cast included also Powell (Hector),
Mills (Agamemnon), Booth (Achilles), Keene (Ajax),
and Mrs Rogers (Andromache). After Betterton's
death there were revivals in five different years—at
Lincoln's Inn Fields (1720, 1721, May and November
1723), and at Covent Garden (20 December and
7 January 1733–4). Ryan was Troilus in all of these.
In the first two Quin played Hector and Boheme
Ulysses, but from 1723 Quin took over Thersites from

[1] On the whole problem, see E. K. Chambers, *William
Shakespeare: Facts and Problems* (1930), I, 441–3; and the
New Variorum Shakespeare ed. by H. N. Hillebrand,
supplemented by T. W. Baldwin (1953), pp. 351–61.

[2] See the New Variorum ed. p. 504.

[3] About April, according to J. R. A. Nicoll, *Restoration
Drama* (1923), p. 360.

William Bullock, and 'was esteemed excellent' as this,
says Davies.[1] Hector was given to Boheme, and in his
place Walker was Ulysses in 1723, succeeding him as
Hector in the Garden productions, where J. Lacy took
Agamemnon. Cressida successively fell to Mrs Boheme
from 1720 to May 1723 (in 1720 and 1721 billed
under her maiden name, Seymour), to Mrs Sterling in
November 1723, and to Mrs Bullock in the two Covent
Garden productions. The last-named had been Andromache in 1720, and in May 1723; in 1721 Mrs Giffard
had had this role; in Covent Garden it was Mrs Buchanan's.[2] The comedian Hippisley played Pandarus
from 1723 on, and 'excited much mirth'.[3]

   Dryden's play redistributes the events of the original,
and achieves a more obvious unity of plot by dint of
excisions and abridgements. But they involve the loss
of much precious poetry; for example in Ulysses'
speech to Achilles on the depredations of Time (3. 3.
145 ff.), and in the impassioned agony of Troilus when
he knows his beloved false (5. 2. 137–60); this last even
the alteration of plot did not require. Everything is
focused on the love story, now remodelled. Cressida is
entirely faithful, and Diomedes is the villain whose lies
bring about the tragic ending. Persuaded by Calchas
that in this way alone can she hope to return to Troy,
though his grounds for the assertion are quite obscure,
Cressida pretends love to the Greek, and even pledges
it with the gift of the ring Troilus had given to her.
In the last scene, all but entirely Dryden's, she intervenes in a combat between Troilus and Diomedes, who

[1] Thomas Davies, *Dramatic Miscellanies* (1783), III, 163
(vol. III has 1784 on title-page).
[2] See C. B. Hogan, *Shakespeare in the Theatre 1701–1800:
London, 1701–50* (1952), pp. 455–6. Davies, *op. cit.* III, 163–4,
names Mrs Buchanan as the Covent Garden Cressida.
[3] *Ibid.* III, 163.

then shows the ring and claims that he has had 'full possession' of her. When Troilus disbelieves her denial she stabs herself, and dies after he is at last convinced of her innocence. He kills the Greek, and is slain by Achilles amid general slaughter of the Trojans; the play is then rounded off by a couplet with the moral of the evil of 'home-bred factions'. One lengthy addition by Dryden (3.2) has been much admired: the quarrel and reconciliation of Troilus with Hector when the former hears of the exchange of Cressida for Antenor. This, his Preface says, 'was hinted' to him by Betterton. It recalls the quarrel of Brutus and Cassius in *Julius Caesar*, 4. 3; but he disclaims the 'honour' of being able to 'imitate the incomparable Shakespeare', and refers to the quarrel of Menelaus and Agamemnon in Euripides' *Iphigenia in Aulis*.[1]

Shakespeare's play was seen after at least more than two and a half centuries on 1 June 1907, when Charles Fry produced it (and acted Thersites) at Great Queen Street Theatre, with Lewis Casson and Olive Kennett in the title parts. *The Times* on 3 June declared that 'the main result was the conviction that it was impossible to arrange the play for the stage'. But William Poel in 1912 on three nights of December showed how with new methods of staging it could be done; this was on the 10th, 15th and 18th with his Elizabethan Stage Society at the King's Hall, Covent Garden. He left the stage bare with blue curtains at the back of it, and there was only one interval of fifteen minutes. For

---

[1] For further analysis and critical comparison of the two plays see G. C. D. Odell, *Shakespeare from Betterton to Irving* (1921), I, 48–51; Hazelton Spencer, *Shakespeare Improved* (1927), pp. 221–37; C. B. Hogan, *op. cit.* pp. 451–2; New Variorum ed. pp. 490–503. Rev. John Genest's discussion in his *Some Account of the English Stage, 1660–1830* (1832), I, 266–9 is relatively of little help.

Cressida he chose a young milliner of twenty-four as
yet unknown to the public theatres; he had seen her
acting in an amateur company at Streatham Town Hall
that spring, and in summer had given her a minor part
in his *Sakuntala* in Cambridge. She was Edith Evans,
and these three nights decided her destiny; a year later
she was playing the Queen in *Hamlet* at Poel's Little
Theatre, and millinery knew her no more. Esmé
Percy was Troilus, Poel Pandarus, Hermione Gingold
Cassandra; Thersites was played by a woman, Elspeth
Keith, and so were also Æneas and Paris. The novelist,
George Moore, was among the audience.[1] The play
was repeated by Poel and his Society at Stratford next
year on 12 May, with Ion Swinley in Percy's place as
Troilus.[2] Poel made extensive cuts in his acting
version—to the loss of some of its best poetry. Ulysses'
great speech on Time he remorselessly abridged; he
excised twelve lines from Troilus' leave-taking of
Cressida in Act 4, sc. 4, including the moving lines
46–8; and his despairing speech on Hector's death at
the end of the play entirely disappeared. As Robert
Speaight has shown, his ear for poetry could be
strangely defective.[3]

The next staging of the play was by the Marlowe
Society at the A.D.C. Theatre in Cambridge in March
1922, under the direction of Frank Birch, when Dennis
Arundell was Ulysses, George Rylands was Diomedes,

[1] See the New Variorum ed., p. 505; J. C. Trewin,
Edith Evans (1953), pp. 11–18, 96; and for the fullest
account of Poel's treatment of the play, Robert Speaight,
William Poel and the Elizabethan Revival (1954), pp. 193–
202, 284.

[2] See J. C. Trewin in T. C. Kemp and J. C. Trewin,
The Stratford Festival (1953), pp. 101–2; Speaight, *op. cit.*
pp. 196, 198–9.

[3] See Speaight, *op. cit.* pp. 196–8.

Dennis (the present Prof. Sir Dennis) Robertson was a brilliant Pandarus, and all the women's parts were played by men; in June the production was taken for a week to the Everyman Theatre in Hampstead, the women now being acted by women—Enid Baddeley the Cressida. *The Times* on both occasions praised the vigour of the acting, but felt the element of comic mockery to be overstressed. The next year, the tercentenary of the First Folio, the Old Vic wound up its staging in ten years of all the plays with *Troilus*, 5–17 November. Robert Atkins, the producer, had a strong cast which included Ion Swinley (again Troilus), Florence Saunders (Cressida), George Hayes (Ajax), Hay Petrie (Thersites). *The Times*, sceptical as at the first revival, wrote that 'the play was dull, as it was bound to be'. Yet the next twenty-five years saw more revivals than ever. In 1928 Nugent Monck with his Norwich Players put on the play at the Maddermarket Theatre, and Frank Birch in May 1932 presented it again at the Festival Theatre in Cambridge, some of his 1922 actors, including Dennis Robertson as Pandarus, figuring in it; Anthony Quayle was Hector. In 1936 it was staged at the Stratford Festival in the New Memorial Theatre with Iden Payne as producer, when Donald Eccles and Pamela Brown personated the lovers, Donald Wolfit was Ulysses, Randle Ayrton Pandarus, James Dale Thersites, and Rosalind Iden Cassandra.[1] Two years later there were two revivals: Nevill Coghill produced the play for the Oxford University Dramatic Society in the Fellows' Garden of Exeter College (13–16 June), and the Mask Theatre Company acted it in modern dress at the Westminster Theatre from 21 September to 15 October—Robert Harris (Troilus), Ruth Lodge (Cressida), Stephen

[1] Cf. T. C. Kemp, *op. cit.* pp. 179–80.

Murray (Thersites), Max Adrian (Pandarus),[1] Robert
Speaight (Ulysses), John Garside (Nestor) and Harry
Andrews (Diomedes). Desmond McCarthy[2] felt the
modernizing brought home to spectators the mood of
'bitter disillusionment' in which he supposed that the
play was written. He praised Murray's and Adrian's
acting, while through Speaight's excellent speaking of
his lines Ulysses 'became a new character' to him, with
meanness added to his adroitness and eloquence. In
March 1940, just eighteen years after their first
revival, the Marlowe Society and A.D.C. gave a
second revival in Cambridge, George Rylands, now a
Lecturer and Fellow of King's College, producing;
Donald Beves was Pandarus. In 1946, from 28 June,
Robert Atkins produced the play at the Open-Air
Theatre in Regent's Park—'a very gallant attempt to
overcome the many difficulties' of 'this bitter play',
wrote *The Times* reviewer on the 29th, and praised the
'tragic intensity' of John Byron's rendering of Troilus'
'illusion of chivalrous youth', but thought Patricia
Hicks 'a little too kind to the hollowness of Cressida'.
Russell Thorndike played Pandarus. 1948 saw two
revivals: in March by the Marlowe Society and A.D.C.
in Cambridge under Rylands with Beves again as
Pandarus (*The Times* on the 9th reviewed it as 'this

---

[1] The full cast is given on the programme now in the
Enthoven Theatre Collection at the Victoria and Albert
Museum. The New Variorum ed. p. 506, apparently
misled by McCarthy's review (see n. 2), assigns Pandarus
to Murray and Thersites to Adrian; but McCarthy has
inadvertently reversed the order of the two characters and
their actors respectively. Cf. *Who's Who in the Theatre*,
eleventh ed. (1953), pp. 248, 1093, and Gordon Crosse,
Shakespearean Playgoing, 1890–1952 (1953), p. 93.

[2] *New Statesman and Nation*, XVI (1 October 1938),
p. 491/2.

comedy'); and at Stratford Festival for the third time
under Anthony Quayle, who again acted Hector as in
1932 in Cambridge. Paul Scofield and Heather Stan-
nard had the title parts; Noel Willman and Esmond
Knight were Pandarus and Thersites; William Squire,
Michael Gwynn, and John Kidd played the Grecians,
Ulysses, Agamemnon and Nestor; Diana Wynyard
was Helen, and Ena Burrill the ill-fated prophetess
Cassandra. Two permanent settings represented Troy
and the Greek camp, but the frequent changes from
one to the other as the action shifted entailed a large
number of black-outs.[1] In June 1953 the Oxford
University Dramatic Society gave *Troilus* in St John's
College garden; in 1954 Byam Shaw produced Stratford's fourth revival, with Laurence Harvey and Muriel
Pavlow in the title parts (Anthony Quayle now
Pandarus and Leo McKern as Ulysses). In September
1954, Rylands, with Douglas Allen of the B.B.C., was
responsible for the first presentation by television. In
1955 Guy Boas with the boys of his Sloane School,
Chelsea showed the play there, with girls from a
neighbouring school taking the women's parts; while
in 1956 the Marlowe Society offered its fourth *Troilus*
at the Arts Theatre, Cambridge, produced jointly by
George Rylands, John Barton and an undergraduate,
Robin Midgley. This same year Tyrone Guthrie
produced for the Old Vic its second revival, cutting
nothing but the Prologue. The costumes were of the
period just before the First World War, the Greek
uniforms recalling those of the Germans and their allies
(Richard Wordsworth as Ulysses was an admiral), and
those of the Trojans like nothing outside Ruritania.
The comic element was stressed to the partial obscuring
of the pathos of the love of Troilus (John Neville)

[1] See Kemp and Trewin, *op. cit.* p. 230.

and Cressida (Rosemary Harris); Wendy Hiller was
a coquettish piano-playing Helen. Pandarus was most
effectively rendered as an elderly roué by Paul Rogers;
and the vile Thersites (Clifford Willlams) ingeniously
represented as a war correspondent with the Greeks.

On the Continent the earliest modern productions
preceded the first in Britain: in Munich a version in
German in 1898, in Berlin in 1899, and in Vienna in
1902. A score of revivals succeeded these in Germany,
Austria and Switzerland, 1904–36, and recently in
Essen in 1953 and in Berlin in 1955. In Hungary the
play translated was staged in 1900; in France in 1920,
and another version twice subsequently; in Prague there
was a production in 1921, and in Florence in 1949.
Altogether the play must be more familiar to Conti-
nental than to British playgoers.[1] In the United States,
university and student circles have had the major share
of productions even more markedly than in Britain.
Thus the credit of the earliest belongs to Yale, where on
17 June 1916 the Dramatic Association under Edgar
M. Woolley performed a *Troilus*, the women's parts
being played by men. The girls of Rockford College in
Illinois followed suit on two nights of April 1927; and
in December 1934, a year and a half before his Stratford
production, Iden Payne directed a presentation by the
Carnegie Institute of Teehnology, at the Little Theatre
in Pittsburgh, Pennsylvania, the costumes and setting
being Elizabethan with an inner, outer and upper
stage. In January 1947 Western Reserve University,
Cleveland, Ohio put on Eric Capon's production; and
at the end of 1948 students of Harvard gave ten performances of the play after a semi-professional company

[1] For most of these facts in fuller detail see the New
Variorum ed. pp. 511–18; the record of productions in
Florence, Essen and Berlin I owe to Mr C. B. Hogan of
Yale.

had mounted it at the Boston Tributary Theatre in the spring. The most prominent professional revival was one by the Players' Club at Moss's Broadway Theatre in New York, 6–11 June 1932. The cast included James Lawler (Troilus), Eugene Powers (Pandarus), Otis Skinner (Thersites), Charles Coburn (Ajax), Edith Barrett (Cressida) and Blanche Yurka (Helen). Critics, however, gave it a poor reception. Those who had some praise for the rendering of Pandarus, Thersites, Cressida and Helen, agreed with the rest in disliking the play—to be read, not staged, was R. Dana Skinner's verdict in the *Commonweal*,[1] while J. W. Krutch in the New York *Nation* declared it 'one continuous discord', unlike any other of Shakespeare's plays. In June 1936 Mr Gilmor Brown offered it at the Pasadena Playhouse, Pasadena, California; and in 1941 two revivals are recorded: one in July in Princeton by the Theatre Intime, another in December at the Civic Theatre, Washington, directed by Leon Askin. This last was in a severely cut version which occupied less than two hours in the acting.[2] The play was acted at Antioch College, Ohio in 1953.[3]

C. B. YOUNG

July 1956

[1] Cf. the critiques of English revivals in *The Times*, *supra*, pp. li–liii.

[2] For this record of U.S.A. revivals, see New Variorum ed. pp. 508–11.

[3] Information from Mr C. B. Hogan.

TO THE READER

A bracket at the beginning of a speech signifies an 'aside'.

THE
Famous Historie of
Troylus *and* Cresseid.

Excellently expressing the beginning
of their loues, with the conceited wooing
of *Pandarus*. Prince of *Licia*.

Written by William Shakespeare.

LONDON
Imprinted by *G. Eld* for *R. Bonian* and *H. Walley,* and
are to be sold at the spred Eagle in Paules-
Church-yeard, ouer against the
great North doore.
1609.

T. &c. — 4

A neuer writer, to an euer reader. Newes.

Ternall reader, you haue heere a new play, neuer stal'd with the Stage, neuer clapper-clawd with the palmes of the vulger, and yet passing full of the palme comicall; for it is a birth of your braine, that neuer vnder-tooke any thing commicall, vainely: And were but the vaine names of commedies changde for the titles of Commodities, or of Playes for Pleas; you should see all those grand censors, that now stile them such vanities, flock to them for the maine grace of their grauities: especially this authors Commedies, that are so fram'd to the life, that they serue for the most common Commentaries, of all the actions of our liues. shewing such a dexteritie, and power of witte, that the most displeased with Playes, are pleasd with his Commedies. And all such dull and heauy-witted worldlings, as were neuer capable of the witte of a Commedie, comming by report of them to his representations, haue found that witte there, 'that they neuer found in them-selues, and haue parted better wittied then they came: feeling an edge of witte set vpon them, more then euer they dreamd they had braine to grinde it on. So much and such sauored salt of witte is in his Commedies, that they seeme (for their height of pleasure) to be borne in that sea that brought forth Venus. Amongst all there is none more witty then this: And had I time I would comment vpon it, though I know it needs not, (for so

¶ 2   much

much as will make you thinke your testerne well be-
stowd) but for so much worth, as euen poore I know to be
stuft in it. It deserues such a labour, as well as the best
Commedy in Terence or Plautus. And beleeue this,
that when hee is gone, and his Commedies out of sale,
you will scramble for them, and set vp a new English
Inquisition. Take this for a warning, and at the perrill
of your pleasures losse, and Iudgements, refuse not, nor
like this the lesse, for not being sullied, with the smoaky
breath of the multitude ; but thinke fortune for the
scape it hath made amongst you. Since by the grand
possessors wills I beleeue you should haue prayd for them
rather then beene prayd. And so I leaue all such to bee
prayd for (for the states of their wits healths)
that will not praise it
Vale.

TROILUS AND CRESSIDA

The scene: Troy, and the Greek camp

CHARACTERS IN THE PLAY

PRIAM, *king of Troy*
HECTOR ⎫
TROILUS ⎪
PARIS ⎬ *his sons*
DEIPHOBUS ⎪
HELENUS ⎭
MARGARELON, *a bastard son of Priam*
ÆNEAS ⎫
ANTENOR ⎭ *Trojan commanders*
CALCHAS, *a Trojan priest, taking part with the Greeks*
PANDARUS, *uncle to Cressida*
AGAMEMNON, *the Greek general*
MENELAUS, *his brother*
ACHILLES ⎫
AJAX ⎪
ULYSSES ⎪
NESTOR ⎬ *Greek commanders*
DIOMEDES ⎪
PATROCLUS ⎭
THERSITES, *a deformed and scurrilous Greek*
ALEXANDER, *servant to Cressida*
Servant to Troilus
Servant to Paris
Servant to Diomedes
The Prologue

HELEN, *wife to Menelaus*
ANDROMACHE, *wife to Hector*
CASSANDRA, *daughter to Priam; a prophetess*
CRESSIDA, *daughter to Calchas*

Trojan and Greek Soldiers, and Attendants

TROILUS AND CRESSIDA

Enter the Prologue in armour

Prologue. In Troy there lies the scene. From isles
   of Greece
The princes orgulous, their high blood chafed,
Have to the port of Athens sent their ships,
Fraught with the ministers and instruments
Of cruel war; sixty and nine, that wore
Their crownets regal, from th'Athenian bay
Put forth toward Phrygia, and their vow is made
To ransack Troy, within whose strong immures
The ravished Helen, Menelaus' queen,
With wanton Paris sleeps—and that's the quarrel.
To Tenedos they come,
And the deep-drawing barks do there disgorge
Their warlike fraughtage; now on Dardan plains
The fresh and yet unbruiséd Greeks do pitch
Their brave pavilions: Priam's six-gated city,
Dardan, and Timbria, Helias, Chetas, Troien,
And Antenorides, with massy staples
And corresponsive and fulfilling bolts,
Sperr up the sons of Troy.
Now expectation, tickling skittish spirits
On one and other side, Trojan and Greek,
Sets all on hazard—and hither am I come
A Prologue armed, but not in confidence
Of author's pen or actor's voice, but suited
In like condition as our argument,
To tell you, fair beholders, that our play
Leaps o'er the vaunt and firstlings of those broils,

Beginning in the middle; starting thence away
To what may be digested in a play.
30 Like or find fault; do as your pleasures are:
Now good or bad, 'tis but the chance of war.   [*goes*

[1. 1.]   *Troy. Before Priam's palace*

Enter PANDARUS *and* TROILUS *in armour*

Troilus. Call here my varlet; I'll unarm again:
Why should I war without the walls of Troy
That find such cruel battle here within?
Each Trojan that is master of his heart,
Let him to field; Troilus, alas, hath none!
Pandarus. Will this gear ne'er be mended?
Troilus. The Greeks are strong, and skilful to
    their strength,
Fierce to their skill, and to their fierceness valiant,
But I am weaker than a woman's tear,
10 Tamer than sleep, fonder than ignorance,
Less valiant than the virgin in the night,
And skilless as unpractised infancy.
Pandarus. Well, I have told you enough of this; for
my part, I'll not meddle nor make no farther. He that
will have a cake out of the wheat must tarry the
grinding.
Troilus. Have I not tarried?
Pandarus. Ay, the grinding; but you must tarry the
bolting.
20 *Troilus.* Have I not tarried?
Pandarus. Ay, the bolting; but you must tarry the
leavening.
Troilus. Still have I tarried.

Pandarus. Ay, to the leavening; but there's yet in the word hereafter, the kneading, the making of the cake, the heating of the oven, and the baking; nay, you must stay the cooling too, or you may chance to burn your lips.

Troilus. Patience herself, what goddess e'er she be,
Doth lesser blench at sufferance than I do; 30
At Priam's royal table do I sit,
And when fair Cressid comes into my thoughts—
So, traitor! 'When she comes!'—When is she thence?

Pandarus. Well, she looked yesternight fairer than ever I saw her look, or any woman else.

Troilus. I was about to tell thee—when my heart,
As wedgéd with a sigh, would rive in twain,
Lest Hector or my father should perceive me,
I have, as when the sun doth light a storm,
Buried this sigh in wrinkle of a smile: 40
But sorrow that is couched in seeming gladness
Is like that mirth fate turns to sudden sadness.

Pandarus. An her hair were not somewhat darker than Helen's—well, go to—there were no more comparison between the women. But, for my part, she is my kinswoman; I would not, as they term it, praise her, but I would somebody had heard her talk yesterday, as I did. I will not dispraise your sister Cassandra's wit, but—

Troilus. O Pandarus! I tell thee, Pandarus— 50
When I do tell thee there my hopes lie drowned,
Reply not in how many fathoms deep
They lie indrenched. I tell thee I am mad
In Cressid's love. Thou answer'st she is fair;
Pour'st in the open ulcer of my heart
Her eyes, her hair, her cheek, her gait, her voice;
Handlest in thy discourse—O, that her hand,

In whose comparison all whites are ink
Writing their own reproach, to whose soft seizure
60 The cygnet's down is harsh, and spirit of sense
Hard as the palm of ploughman! this thou tell'st me,
As true thou tell'st me, when I say I love her;
But saying thus, instead of oil and balm,
Thou lay'st in every gash that love hath given me
The knife that made it.

Pandarus. I speak no more than truth.

Troilus. Thou dost not speak so much.

Pandarus. Faith, I'll not meddle in 't. Let her be as
she is. If she be fair, 'tis the better for her; an she be
70 not, she has the mends in her own hands.

Troilus. Good Pandarus, how now, Pandarus!

Pandarus. I have had my labour for my travail:
ill thought on of her, and ill thought on of you; gone
between and between, but small thanks for my labour.

Troilus. What, art thou angry, Pandarus? what,
with me?

Pandarus. Because she's kin to me, therefore she's not
so fair as Helen; an she were not kin to me, she would
be as fair o' Friday as Helen is o' Sunday. But what
care I? I care not an she were a blackamoor; 'tis all
80 one to me.

Troilus. Say I she is not fair?

Pandarus. I do not care whether you do or no.
She's a fool to stay behind her father. Let her to the
Greeks, and so I'll tell her the next time I see her. For
my part, I'll meddle nor make no more i'th' matter.

Troilus. Pandarus—

Pandarus. Not I.

Troilus. Sweet Pandarus—

Pandarus. Pray you, speak no more to me: I will
90 leave all as I found it, and there an end. [*goes; alarum*

Troilus. Peace, you ungracious clamours! peace,
    rude sounds!
Fools on both sides! Helen must needs be fair,
When with your blood you daily paint her thus.
I cannot fight upon this argument;
It is too starved a subject for my sword.
But Pandarus—O gods, how do you plague me!
I cannot come to Cressid but by Pandar,
And he's as tetchy to be wooed to woo
As she is stubborn-chaste against all suit.
Tell me, Apollo, for thy Daphne's love,   100
What Cressid is, what Pandar, and what we?
Her bed is India; there she lies, a pearl;
Between our Ilium and where she resides
Let it be called the wild and wandering flood;
Ourself the merchant, and this sailing Pandar,
Our doubtful hope, our convoy and our bark.

Alarum. Enter ÆNEAS

Æneas. How now, Prince Troilus! Wherefore
    not afield?
Troilus. Because not there; this woman's answer sorts,
For womanish it is to be from thence.
What news, Æneas, from the field today?   110
Æneas. That Paris is returnéd home, and hurt.
Troilus. By whom, Æneas?
Æneas.   Troilus, by Menelaus.
Troilus. Let Paris bleed: 'tis but a scar to scorn;
Paris is gored with Menelaus' horn.   *[alarum*
Æneas. Hark what good sport is out of town today!
Troilus. Better at home, if 'would I might' were 'may'.
But to the sport abroad: are you bound thither?
Æneas. In all swift haste.
Troilus.   Come, go we then together. *[they go*

[1. 2.]   *The same. A street*

Enter CRESSIDA *and* ALEXANDER, *her man*

Cressida. Who were those went by?
Alexander.   Queen Hecuba and Helen.
Cressida. And whither go they?
Alexander.   Up to the eastern tower,
Whose height commands as subject all the vale,
To see the battle. Hector, whose patience
Is as a virtue fixed, today was moved:
He chid Andromache and struck his armourer;
And, like as there were husbandry in war,
Before the sun rose he was harnessed light,
And to the field goes he; where every flower
10 Did, as a prophet, weep what it foresaw
In Hector's wrath.
Cressida.   What was his cause of anger?
Alexander. The noise goes this: there is among
        the Greeks
A lord of Trojan blood, nephew to Hector;
They call him Ajax.
Cressida.   Good; and what of him?
Alexander. They say he is a very man per se,
And stands alone.
Cressida. So do all men, unless they are drunk, sick,
or have no legs.
Alexander. This man, lady, hath robbed many beasts
20 of their particular additions: he is as valiant as the lion,
churlish as the bear, slow as the elephant—a man into
whom nature hath so crowded humours that his valour
is crushed into folly, his folly forced with discretion.
There is no man hath a virtue that he hath not a glimpse
of, nor any man an attaint but he carries some stain of

it; he is melancholy without cause and merry against the hair; he hath the joints of everything, but everything so out of joint that he is a gouty Briareus, many hands and no use, or a purblind Argus, all eyes and no sight. 30

Cressida. But how should this man, that makes me smile, make Hector angry?

Alexander. They say he yesterday coped Hector in the battle and struck him down, the disdain and shame whereof hath ever since kept Hector fasting and waking.

Cressida. Who comes here?

Alexander. Madam, your uncle Pandarus.

Enter PANDARUS

Cressida. Hector's a gallant man.

Alexander. As may be in the world, lady.

Pandarus. What's that? what's that? 40

Cressida. Good morrow, uncle Pandarus.

Pandarus. Good morrow, cousin Cressid. What do you talk of? Good morrow, Alexander. How do you, cousin? When were you at Ilium?

Cressida. This morning, uncle.

Pandarus. What were you talking of when I came? Was Hector armed and gone ere you came to Ilium? Helen was not up, was she?

Cressida. Hector was gone; but Helen was not up.

Pandarus. E'en so: Hector was stirring early. 50

Cressida. That were we talking of, and of his anger.

Pandarus. Was he angry?

Cressida. So he says here.

Pandarus. True, he was so; I know the cause too; he'll lay about him today, I can tell them that. And there's Troilus will not come far behind him; let them take heed of Troilus, I can tell them that too.

Cressida. What, is he angry too?

Pandarus. Who, Troilus? Troilus is the better man
60 of the two.

Cressida. O Jupiter! there's no comparison.

Pandarus. What, not between Troilus and Hector?
Do you know a man if you see him?

Cressida. Ay, if I ever saw him before and knew him.

Pandarus. Well, I say Troilus is Troilus.

Cressida. Then you say as I say; for I am sure he is
not Hector.

Pandarus. No, nor Hector is not Troilus in some
degrees.

70 *Cressida.* 'Tis just to each of them; he is himself.

Pandarus. Himself! Alas, poor Troilus! I would he
were—

Cressida. So he is.

Pandarus. Condition I had gone barefoot to India.

Cressida. He is not Hector.

Pandarus. Himself! no, he's not himself. Would
'a were himself! Well, the gods are above; time must
friend or end. Well, Troilus, well, I would my heart
were in her body! No, Hector is not a better man than
80 Troilus.

Cressida. Excuse me.

Pandarus. He is elder.

Cressida. Pardon me, pardon me.

Pandarus. Th'other's not come to't. You shall tell me
another tale when th'other's come to't. Hector shall
not have his wit this year.

Cressida. He shall not need it, if he have his own.

Pandarus. Nor his qualities.

Cressida. No matter.

90 *Pandarus.* Nor his beauty.

Cressida. 'Twould not become him; his own's better.

Pandarus. You have no judgement, niece. Helen herself swore th'other day that Troilus for a brown favour, for so 'tis, I must confess—not brown neither—

Cressida. No, but brown.

Pandarus. Faith, to say the truth, brown and not brown.

Cressida. To say the truth, true and not true.

Pandarus. She praised his complexion above Paris.

Cressida. Why, Paris hath colour enough.   100

Pandarus. So he has.

Cressida. Then Troilus should have too much: if she praised him above, his complexion is higher than his; he having colour enough, and the other higher, is too flaming a praise for a good complexion. I had as lief Helen's golden tongue had commended Troilus for a copper nose.

Pandarus. I swear to you, I think Helen loves him better than Paris.

Cressida. Then she's a merry Greek indeed.   110

Pandarus. Nay, I am sure she does. She came to him th'other day into the compassed window—and, you know, he has not past three or four hairs on his chin—

Cressida. Indeed, a tapster's arithmetic may soon bring his particulars therein to a total.

Pandarus. Why, he is very young; and yet will he within three pound lift as much as his brother Hector.

Cressida. Is he so young a man and so old a lifter?

Pandarus. But to prove to you that Helen loves him: she came and puts me her white hand to his cloven 120 chin—

Cressida. Juno have mercy! how came it cloven?

Pandarus. Why, you know, 'tis dimpled. I think his smiling becomes him better than any man in all Phrygia.

Cressida. O, he smiles valiantly.

Pandarus. Does he not?

Cressida. O yes, an 'twere a cloud in autumn.

Pandarus. Why, go to, then! But to prove to you that Helen loves Troilus—

130 *Cressida.* Troilus will stand to the proof, if you'll prove it so.

Pandarus. Troilus! Why, he esteems her no more than I esteem an addle egg.

Cressida. If you love an addle egg as well as you love an idle head, you would eat chickens i'th'shell.

Pandarus. I cannot choose but laugh to think how she tickled his chin; indeed, she has a marvellous white hand, I must needs confess—

Cressida. Without the rack.

140 *Pandarus.* And she takes upon her to spy a white hair on his chin.

Cressida. Alas, poor chin! many a wart is richer.

Pandarus. But there was such laughing! Queen Hecuba laughed, that her eyes ran o'er.

Cressida. With millstones.

Pandarus. And Cassandra laughed.

Cressida. But there was a more temperate fire under the pot of her eyes. Did her eyes run o'er too?

Pandarus. And Hector laughed.

150 *Cressida.* At what was all this laughing?

Pandarus. Marry, at the white hair that Helen spied on Troilus' chin.

Cressida. An't had been a green hair, I should have laughed too.

Pandarus. They laughed not so much at the hair as at his pretty answer.

Cressida. What was his answer?

Pandarus. Quoth she, 'Here's but two and fifty hairs on your chin, and one of them is white'.

Cressida. This is her question. 160

Pandarus. That's true; make no question of that. 'Two and fifty hairs', quoth he, 'and one white; that white hair is my father, and all the rest are his sons.' 'Jupiter!' quoth she, 'which of these hairs is Paris my husband?' 'The forked one,' quoth he; 'pluck't out, and give it him.' But there was such laughing, and Helen so blushed, and Paris so chafed, and all the rest so laughed, that it passed!

Cressida. So let it now; for it has been a great while going by. 170

Pandarus. Well, cousin, I told you a thing yesterday; think on't.

Cressida. So I do.

Pandarus. I'll be sworn 'tis true; he will weep you an 'twere a man born in April.

Cressida. And I'll spring up in his tears an 'twere a nettle against May. [*retreat sounded*

Pandarus. Hark! they are coming from the field. Shall we stand up here and see them as they pass toward Ilion? Good niece, do, sweet niece Cressida. 180

Cressida. At your pleasure.

Pandarus. Here, here, here's an excellent place; here we may see most bravely. I'll tell you them all by their names as they pass by. But mark Troilus above the rest.

Cressida. Speak not so loud.

ÆNEAS passes

Pandarus. That's Æneas. Is not that a brave man? He's one of the flowers of Troy, I can tell you. But mark Troilus; you shall see Troilus anon.

ANTENOR passes

Cressida. Who's that?

Pandarus. That's Antenor. He has a shrewd wit, 190

I can tell you, and he's a man good enough: he's one
o'th' soundest judgements in Troy whosoever, and a
proper man of person. When comes Troilus? I'll show
you Troilus anon. If he see me, you shall see him nod
at me.

Cressida. Will he give you the nod?

Pandarus. You shall see.

Cressida. If he do, the rich shall have more.

HECTOR passes

Pandarus. That's Hector, that, that, look you, that;
200 there's a fellow! Go thy way, Hector! There's a brave
man, niece. O brave Hector! Look how he looks!
There's a countenance! Is't not a brave man?

Cressida. O, a brave man!

Pandarus. Is 'a not? It does a man's heart good. Look
you what hacks are on his helmet! Look you yonder,
do you see? look you there: there's no jesting; there's
laying on, take't off who will, as they say; there be
hacks!

Cressida. Be those with swords?

210 *Pandarus.* Swords! anything, he cares not; an the
devil come to him, it's all one. By God's lid, it does
one's heart good. Yonder comes Paris, yonder comes
Paris.

PARIS passes

Look ye yonder, niece; is't not a gallant man too, is't not?
Why, this is brave now. Who said he came home hurt
today? He's not hurt. Why, this will do Helen's heart
good now, ha! Would I could see Troilus now! You
shall see Troilus anon.

HELENUS passes

Cressida. Who's that?

Pandarus. That's Helenus. I marvel where Troilus 220
is. That's Helenus. I think he went not forth today.
That's Helenus.

Cressida. Can Helenus fight, uncle?

Pandarus. Helenus! no—yes, he'll fight indifferent
well. I marvel where Troilus is. Hark! do you not
hear the people cry 'Troilus'? Helenus is a priest.

Cressida. What sneaking fellow comes yonder?

TROILUS passes

Pandarus. Where? yonder? that's Deiphobus. 'Tis
Troilus! there's a man, niece! Hem! Brave Troilus! the
prince of chivalry!   230

Cressida. Peace, for shame, peace!

Pandarus. Mark him; note him. O brave Troilus!
Look well upon him, niece; look you how his sword is
bloodied, and his helm more hacked than Hector's, and
how he looks, and how he goes! O admirable youth!
he ne'er saw three and twenty. Go thy way, Troilus,
go thy way! Had I a sister were a grace, or a daughter
a goddess, he should take his choice. O admirable man!
Paris? Paris is dirt to him; and, I warrant, Helen, to
change, would give an eye to boot.   240

Common Soldiers pass

Cressida. Here come more.

Pandarus. Asses, fools, dolts! chaff and bran, chaff and
bran! porridge after meat! I could live and die i' th'
eyes of Troilus. Ne'er look, ne'er look; the eagles are
gone: crows and daws, crows and daws! I had rather
be such a man as Troilus than Agamemnon and all
Greece.

Cressida. There is among the Greeks Achilles, a
better man than Troilus.

250 *Pandarus.* Achilles! a drayman, a porter, a very camel.

Cressida. Well, well.

Pandarus. Well, well! Why, have you any discretion? have you any eyes? do you know what a man is? Is not birth, beauty, good shape, discourse, manhood, learning, gentleness, virtue, youth, liberality, and such like, the spice and salt that season a man?

Cressida. Ay, a minced man; and then to be baked with no date in the pie, for then the man's date is out.

Pandarus. You are such another woman, a man
260 knows not at what ward you lie.

Cressida. Upon my back, to defend my belly; upon my wit, to defend my wiles; upon my secrecy, to defend mine honesty; my mask, to defend my beauty; and you, to defend all these: and at all these wards I lie, at a thousand watches.

Pandarus. Say one of your watches.

Cressida. Nay, I'll watch you for that; and that's one of the chiefest of them too: if I cannot ward what I would not have hit, I can watch you for telling how
270 I took the blow; unless it swell past hiding, and then it's past watching.

Pandarus. You are such another!

Enter Troilus' Boy

Boy. Sir, my lord would instantly speak with you.

Pandarus. Where?

Boy. At your own house; there he unarms him.

Pandarus. Good boy, tell him I come. [*Boy goes*] I doubt he be hurt. Fare ye well, good niece.

Cressida. Adieu, uncle.

Pandarus. I'll be with you, niece, by and by.
280 *Cressida.* To bring, uncle?

Pandarus. Ay, a token from Troilus.

Cressida. By the same token, you are a bawd.

                               [Pandarus goes

Words, vows, gifts, tears, and love's full sacrifice,
He offers in another's enterprise;
But more in Troilus thousandfold I see
Than in the glass of Pandar's praise may be.
Yet hold I off: women are angels, wooing;
Things won are done—joy's soul lies in the doing.
That she beloved knows nought that knows not this:
Men prize the thing ungained more than it is.   290
That she was never yet that ever knew
Love got so sweet as when desire did sue.
Therefore this maxim out of love I teach:
'Achievement is command; ungained, beseech.'
Then though my heart's content firm love doth bear,
Nothing of that shall from mine eyes appear. *[they go*

[1. 3.]   *The Greek camp. Before Agamemnon's tent*

  Sennet. Enter AGAMEMNON, NESTOR, ULYSSES,
             MENELAUS, *with others*

Agamemnon. Princes,
What grief hath set this jaundice on your cheeks?
The ample proposition that hope makes
In all designs begun on earth below
Fails in the promised largeness: checks
    and disasters
Grow in the veins of actions highest reared,
As knots, by the conflux of meeting sap,
Infect the sound pine and divert his grain
Tortive and errant from his course of growth
Nor, princes, is it matter new to us   10

    T. & C. – 5

That we come short of our suppose so far
That after seven years' siege yet Troy walls stand;
Sith every action that hath gone before
Whereof we have record, trial did draw
Bias and thwart, not answering the aim
And that unbodied figure of the thought
That gave't surmiséd shape. Why then, you princes,
Do you with cheeks abashed behold our works,
And call them shames, which are indeed nought else
20 But the protractive trials of great Jove
To find persistive constancy in men?
The fineness of which metal is not found
In fortune's love: for then the bold and coward,
The wise and fool, the artist and unread,
The hard and soft, seem all affined and kin;
But, in the wind and tempest of her frown,
Distinction with a broad and powerful fan,
Puffing at all, winnows the light away,
And what hath mass or matter, by itself
30 Lies rich in virtue and unmingléd.
   Nestor. With due observance of thy godlike seat,
Great Agamemnon, Nestor shall apply
Thy latest words. In the reproof of chance
Lies the true proof of men: the sea being smooth,
How many shallow bauble boats dare sail
Upon her patient breast, making their way
With those of nobler bulk!
But let the ruffian Boreas once enrage
The gentle Thetis, and anon behold
40 The strong-ribbed bark through liquid mountains cut,
Bounding between the two moist elements
Like Perseus' horse; where's then the saucy boat
Whose weak untimbered sides but even now
Co-rivalled greatness?—either to harbour fled,

Or made a toast for Neptune. Even so
Doth valour's show and valour's worth divide
In storms of fortune: for in her ray and brightness
The herd hath more annoyance by the breese
Than by the tiger; but when the splitting wind
Makes flexible the knees of knotted oaks 50
And flies flee under shade, why then the thing of courage,
As roused with rage, with rage doth sympathize,
And with an accent tuned in selfsame key
Retorts to chiding fortune.
  Ulysses.   Agamemnon,
Thou great commander, nerve and bone of Greece,
Heart of our numbers, soul and only spirit,
In whom the tempers and the minds of all
Should be shut up, hear what Ulysses speaks.
Besides th'applause and approbation
The which, [*to Agamemnon*] most mighty for thy place
    and sway, 60
[*to Nestor*] And thou most reverend for thy stretched-
    out life,
I give to both your speeches, which were such
As, Agamemnon, all the hands of Greece
Should hold up high in brass, and such again
As, venerable Nestor, hatched in silver,
Should with a bond of air, strong as the axletree
On which heaven rides, knit all the Greekish ears
To his experienced tongue—yet let it please both,
Thou great, and wise, to hear Ulysses speak.
  Agamemnon. Speak, Prince of Ithaca; and be't of
    less expect
                  70
That matter needless, of importless burden,
Divide thy lips than we are confident,
When rank Thersites opes his mastic jaws,
We shall hear music, wit and oracle.

Ulysses. Troy, yet upon his basis, had been down,
And the great Hector's sword had lacked a master,
But for these instances:
The specialty of rule hath been neglected;
And look how many Grecian tents do stand
80 Hollow upon this plain, so many hollow factions.
When that the general is not like the hive
To whom the foragers shall all repair,
What honey is expected? Degree being vizarded,
Th'unworthiest shows as fairly in the mask.
The heavens themselves, the planets, and this centre,
Observe degree, priority, and place,
Insisture, course, proportion, season, form,
Office, and custom, in all line of order;
And therefore is the glorious planet Sol
90 In noble eminence enthroned and sphered
Amidst the other; whose medicinable eye
Corrects the influence of evil planets,
And posts, like the commandment of a king,
Sans check to good and bad. But when the planets
In evil mixture to disorder wander,
What plagues and what portents, what mutiny,
What raging of the sea, shaking of earth,
Commotion in the winds, frights, changes, horrors,
Divert and crack, rend and deracinate
100 The unity and married calm of states
Quite from their fixure! O, when degree is shaked,
Which is the ladder of all high designs,
The enterprise is sick! How could communities,
Degrees in schools, and brotherhoods in cities,
Peaceful commerce from dividable shores,
The primogenitive and due of birth,
Prerogative of age, crowns, sceptres, laurels,
But by degree, stand in authentic place?

Take but degree away, untune that string,
And hark what discord follows! each thing meets   110
In mere oppugnancy: the bounded waters
Should lift their bosoms higher than the shores,
And make a sop of all this solid globe;
Strength should be lord of imbecility,
And the rude son should strike his father dead;
Force should be right; or rather, right and wrong,
Between whose endless jar justice resides,
Should lose their names, and so should justice too.
Then everything includes itself in power,
Power into will, will into appetite;   120
And appetite, an universal wolf,
So doubly seconded with will and power,
Must make perforce an universal prey,
And last eat up himself. Great Agamemnon,
This chaos, when degree is suffocate,
Follows the choking.
And this neglection of degree it is
That by a pace goes backward, with a purpose
It hath to climb. The general's disdained
By him one step below, he by the next,   130
That next by him beneath; so every step,
Exampled by the first pace that is sick
Of his superior, grows to an envious fever
Of pale and bloodless emulation—
And 'tis this fever that keeps Troy on foot,
Not her own sinews: to end a tale of length,
Troy in our weakness stands, not in her strength.

Nestor. Most wisely hath Ulysses here discovered
The fever whereof all our power is sick.

Agamemnon. The nature of the sickness found, Ulysses,   140
What is the remedy?

Ulysses. The great Achilles, whom opinion crowns

The sinew and the forehand of our host,
Having his ear full of his airy fame,
Grows dainty of his worth, and in his tent
Lies mocking our designs. With him, Patroclus,
Upon a lazy bed, the livelong day
Breaks scurril jests,
And with ridiculous and awkward action,
150 Which, slanderer, he imitation calls,
He pageants us. Sometime, great Agamemnon,
Thy topless deputation he puts on,
And, like a strutting player whose conceit
Lies in his hamstring, and doth think it rich
To hear the wooden dialogue and sound
'Twixt his stretched footing and the scaffoldage,
Such to-be-pitied and o'er-wrested seeming
He acts thy greatness in; and, when he speaks,
'Tis like a chime a-mending; with terms unsquared,
160 Which, from the tongue of roaring Typhon dropped,
Would seem hyperboles. At this fusty stuff,
The large Achilles, on his pressed bed lolling,
From his deep chest laughs out a loud applause,
Cries 'Excellent! 'tis Agamemnon right!
Now play me Nestor: hem, and stroke thy beard,
As he being dressed to some oration.'
That's done—as near as the extremest ends
Of parallels, as like as Vulcan and his wife.
Yet god Achilles still cries 'Excellent!
170 'Tis Nestor right! Now play him me, Patroclus,
Arming to answer in a night alarm.'
And then, forsooth, the faint defects of age
Must be the scene of mirth: to cough and spit,
And, with a palsy fumbling on his gorget,
Shake in and out the rivet. And at this sport
Sir Valour dies; cries 'O, enough, Patroclus,

Or give me ribs of steel! I shall split all
In pleasure of my spleen!' And in this fashion,
All our abilities, gifts, natures, shapes,
Severals and generals of grace exact,   180
Achievements, plots, orders, preventions,
Excitements to the field or speech for truce,
Success or loss, what is or is not, serves
As stuff for these two to make paradoxes.
  Nestor. And in the imitation of these twain,
Who, as Ulysses says, opinion crowns
With an imperial voice, many are infect.
Ajax is grown self-willed and bears his head
In such a rein, in full as proud a place
As broad Achilles; keeps his tent like him;   190
Makes factious feasts; rails on our state of war
Bold as an oracle; and sets Thersites,
A slave whose gall coins slanders like a mint,
To match us in comparisons with dirt,
To weaken and discredit our exposure,
How rank soever rounded in with danger.
  Ulysses. They tax our policy and call it cowardice,
Count wisdom as no member of the war,
Forestall prescience, and esteem no act
But that of hand; the still and mental parts   200
That do contrive how many hands shall strike
When fitness calls them on, and know by measure
Of their observant toil the enemy's weight—
Why, this hath not a finger's dignity:
They call this bed-work, mappery, closet-war;
So that the ram that batters down the wall,
For the great swing and rudeness of his poise,
They place before his hand that made the engine
Or those that with the fineness of their souls
By reason guide his execution.   210

Nestor. Let this be granted, and Achilles' horse
Makes many Thetis' sons.   [*tucket*
Agamemnon. What trumpet? look, Menelaus.
Menelaus. From Troy.

Enter ÆNEAS

Agamemnon. What would you 'fore our tent?
Æneas. Is this great Agamemnon's tent, I pray you?
Agamemnon. Even this.
Æneas. May one that is a herald and a prince
Do a fair message to his kingly eyes?
220 *Agamemnon.* With surety stronger than Achilles' arms
'Fore all the Greekish heads, which with one voice
Call Agamemnon head and general.
Æneas. Fair leave and large security. How may
A stranger to those most imperial looks
Know them from eyes of other mortals?
Agamemnon.   How?
Æneas. Ay:
I ask, that I might waken reverence,
And bid the cheek be ready with a blush
Modest as morning when she coldly eyes
230 The youthful Phoebus.
Which is that god in office, guiding men?
Which is the high and mighty Agamemnon?
Agamemnon. This Trojan scorns us, or the men
of Troy
Are ceremonious courtiers.
Æneas. Courtiers as free, as debonair, unarmed,
As bending angels: that's their fame in peace.
But when they would seem soldiers, they have galls,
Good arms, strong joints, true swords, and—
Jove's accord—
Nothing so full of heart. But peace, Æneas,

Peace, Trojan; lay thy finger on thy lips! 240
The worthiness of praise distains his worth,
If that the praised himself bring the praise forth:
But what the repining enemy commends,
That breath fame blows; that praise, sole
    pure, transcends.
  Agamemnon. Sir you of Troy, call you
    yourself Æneas?
  Æneas. Ay, Greek, that is my name.
  Agamemnon. What's your affair, I pray you?
  Æneas. Sir, pardon: 'tis for Agamemnon's ears.
  Agamemnon. He hears nought privately that comes
    from Troy.
  Æneas. Nor I from Troy come not to whisper him; 250
I bring a trumpet to awake his ear,
To set his sense on the attentive bent,
And then to speak.
  Agamemnon.   Speak frankly as the wind;
It is not Agamemnon's sleeping hour.
That thou shalt know, Trojan, he is awake,
He tells thee so himself.
  Æneas.   Trumpet, blow loud,
Send thy brass voice through all these lazy tents;
And every Greek of mettle, let him know,
What Troy means fairly shall be spoke aloud.
                            [*trumpet sounds*
We have, great Agamemnon, here in Troy 260
A prince called Hector—Priam is his father—
Who in this dull and long-continued truce
Is resty grown. He bade me take a trumpet,
And to this purpose speak: kings, princes, lords!
If there be one among the fair'st of Greece,
That holds his honour higher than his ease,
That seeks his praise more than he fears his peril,

That knows his valour and knows not his fear,
That loves his mistress more than in confession
270 With truant vows to her own lips he loves,
And dare avow her beauty and her worth
In other arms than hers—to him this challenge!
Hector, in view of Trojans and of Greeks,
Shall make it good, or do his best to do it,
He hath a lady, wiser, fairer, truer,
Than ever Greek did couple in his arms;
And will tomorrow with his trumpet call
Midway between your tents and walls of Troy,
To rouse a Grecian that is true in love.
280 If any come, Hector shall honour him;
If none, he'll say in Troy when he retires,
The Grecian dames are sunburnt and not worth
The splinter of a lance. Even so much.
    Agamemnon. This shall be told our lovers, Lord Æneas.
If none of them have soul in such a kind,
We left them all at home. But we are soldiers;
And may that soldier a mere recreant prove,
That means not, hath not, or is not in love!
If then one is, or hath, or means to be,
290 That one meets Hector; if none else, I am he.
    Nestor. Tell him of Nestor, one that was a man
When Hector's grandsire sucked. He is old now;
But if there be not in our Grecian host
One noble man that hath one spark of fire,
To answer for his love, tell him from me
I'll hide my silver beard in a gold beaver
And in my vantbrace put this withered brawn,
And, meeting him, will tell him that my lady
Was fairer than his grandam and as chaste
300 As may be in the world: his youth in flood,
I'll prove this truth with my three drops of blood.

Æneas. Now heavens forfend such scarcity of youth!

Ulysses. Amen.

Agamemnon. Fair Lord Æneas, let me touch
    your hand;
To our pavilion shall I lead you first.
Achilles shall have word of this intent;
So shall each lord of Greece, from tent to tent.
Yourself shall feast with us before you go,
And find the welcome of a noble foe.

                  [they go; Ulysses detains Nestor

Ulysses. Nestor!   310

Nestor. What says Ulysses?

Ulysses. I have a young conception in my brain;
Be you my time to bring it to some shape.

Nestor. What is't?

Ulysses. This 'tis:
Blunt wedges rive hard knots; the seeded pride
That hath to this maturity blown up
In rank Achilles must or now be cropped,
Or, shedding, breed a nursery of like evil
To overbulk us all.

Nestor.   Well, and how?   320

Ulysses. This challenge that the gallant Hector sends,
However it is spread in general name,
Relates in purpose only to Achilles.

Nestor. True: the purpose is perspicuous
    as substance,
Whose grossness little characters sum up;
And, in the publication, make no strain
But that Achilles, were his brain as barren
As banks of Libya—though, Apollo knows,
'Tis dry enough—will, with great speed of judgement,
Ay, with celerity, find Hector's purpose   330
Pointing on him.

Ulysses. And wake him to the answer, think you?
Nestor. Why, 'tis most meet. Who may you
    else oppose
That can from Hector bring his honour off,
If not Achilles? Though't be a sportful combat,
Yet in this trial much opinion dwells:
For here the Trojans taste our dear'st repute
With their fin'st palate—and trust to me, Ulysses,
Our imputation shall be oddly poised
340 In this wild action; for the success,
Although particular, shall give a scantling
Of good or bad unto the general;
And in such indexes, although small pricks
To their subsequent volumes, there is seen
The baby figure of the giant mass
Of things to come at large. It is supposed
He that meets Hector issues from our choice;
And choice, being mutual act of all our souls,
Makes merit her election, and doth boil,
350 As 'twere from forth us all, a man distilled
Out of our virtues; who miscarrying,
What heart receives from hence a conquering part,
To steel a strong opinion to themselves?
Which entertained, limbs are his instruments,
E'en no less working than are swords and bows
Directive by the limbs.
    Ulysses. Give pardon to my speech: therefore 'tis meet
Achilles meet not Hector. Let us, like merchants,
First show foul wares, and think perchance they'll sell.
360 If not, the lustre of the better shall exceed
By showing the worse first. Do not consent
That ever Hector and Achilles meet;
For both our honour and our shame in this
Are dogged with two strange followers.

Nestor. I see them not with my old eyes: what
  are they?
Ulysses. What glory our Achilles shares
  from Hector,
Were he not proud, we all should share with him.
But he already is too insolent;
And we were better parch in Afric sun
Than in the pride and salt scorn of his eyes,   370
Should he scape Hector fair: if he were foiled,
Why, then we did our main opinion crush
In taint of our best man. No, make a lottery,
And by device let blockish Ajax draw
The sort to fight with Hector; 'mong ourselves
Give him allowance as the better man;
For that will physic the great Myrmidon,
Who broils in loud applause, and make him fall
His crest that prouder than blue Iris bends.
If the dull brainless Ajax come safe off,   380
We'll dress him up in voices; if he fail,
Yet go we under our opinion still
That we have better men. But, hit or miss,
Our project's life this shape of sense assumes—
Ajax employed plucks down Achilles' plumes.
 Nestor. Ulysses,
Now I begin to relish thy advice,
And I will give a taste thereof forthwith
To Agamemnon. Go we to him straight.
Two curs shall tame each other: pride alone   390
Must tarre the mastiffs on, as 'twere their bone.
             [they go

[2. 1.]   *The Greek camp*

Enter AJAX *and* THERSITES

Ajax. Thersites!

Thersites. Agamemnon—how if he had boils, full, all over, generally?

Ajax. Thersites!

Thersites. And those boils did run? Say so: did not the general run then? were not that a botchy core?

Ajax. Dog!

Thersites. Then would come some matter from him; I see none now.

10 *Ajax.* Thou bitch-wolf's son, canst thou not hear? Feel, then.   [*strikes him*

Thersites. The plague of Greece upon thee, thou mongrel beef-witted lord!

Ajax. Speak then, thou vinewed'st leaven, speak! I will beat thee into handsomeness!

Thersites. I shall sooner rail thee into wit and holiness; but I think thy horse will sooner con an oration than thou learn a prayer without book. Thou canst strike, canst thou? A red murrain o' thy jade's tricks!

20 *Ajax.* Toadstool, learn me the proclamation.

Thersites. Dost thou think I have no sense, thou strikest me thus?

Ajax. The proclamation!

Thersites. Thou art proclaimed a fool, I think.

Ajax. Do not, porpentine, do not; my fingers itch.

Thersites. I would thou didst itch from head to foot and I had the scratching of thee; I would make thee the loathsomest scab in Greece. When thou art forth in the incursions, thou strikest as slow as another.

30 *Ajax.* I say, the proclamation!

Thersites. Thou grumblest and railest every hour on Achilles, and thou art as full of envy at his greatness as Cerberus is at Proserpina's beauty, ay, that thou barkest at him.

Ajax. Mistress Thersites!

Thersites. Thou shouldst strike him.

Ajax. Cobloaf!

Thersites. He would pun thee into shivers with his fist, as a sailor breaks a biscuit.

Ajax. You whoreson cur!   [*strikes him* 40

Thersites. Do, do, thou stool for a witch! ay, do, do, thou sodden-witted lord! Thou hast no more brain in thy head than I have in mine elbows; an assinego may tutor thee. Thou scurvy-valiant ass! thou art here but to thrash Trojans; and thou art bought and sold among those of any wit, like a barbarian slave. If thou use to beat me, I will begin at thy heel and tell what thou art by inches, thou thing of no bowels, thou!

Ajax. You dog!

Thersites. You scurvy lord!   50

Ajax. You cur!   [*strikes him*

Thersites. Mars his idiot! do, rudeness; do, camel, do, do.

Enter ACHILLES *and* PATROCLUS

Achilles. Why, how now, Ajax! Wherefore do you thus? How now, Thersites! What's the matter, man?

Thersites. You see him there, do you?

Achilles. Ay; what's the matter?

Thersites. Nay, look upon him.

Achilles. So I do; what's the matter?

Thersites. Nay, but regard him well.   60

Achilles. 'Well!'—why, so I do.

Thersites. But yet you look not well upon him: for whosoever you take him to be, he is Ajax.

Achilles. I know that, fool.

Thersites. Ay, but that fool knows not himself.

Ajax. Therefore I beat thee.

Thersites. Lo, lo, lo, lo, what modicums of wit he utters! His evasions have ears thus long. I have bobbed his brain more than he has beat my bones. I will buy 70 nine sparrows for a penny, and his pia mater is not worth the ninth part of a sparrow. This lord, Achilles— Ajax, who wears his wit in his belly and his guts in his head—I'll tell you what I say of him.

Achilles. What?

Thersites. I say this Ajax— [*Ajax offers to strike him*

Achilles. Nay, good Ajax.

Thersites. Has not so much wit—

Achilles. Nay, I must hold you.

Thersites. As will stop the eye of Helen's needle, for 80 whom he comes to fight.

Achilles. Peace, fool!

Thersites. I would have peace and quietness, but the fool will not—he there; that he; look you there!

Ajax. O thou damned cur! I shall—

Achilles. Will you set your wit to a fool's?

Thersites. No, I warrant you; for the fool's will shame it.

Patroclus. Good words, Thersites.

Achilles. What's the quarrel?

90 *Ajax.* I bade the vile owl go learn me the tenour of the proclamation, and he rails upon me.

Thersites. I serve thee not.

Ajax. Well, go to, go to.

Thersites. I serve here voluntary.

Achilles. Your last service was sufferance, 'twas not voluntary. No man is beaten voluntary. Ajax was here the voluntary, and you as under an impress.

Thersites. E'en so; a great deal of your wit too lies in your sinews, or else there be liars. Hector shall have a great catch an 'a knock out either of your brains: 'a were 100 as good crack a fusty nut with no kernel.

Achilles. What, with me too, Thersites?

Thersites. There's Ulysses and old Nestor, whose wit was mouldy ere your grandsires had nails on their toes, yoke you like draught-oxen, and make you plough up the wars.

Achilles. What? what?

Thersites. Yes, good sooth: to, Achilles! to, Ajax, to!

Ajax. I shall cut out your tongue.

Thersites. 'Tis no matter; I shall speak as much wit 110 as thou afterwards.

Patroclus. No more words, Thersites; peace!

Thersites. I will hold my peace when Achilles' brach bids me, shall I?

Achilles. There's for you, Patroclus.

Thersites. I will see you hanged, like clotpolls, ere I come any more to your tents. I will keep where there is wit stirring, and leave the faction of fools.   [*goes*

Patroclus. A good riddance.

Achilles. Marry, this, sir, is proclaimed through all 120
    our host:
That Hector, by the fifth hour of the sun,
Will with a trumpet 'twixt our tents and Troy
Tomorrow morning call some knight to arms
That hath a stomach, and such a one that dare
Maintain—I know not what; 'tis trash. Farewell.

Ajax. Farewell. Who shall answer him?

Achilles. I know not. 'Tis put to lottery; otherwise
He knew his man.

Ajax. O, meaning you. I'll go learn more of it.
                                        [*they go*

[2. 2.]   *Troy. Priam's palace*

Enter PRIAM, HECTOR, TROILUS, PARIS,
and HELENUS

Priam. After so many hours, lives, speeches spent,
Thus once again says Nestor from the Greeks:
'Deliver Helen, and all damage else—
As honour, loss of time, travail, expense,
Wounds, friends, and what else dear that
        is consumed
In hot digestion of this cormorant war—
Shall be struck off.' Hector, what say you to't?
  Hector. Though no man lesser fears the Greeks
        than I
As far as toucheth my particular,
10 Yet, dread Priam,
There is no lady of more softer bowels,
More spongy to suck in the sense of fear,
More ready to cry out 'Who knows what follows?'
Than Hector is. The wound of peace is surety,
Surety secure; but modest doubt is called
The beacon of the wise, the tent that searches
To th'bottom of the worst. Let Helen go.
Since the first sword was drawn about this question,
Every tithe-soul 'mongst many thousand dismes
20 Hath been as dear as Helen—I mean, of ours.
If we have lost so many tenths of ours
To guard a thing not ours, nor worth to us—
Had it our name—the value of one ten,
What merit's in that reason which denies
The yielding of her up?
  Troilus.   Fie, fie, my brother!
Weigh you the worth and honour of a king
So great as our dread father in a scale

Of common ounces? Will you with counters sum
The past-proportion of his infinite,
And buckle in a waist most fathomless   30
With spans and inches so diminutive
As fears and reasons? Fie, for godly shame!
  Helenus. No marvel though you bite so sharp
      at reasons,
You are so empty of them. Should not our father
Bear the great sway of his affairs with reasons,
Because your speech hath none that tells him so?
  Troilus. You are for dreams and slumbers,
      brother priest.
You fur your gloves with reasons. Here are
      your reasons:
You know an enemy intends you harm;
You know a sword employed is perilous,   40
And reason flies the object of all harm;
Who marvels then, when Helenus beholds
A Grecian and his sword, if he do set
The very wings of reason to his heels
And fly, like chidden Mercury from Jove
Or like a star disorbed? Nay, if we talk of reason,
Let's shut our gates and sleep. Manhood
      and honour
Should have hare hearts, would they but fat
      their thoughts
With this crammed reason; reason and respect
Make livers pale and lustihood deject.   50
  Hector. Brother, she is not worth what she doth cost
The keeping.
  Troilus.   What's aught, but as 'tis valued?
  Hector. But value dwells not in particular will:
It holds his estimate and dignity
As well wherein 'tis precious of itself

As in the prizer. 'Tis mad idolatry
To make the service greater than the god;
And the will dotes that is attributive
To what infectiously itself affects,
60 Without some image of th'affected merit.
   Troilus. I take today a wife, and my election
Is led on in the conduct of my will;
My will enkindled by mine eyes and ears—
Two traded pilots 'twixt the dangerous shores
Of will and judgement—how may I avoid,
Although my will distaste what it elected,
The wife I chose? There can be no evasion
To blench from this and to stand firm by honour.
We turn not back the silks upon the merchant
70 When we have soiled them; nor the remainder viands
We do not throw in unrespective sieve
Because we now are full. It was thought meet
Paris should do some vengeance on the Greeks;
Your breath of full consent bellied his sails;
The seas and winds, old wranglers, took a truce,
And did him service; he touched the ports desired;
And for an old aunt whom the Greeks held captive
He brought a Grecian queen, whose youth
    and freshness
Wrinkles Apollo's and makes pale the morning.
80 Why keep we her?—the Grecians keep our aunt;
Is she worth keeping?—why, she is a pearl
Whose price hath launched above a thousand ships
And turned crowned kings to merchants.
If you'll avouch 'twas wisdom Paris went—
As you must needs, for you all cried 'Go, go';
If you'll confess he brought home worthy prize—
As you must needs, for you all clapped your hands
And cried 'Inestimable!'; why do you now

The issue of your proper wisdoms rate,
And do a deed that Fortune never did,   90
Beggar the estimation which you prized
Richer than sea and land? O, theft most base,
That we have stolen what we do fear to keep!
But thieves unworthy of a thing so stolen,
That in their country did them that disgrace
We fear to warrant in our native place!

Cassandra [*within*]. Cry, Trojans, cry!
Priam.   What noise, what shriek is this?
Troilus. 'Tis our mad sister, I do know her voice.
Cassandra [*within*]. Cry, Trojans!
Hector. It is Cassandra.   100

Enter CASSANDRA, *raving, with her hair
about her ears*

Cassandra. Cry, Trojans, cry! lend me ten
        thousand eyes,
And I will fill them with prophetic tears.
Hector. Peace, sister, peace!
Cassandra. Virgins and boys, mid-age and
        wrinkled eld,
Soft infancy, that nothing canst but cry,
Add to my clamours! Let us pay betimes
A moiety of that mass of moan to come.
Cry, Trojans, cry! Practise your eyes with tears!
Troy must not be, nor goodly Ilion stand;
Our firebrand brother, Paris, burns us all.   110
Cry, Trojans, cry! a Helen and a woe:
Cry, cry! Troy burns, or else let Helen go.   [*goes*
    Hector. Now youthful Troilus, do not these
        high strains
Of divination in our sister work
Some touches of remorse, or is your blood

So madly hot that no discourse of reason,
Nor fear of bad success in a bad cause,
Can qualify the same?
   Troilus.   Why, brother Hector,
We may not think the justness of each act
120 Such and no other than event doth form it,
Nor once deject the courage of our minds
Because Cassandra's mad. Her brainsick raptures
Cannot distaste the goodness of a quarrel
Which hath our several honours all engaged
To make it gracious. For my private part,
I am no more touched than all Priam's sons;
And Jove forbid there should be done amongst us
Such things as might offend the weakest spleen
To fight for and maintain!
130   *Paris.* Else might the world convince of levity
As well my undertakings as your counsels;
But I attest the gods, your full consent
Gave wings to my propension and cut off
All fears attending on so dire a project.
For what, alas, can these my single arms?
What propugnation is in one man's valour
To stand the push and enmity of those
This quarrel would excite? Yet, I protest,
Were I alone to pass the difficulties
140 And had as ample power as I have will,
Paris should ne'er retract what he hath done,
Nor faint in the pursuit.
   Priam.   Paris, you speak
Like one besotted on your sweet delights;
You have the honey still, but these the gall:
So to be valiant is no praise at all.
   Paris. Sir, I propose not merely to myself
The pleasures such a beauty brings with it,

But I would have the soil of her fair rape
Wiped off in honourable keeping her.
What treason were it to the ransacked queen,   150
Disgrace to your great worths, and shame to me.
Now to deliver her possession up
On terms of base compulsion! Can it be
That so degenerate a strain as this
Should once set footing in your generous bosoms?
There's not the meanest spirit on our party
Without a heart to dare or sword to draw
When Helen is defended; nor none so noble
Whose life were ill bestowed or death unfamed
Where Helen is the subject. Then, I say,   160
Well may we fight for her whom we know well
The world's large spaces cannot parallel.
  Hector. Paris and Troilus, you have both said well,
And on the cause and question now in hand
Have glozed—but superficially; not much
Unlike young men, whom Aristotle thought
Unfit to hear moral philosophy.
The reasons you allege do more conduce
To the hot passion of distempered blood
Than to make up a free determination   170
'Twixt right and wrong: for pleasure and revenge
Have ears more deaf than adders to the voice
Of any true decision. Nature craves
All dues be rendered to their owners: now,
What nearer debt in all humanity
Than wife is to the husband? If this law
Of nature be corrupted through affection,
And that great minds, of partial indulgence
To their benumbéd wills, resist the same,
There is a law in each well-ordered nation   180
To curb those raging appetites that are

Most disobedient and refractory.
If Helen then be wife to Sparta's king,
As it is known she is, these moral laws
Of nature and of nations speak aloud
To have her back returned. Thus to persist
In doing wrong extenuates not wrong,
But makes it much more heavy. Hector's opinion
Is this in way of truth. Yet, ne'ertheless,

190 My sprightly brethren, I propend to you
In resolution to keep Helen still;
For 'tis a cause that hath no mean dependence
Upon our joint and several dignities.

   Troilus. Why, there you touched the life of
      our design:
Were it not glory that we more affected
Than the performance of our heaving spleens,
I would not wish a drop of Trojan blood
Spent more in her defence. But, worthy Hector,
She is a theme of honour and renown,

200 A spur to valiant and magnanimous deeds,
Whose present courage may beat down our foes,
And fame in time to come canonize us;
For I presume brave Hector would not lose
So rich advantage of a promised glory
As smiles upon the forehead of this action
For the wide world's revenue.

   Hector.   I am yours,
You valiant offspring of great Priamus.
I have a roisting challenge sent amongst
The dull and factious nobles of the Greeks

210 Will strike amazement to their drowsy spirits.
I was advertised their great general slept,
Whilst emulation in the army crept:
This, I presume, will wake him.   *[they go*

[2. 3.]   *The Greek camp.   Before the tent
of Achilles*

Enter THERSITES, *solus*

Thersites. How now, Thersites! What, lost in the
labyrinth of thy fury! Shall the elephant Ajax carry it
thus? He beats me, and I rail at him. O worthy
satisfaction! Would it were otherwise: that I could
beat him, whilst he railed at me. 'Sfoot, I'll learn to
conjure and raise devils but I'll see some issue of my
spiteful execrations. Then there's Achilles—a rare
enginer. If Troy be not taken till these two undermine
it, the walls will stand till they fall of themselves.
O thou great thunder-darter of Olympus, forget that   10
thou art Jove, the king of gods, and, Mercury, lose all
the serpentine craft of thy caduceus, if ye take not that
little little less than little wit from them that they have!
which short-armed ignorance itself knows is so abun-
dant scarce, it will not in circumvention deliver a fly
from a spider without drawing their massy irons and
cutting the web. After this, the vengeance on the whole
camp! or, rather, the Neapolitan bone-ache! for that,
methinks, is the curse dependent on those that war for
a placket. I have said my prayers; and devil Envy say   20
'Amen'. What ho! my Lord Achilles!

Patroclus [*within*]. Who's there? Thersites? Good
Thersites, come in and rail.

Thersites. If I could a' remembered a gilt counterfeit,
thou wouldst not have slipped out of my contempla-
tion; but it is no matter—thyself upon thyself! The
common curse of mankind, folly and ignorance, be
thine in great revenue! Heaven bless thee from a tutor,
and discipline come not near thee! Let thy blood be

30 thy direction till thy death! Then if she that lays thee
out says thou art a fair corpse, I'll be sworn and sworn
upon't she never shrouded any but lazars. Amen.

Enter PATROCLUS

Where's Achilles?
   Patroclus. What, art thou devout? Wast thou in
prayer?
   Thersites. Ay; the heavens hear me!
   Patroclus. Amen.
   Achilles [*within*]. Who's there?
   Patroclus. Thersites, my lord.

Enter ACHILLES

40 *Achilles.* Where, where? O where? Art thou come?
Why, my cheese, my digestion, why hast thou not
served thyself in to my table so many meals? Come,
what's Agamemnon?
   Thersites. Thy commander, Achilles; then tell me,
Patroclus, what's Achilles?
   Patroclus. Thy lord, Thersites; then tell me, I pray
thee, what's thyself?
   Thersites. Thy knower, Patroclus; then tell me,
Patroclus, what art thou?
50 *Patroclus.* Thou mayst tell that knowest.
   Achilles. O tell, tell.
   Thersites. I'll decline the whole question. Aga-
memnon commands Achilles; Achilles is my lord; I am
Patroclus' knower, and Patroclus is a fool.
   Patroclus. You rascal!
   Thersites. Peace, fool! I have not done.
   Achilles. He is a privileged man. Proceed, Thersites.
   Thersites. Agamemnon is a fool; Achilles is a fool;
Thersites is a fool, and, as aforesaid, Patroclus is a fool.

Achilles. Derive this; come.   60

Thersites. Agamemnon is a fool to offer to command
Achilles; Achilles is a fool to be commanded of
Agamemnon; Thersites is a fool to serve such a fool;
and Patroclus is a fool positive.

Patroclus. Why am I a fool?

Thersites. Make that demand of the Creator. It
suffices me thou art. Look you, who comes here?

Achilles. Patroclus, I'll speak with nobody. Come in
with me, Thersites.   [*enters his tent*

Thersites. Here is such patchery, such juggling and 70
such knavery! All the argument is a whore and a
cuckold—a good quarrel to draw emulous factions and
bleed to death upon. Now, the dry serpigo on the
subject, and war and lechery confound all!

                                   [*enters the tent*

Enter AGAMEMNON, ULYSSES, NESTOR, DIOMEDES, *and* AJAX

Agamemnon. Where is Achilles?

Patroclus. Within his tent; but ill-disposed, my lord.

Agamemnon. Let it be known to him that we are here.
We sent our messengers, and we lay by
Our appertainments, visiting of him.
Let him be told so, lest perchance he think   80
We dare not move the question of our place,
Or know not what we are.

Patroclus.   I shall say so to him.   [*goes in*

Ulysses. We saw him at the opening of his tent:
He is not sick.

Ajax. Yes, lion-sick, sick of proud heart. You may
call it melancholy, if you will favour the man; but, by
my head, 'tis pride. But why, why? Let him show us
the cause. A word, my lord. [*takes Agamemnon aside*

Nestor. What moves Ajax thus to bay at him?

90   *Ulysses.* Achilles hath inveigled his fool from him.

Nestor. Who, Thersites?

Ulysses. He.

Nestor. Then will Ajax lack matter, if he have lost his argument.

Ulysses. No, you see, he is his argument that has his argument—Achilles.

Nestor. All the better: their fraction is more our wish than their faction. But it was a strong composure a fool could disunite!

100   *Ulysses.* The amity that wisdom knits not, folly may easily untie.

Re-enter PATROCLUS

Here comes Patroclus.

Nestor. No Achilles with him.

Ulysses. The elephant hath joints, but none for courtesy: his legs are legs for necessity, not for flexure.

Patroclus. Achilles bids me say he is much sorry
If anything more than your sport and pleasure
Did move your greatness and this noble state
To call upon him; he hopes it is no other
110 But for your health and your digestion's sake,
An after-dinner's breath.

Agamemnon.   Hear you, Patroclus:
We are too well acquainted with these answers;
But his evasion, winged thus swift with scorn,
Cannot outfly our apprehensions.
Much attribute he hath, and much the reason
Why we ascribe it to him; yet all his virtues,
Not virtuously on his own part beheld,
Do in our eyes begin to lose their gloss,
Yea, like fair fruit in an unwholesome dish,
120 Are like to rot untasted. Go and tell him

We come to speak with him; and you shall not sin
If you do say we think him over-proud
And under-honest, in self-assumption greater
Than in the note of judgement; and worthier
    than himself
Here tend the savage strangeness he puts on,
Disguise the holy strength of their command,
And underwrite in an observing kind
His humorous predominance; yea, watch
His pettish lunes, his ebbs and flows, as if
The passage and whole carriage of this action   130
Rode on his tide. Go tell him this, and add
That if he overhold his price so much
We'll none of him but let him, like an engine
Not portable, lie under this report:
'Bring action hither; this cannot go to war:
A stirring dwarf we do allowance give
Before a sleeping giant.' Tell him so.
   Patroclus. I shall; and bring his answer presently.
                                 [enters the tent
   Agamemnon. In second voice we'll not be satisfied;
We come to speak with him. Ulysses, enter you.   140
                                 [Ulysses follows
   Ajax. What is he more than another?
   Agamemnon. No more than what he thinks he is.
   Ajax. Is he so much? Do you not think he thinks
himself a better man than I am?
   Agamemnon. No question.
   Ajax. Will you subscribe his thought and say he is?
   Agamemnon. No, noble Ajax; you are as strong, as
valiant, as wise, no less noble, much more gentle, and
altogether more tractable.
   Ajax. Why should a man be proud? How doth pride   150
grow? I know not what pride is.

Agamemnon. Your mind is the clearer, Ajax, and your virtues the fairer. He that is proud eats up himself: pride is his own glass, his own trumpet, his own chronicle; and whatever praises itself but in the deed, devours the deed in the praise.

Ajax. I do hate a proud man as I do hate the engendering of toads.

(*Nestor.* And yet he loves himself: is it not strange?

Re-enter ULYSSES

160   *Ulysses.* Achilles will not to the field tomorrow.

   Agamemnon. What's his excuse?

   Ulysses.   He doth rely on none,
But carries on the stream of his dispose
Without observance or respect of any,
In will peculiar and in self-admission.

   Agamemnon. Why will he not, upon our fair request,
Untent his person and share th'air with us?

   Ulysses. Things small as nothing, for request's
      sake only,
He makes important; possessed he is with greatness,
And speaks not to himself but with a pride
170 That quarrels at self-breath: imagined worth
Holds in his blood such swollen and hot discourse
That 'twixt his mental and his active parts
Kingdomed Achilles in commotion rages
And batters down himself. What should I say?
He is so plaguey proud that the death-tokens of it
Cry 'No recovery'.

   Agamemnon.   Let Ajax go to him.
Dear lord, go you and greet him in his tent.
'Tis said he holds you well, and will be led,
At your request, a little from himself.

180   *Ulysses.* O Agamemnon, let it not be so!

We'll consecrate the steps that Ajax makes
When they go from Achilles. Shall the proud lord
That bastes his arrogance with his own seam
And never suffers matter of the world
Enter his thoughts, save such as doth revolve
And ruminate himself, shall he be worshipped
Of that we hold an idol more than he?
No, this thrice-worthy and right valiant lord
Must not so stale his palm, nobly acquired,
Nor, by my will, assubjugate his merit—   190
As amply titled as Achilles is—
By going to Achilles:
That were to enlard his fat-already pride,
And add more coals to Cancer when he burns
With entertaining great Hyperion.
This lord go to him! Jupiter forbid,
And say in thunder 'Achilles go to him'.
  (*Nestor.* O, this is well; he rubs the vein of him.
  (*Diomedes.* And how his silence drinks up
    this applause!
  Ajax. If I go to him, with my arméd fist   200
I'll pash him o'er the face.
  Agamemnon. O, no, you shall not go.
  Ajax. An 'a be proud with me, I'll feeze his pride:
Let me go to him.
  Ulysses. Not for the worth that hangs upon
    our quarrel.
  Ajax. A paltry, insolent fellow!
  (*Nestor.* How he describes himself!
  Ajax. Can he not be sociable?
  (*Ulysses.* The raven chides blackness.
  Ajax. I'll let his humour's blood.   210
  (*Agamemnon.* He will be the physician that should be
the patient.

Ajax. An all men were o' my mind—

(*Ulysses.* Wit would be out of fashion.

Ajax. 'A should not bear it so; 'a should eat swords
first. Shall pride carry it?

(*Nestor.* An 'twould, you'ld carry half.

(*Ulysses.* 'A would have ten shares.

Ajax. I'll knead him, I'll make him supple.

220 (*Nestor.* He's not yet through warm. Force him with
praises: pour in, pour in; his ambition is dry.

    Ulysses [*to Agamemnon*]. My lord, you feed too much
      on this dislike.

Nestor. Our noble general, do not do so.

Diomedes. You must prepare to fight
      without Achilles.

    Ulysses. Why, 'tis this naming of him does him harm.
Here is a man—but 'tis before his face:
I will be silent.

    Nestor.   Wherefore should you so?
He is not emulous, as Achilles is.

Ulysses. Know the whole world, he is as valiant.

230 *Ajax.* A whoreson dog, that shall palter thus
      with us!
Would he were a Trojan!

Nestor. What a vice were it in Ajax now—

Ulysses. If he were proud—

Diomedes. Or covetous of praise—

Ulysses. Ay, or surly borne—

Diomedes. Or strange, or self-affected!

Ulysses. Thank the heavens, lord, thou art of
      sweet composure;
Praise him that got thee, she that gave thee suck;
Famed be thy tutor, and thy parts of nature

240 Thrice-famed beyond, beyond all erudition:
But he that disciplined thine arms to fight,

Let Mars divide eternity in twain,
And give him half; and, for thy vigour,
Bull-bearing Milo his addition yield
To sinewy Ajax. I will not praise thy wisdom,
Which, like a bourn, a pale, a shore, confines
Thy spacious and dilated parts. Here's Nestor,
Instructed by the antiquary times;
He must, he is, he cannot but be wise:
But pardon, father Nestor, were your days   250
As green as Ajax', and your brain so tempered,
You should not have the eminence of him,
But be as Ajax.
  Ajax.   Shall I call you father?
  Nestor. Ay, my good son.
  Diomedes.   Be ruled by him, Lord Ajax.
  Ulysses. There is no tarrying here: the
          hart Achilles
Keeps thicket. Please it our great general
To call together all his state of war:
Fresh kings are come to Troy; tomorrow
We must with all our main of power stand fast;
And here's a lord, come knights from east to west,   260
And cull their flower, Ajax shall cope the best.
  Agamemnon. Go we to council. Let Achilles sleep:
Light boats sail swift, though greater hulks draw deep.
                                        [*they go*

[3. 1.]   *Troy. Priam's palace*

          Enter PANDARUS *and a Servant*

  Pandarus. Friend, you, pray you, a word: do you not
follow the young Lord Paris?
  Servant. Ay sir, when he goes before me.

Pandarus. You depend upon him, I mean?

Servant. Sir, I do depend upon the Lord.

Pandarus. You depend upon a noble gentleman; I must needs praise him.

Servant. The Lord be praised!

Pandarus. You know me, do you not?

10   *Servant.* Faith, sir, superficially.

Pandarus. Friend, know me better: I am the Lord Pandarus.

Servant. I hope I shall know your honour better.

Pandarus. I do desire it.

Servant. You are in the state of grace.

Pandarus. Grace! not so, friend: honour and lordship are my titles. [*music within*] What music is this?

Servant. I do but partly know, sir: it is music in parts.

20   *Pandarus.* Know you the musicians?

Servant. Wholly, sir.

Pandarus. Who play they to?

Servant. To the hearers, sir.

Pandarus. At whose pleasure, friend?

Servant. At mine, sir, and theirs that love music.

Pandarus. Command, I mean, friend.

Servant. Who shall I command, sir?

Pandarus. Friend, we understand not one another: I am too courtly, and thou art too cunning. At whose

30   request do these men play?

Servant. That's to't, indeed, sir: marry, sir, at the request of Paris my lord, who is there in person; with him, the mortal Venus, the heart-blood of beauty, love's indivisible soul.

Pandarus. Who, my cousin Cressida?

Servant. No, sir, Helen. Could you not find out that by her attributes?

Pandarus. It should seem, fellow, that thou hast not seen the Lady Cressida. I come to speak with Paris from the Prince Troilus; I will make a complimental 40 assault upon him, for my business seethes.

(*Servant.* Sodden business! There's a stewed phrase indeed!

Enter PARIS and HELEN, attended

Pandarus. Fair be to you, my lord, and to all this fair company! Fair desires, in all fair measure, fairly guide them! Especially to you, fair queen, fair thoughts be your fair pillow!

Helen. Dear lord, you are full of fair words.

Pandarus. You speak your fair pleasure, sweet queen. Fair prince, here is good broken music. 50

Paris. You have broke it, cousin; and, by my life, you shall make it whole again: you shall piece it out with a piece of your performance. Nell, he is full of harmony.

Pandarus. Truly, lady, no.

Helen. O, sir—

Pandarus. Rude, in sooth; in good sooth, very rude.

Paris. Well said, my lord! well, you say so in fits.

Pandarus. I have business to my lord, dear queen. My lord, will you vouchsafe me a word? 60

Helen. Nay, this shall not hedge us out; we'll hear you sing, certainly.

Pandarus. Well, sweet queen, you are pleasant with me.—But, marry, thus, my lord: my dear lord, and most esteemed friend, your brother Troilus—

Helen. My Lord Pandarus; honey-sweet lord—

Pandarus. Go to, sweet queen, go to—commends himself most affectionately to you—

Helen. You shall not bob us out of our melody. If you do, our melancholy upon your head! 70

Pandarus. Sweet queen, sweet queen; that's a sweet queen, i'faith.

Helen. And to make a sweet lady sad is a sour offence.

Pandarus. Nay, that shall not serve your turn; that shall it not, in truth, la. Nay, I care not for such words; no, no.—And, my lord, he desires you, that if the king call for him at supper you will make his excuse.

Helen. My Lord Pandarus—

Pandarus. What says my sweet queen, my very very
80 sweet queen?

Paris. What exploit's in hand? where sups he tonight?

Helen. Nay, but, my lord—

Pandarus. What says my sweet queen?—My cousin will fall out with you. You must not know where he sups.

Paris. I'll lay my life, with my disposer Cressida.

Pandarus. No, no, no such matter; you are wide: come, your disposer is sick.

90 *Paris.* Well, I'll make's excuse.

Pandarus. Ay, good my lord. Why should you say Cressida? no, your poor disposer's sick.

Paris. I spy.

Pandarus. You spy! What do you spy? Come, give me an instrument. Now, sweet queen.

Helen. Why, this is kindly done.

Pandarus. My niece is horribly in love with a thing you have, sweet queen.

Helen. She shall have it, my lord, if it be not my
100 lord Paris.

Pandarus. He! no, she'll none of him; they two are twain.

Helen. Falling in, after falling out, may make them three.

Pandarus. Come, come, I'll hear no more of this.
I'll sing you a song now.

Helen. Ay, ay, prithee now. By my troth, sweet lord,
thou hast a fine forehead.

Pandarus. Ay, you may, you may.

Helen. Let thy song be love; this love will undo us all. 110
O Cupid, Cupid, Cupid!

Pandarus. Love! ay, that it shall, i'faith.

Paris. Ay, good now, love, love, nothing but love.

Pandarus. In good troth, it begins so.   [*sings*

Love, love, nothing but love, still love, still more!
     For, O, love's bow
     Shoots buck and doe;
     The shaft confounds
     Not that it wounds,
But tickles still the sore.   120
These lovers cry Oh, oh, they die!
     Yet that which seems the wound to kill,
Doth turn oh! oh! to ha! ha! he!
     So dying love lives still.
Oh! oh! a while, but ha! ha! ha!
Oh! oh! groans out for ha! ha! ha!

Heigh-ho!

Helen. In love, i'faith, to the very tip of the nose.

Paris. He eats nothing but doves, love, and that
breeds hot blood, and hot blood begets hot thoughts, 130
and hot thoughts beget hot deeds, and hot deeds is love.

Pandarus. Is this the generation of love?—hot blood,
hot thoughts, and hot deeds? Why, they are vipers. Is
love a generation of vipers? Sweet lord, who's afield
today?

Paris. Hector, Deiphobus, Helenus, Antenor, and
all the gallantry of Troy. I would fain have armed

today, but my Nell would not have it so. How chance
my brother Troilus went not?

140   *Helen.* He hangs the lip at something; you know all,
Lord Pandarus.

    Pandarus. Not I, honey-sweet queen. I long to hear
how they sped today.—You'll remember your brother's
excuse?

    Paris. To a hair.

    Pandarus. Farewell, sweet queen.

    Helen. Commend me to your niece.

    Pandarus. I will, sweet queen.   *[goes*
                                [retreat sounded

    Paris. They're come from th'field: let us to
        Priam's hall,

150 To greet the warriors. Sweet Helen, I must woo you
To help unarm our Hector. His stubborn buckles,
With these your white enchanting fingers touched,
Shall more obey than to the edge of steel
Or force of Greekish sinews. You shall do more
Than all the island kings—disarm great Hector.

    Helen. 'Twill make us proud to be his
        servant, Paris;
Yea, what he shall receive of us in duty
Gives us more palm in beauty than we have,
Yea, overshines ourself.

160   *Paris.* Sweet, above thought I love thee.   *[they go*

    [3. 2.]   *The same. Pandarus' orchard*

      Enter PANDARUS *and Troilus' Boy, meeting*

    Pandarus. How now! Where's thy master? At my
cousin Cressida's?

Boy. No, sir; he stays for you to conduct him thither.
Pandarus. O, here he comes.

Enter TROILUS

How now, how now!
  Troilus. Sirrah, walk off.   [*Boy goes*
  Pandarus. Have you seen my cousin?
  Troilus. No, Pandarus; I stalk about her door,
Like a strange soul upon the Stygian banks
Staying for waftage. O, be thou my Charon,   10
And give me swift transportance to those fields
Where I may wallow in the lily beds
Proposed for the deserver! O gentle Pandar,
From Cupid's shoulder pluck his painted wings,
And fly with me to Cressid!
  Pandarus. Walk here i'th'orchard; I'll bring her
straight.   [*goes*
  Troilus. I am giddy: expectation whirls me round.
Th'imaginary relish is so sweet
That it enchants my sense. What will it be   20
When that the watery palate tastes indeed
Love's thrice repuréd nectar?—death, I fear me,
Swooning distraction, or some joy too fine,
Too subtle-potent, tuned too sharp in sweetness,
For the capacity of my ruder powers;
I fear it much, and I do fear besides
That I shall lose distinction in my joys,
As doth a battle, when they charge on heaps
The enemy flying.

Re-enter PANDARUS

  Pandarus. She's making her ready; she'll come 30
straight. You must be witty now: she does so blush,
and fetches her wind so short as if she were frayed with

a sprite. I'll fetch her. It is the prettiest villain; she
fetches her breath as short as a new-ta'en sparrow.

[*goes*

Troilus. Even such a passion doth embrace my bosom:
My heart beats thicker than a feverous pulse;
And all my powers do their bestowing lose,
Like vassalage at unawares encountering
The eye of majesty.

Re-enter PANDARUS *and* CRESSIDA

40 *Pandarus.* Come, come, what need you blush?
Shame's a baby. Here she is now. Swear the oaths
now to her that you have sworn to me. What, are you
gone again? You must be watched ere you be made tame,
must you? Come your ways, come your ways; an you
draw backward, we'll put you i'th' fills. Why do you not
speak to her? Come, draw this curtain, and let's see
your picture. Alas the day, how loath you are to offend
daylight! An 'twere dark, you'ld close sooner. So, so;
rub on, and kiss the mistress. How now! a kiss in fee-
50 farm!—build there, carpenter; the air is sweet. Nay,
you shall fight your hearts out ere I part you—the falcon
as the tercel, for all the ducks i'th'river. Go to, go to.
Troilus. You have bereft me of all words, lady.
Pandarus. Words pay no debts, give her deeds; but
she'll bereave you o'th'deeds too, if she call your
activity in question. What, billing again? Here's 'In
witness whereof the parties interchangeably'—Come in,
come in; I'll go get a fire.   [*goes*
Cressida. Will you walk in, my lord?
60 *Troilus.* O Cressida, how often have I wished me
thus!
Cressida. Wished, my lord?—The gods grant—O,
my lord!

Troilus. What should they grant? What makes this pretty abruption? What too curious dreg espies my sweet lady in the fountain of our love?

Cressida. More dregs than water, if my fears have eyes.

Troilus. Fears make devils of cherubins; they never see truly.

Cressida. Blind fear, that seeing reason leads, finds 70 safer footing than blind reason stumbling without fear: to fear the worst oft cures the worse.

Troilus. O, let my lady apprehend no fear: in all Cupid's pageant there is presented no monster.

Cressida. Nor nothing monstrous neither?

Troilus. Nothing but our undertakings, when we vow to weep seas, live in fire, eat rocks, tame tigers; thinking it harder for our mistress to devise imposition enough than for us to undergo any difficulty imposed. This is the monstruosity in love, lady—that the will is infinite 80 and the execution confined; that the desire is boundless and the act a slave to limit.

Cressida. They say all lovers swear more performance than they are able, and yet reserve an ability that they never perform; vowing more than the perfection of ten, and discharging less than the tenth part of one. They that have the voice of lions and the act of hares, are they not monsters?

Troilus. Are there such? Such are not we. Praise us as we are tasted, allow us as we prove. Our head shall 90 go bare till merit crown it: no perfection in reversion shall have a praise in present. We will not name desert before his birth; and, being born, his addition shall be humble. Few words to fair faith: Troilus shall be such to Cressid as what envy can say worst shall be a mock for his truth; and what truth can speak truest, not truer than Troilus.

Cressida. Will you walk in, my lord?

Re-enter PANDARUS

Pandarus. What, blushing still? Have you not done
100 talking yet?

Cressida. Well, uncle, what folly I commit, I dedicate
to you.

Pandarus. I thank you for that: if my lord get a boy
of you, you'll give him me. Be true to my lord; if he
flinch, chide me for it.

Troilus. You know now your hostages: your uncle's
word and my firm faith.

Pandarus. Nay, I'll give my word for her too. Our
kindred, though they be long ere they are wooed, they
110 are constant being won. They are burs, I can tell you;
they'll stick where they are thrown.

Cressida. Boldness comes to me now and brings
    me heart:
Prince Troilus, I have loved you night and day
For many weary months.

Troilus. Why was my Cressid then so hard to win?

Cressida. Hard to seem won; but I was won,
    my lord,
With the first glance that ever—pardon me;
If I confess much, you will play the tyrant.
I love you now; but not, till now, so much
120 But I might master it. In faith, I lie!
My thoughts were like unbridled children, grown
Too headstrong for their mother. See, we fools!
Why have I blabbed? Who shall be true to us,
When we are so unsecret to ourselves?
But, though I loved you well, I wooed you not;
And yet, good faith, I wished myself a man,
Or that we women had men's privilege

Of speaking first. Sweet, bid me hold my tongue;
For in this rapture I shall surely speak
The thing I shall repent. See, see, your silence,   130
Cunning in dumbness, from my weakness draws
My very soul of counsel! Stop my mouth.
  Troilus. And shall, albeit sweet music issues thence.
                                        [*kisses her*
  Pandarus. Pretty, i'faith.
  Cressida. My lord, I do beseech you, pardon me:
'Twas not my purpose thus to beg a kiss.
I am ashamed. O heavens! what have I done?
For this time will I take my leave, my lord.
  Troilus. Your leave, sweet Cressid?
  Pandarus. Leave! An you take leave till tomorrow 140
morning—
  Cressida. Pray you, content you.
  Troilus. What offends you, lady?
  Cressida. Sir, mine own company.
  Troilus. You cannot shun yourself.
  Cressida. Let me go and try.
I have a kind of self resides with you,
But an unkind self that itself will leave
To be another's fool. I would be gone.
Where is my wit? I know not what I speak.   150
  Troilus. Well know they what they speak that speak
      so wisely.
  Cressida. Perchance, my lord, I show more craft
      than love,
And fell so roundly to a large confession
To angle for your thoughts; but you are wise,
Or else you love not: for to be wise and love
Exceeds man's might; that dwells with gods above.
  Troilus. O that I thought it could be in a woman—
As, if it can, I will presume in you—

To feed for aye her lamp and flame of love;
160 To keep her constancy in plight and youth,
Outliving beauties outward, with a mind
That doth renew swifter than blood decays!
Or that persuasion could but thus convince me
That my integrity and truth to you
Might be affronted with the match and weight
Of such a winnowed purity in love—
How were I then uplifted! But, alas,
I am as true as truth's simplicity,
And simpler than the infancy of truth!

170 *Cressida.* In that I'll war with you.
    Troilus.   O virtuous fight,
When right with right wars who shall be most right!
True swains in love shall in the world to come
Approve their truths by Troilus. When their rhymes,
Full of protest, of oath, and big compare,
Want similes, truth tired with iteration—
'As true as steel, as plantage to the moon,
As sun to day, as turtle to her mate,
As iron to adamant, as earth to th'centre'—
Yet, after all comparisons of truth,
180 As truth's authentic author to be cited,
'As true as Troilus' shall crown up the verse
And sanctify the numbers.
    Cressida.   Prophet may you be!
If I be false, or swerve a hair from truth,
When time is old and hath forgot itself,
When waterdrops have worn the stones of Troy,
And blind oblivion swallowed cities up,
And mighty states characterless are grated
To dusty nothing, yet let memory,
From false to false, among false maids in love,
190 Upbraid my falsehood! When they've said 'as false

As air, as water, wind or sandy earth,
As fox to lamb, or wolf to heifer's calf,
Pard to the hind, or stepdame to her son',
Yea let them say, to stick the heart of falsehood,
'As false as Cressid'.

Pandarus. Go to, a bargain made. Seal it, seal it.
I'll be the witness. Here I hold your hand; here my
cousin's. If ever you prove false one to another, since
I have taken such pains to bring you together, let all
pitiful goers-between be called to the world's end after 200
my name—call them all Pandars: let all constant men
be Troiluses, all false women Cressids, and all brokers-
between Pandars! Say 'amen'.

Troilus. Amen.

Cressida. Amen.

Pandarus. Amen. Whereupon I will show you a
chamber with a bed; which bed, because it shall not
speak of your pretty encounters, press it to death. Away!
                                                    [*they go*

And Cupid grant all tongue-tied maidens here
Bed, chamber, pandar, to provide this gear!   [*goes* 210

[3. 3.]   *The Greek camp*

Flourish. Enter AGAMEMNON, ULYSSES, DIOMEDES,
    NESTOR, AJAX, MENELAUS, *and* CALCHAS

Calchas. Now, princes, for the service I have done,
Th'advantage of the time prompts me aloud
To call for recompense. Appear it to your minds
That, through the sight I bear in things to come,
I have abandoned Troy, left my possession,
Incurred a traitor's name, exposed myself,

From certain and possessed conveniences,
To doubtful fortunes; sequestering from me all
That time, acquaintance, custom and condition
10 Made tame and most familiar to my nature;
And here, to do you service, am become
As new into the world, strange, unacquainted.
I do beseech you, as in way of taste,
To give me now a little benefit
Out of those many registered in promise,
Which, you say, live to come in my behalf.
 Agamemnon. What wouldst thou of us, Trojan?
  Make demand.
 Calchas. You have a Trojan prisoner
  called Antenor,
Yesterday took; Troy holds him very dear.
20 Oft have you—often have you thanks therefore—
Desired my Cressid in right great exchange,
Whom Troy hath still denied; but this Antenor
I know is such a wrest in their affairs.
That their negotiations all must slack,
Wanting his manage; and they will almost
Give us a prince of blood, a son of Priam,
In change of him. Let him be sent, great princes,
And he shall buy my daughter; and her presence
Shall quite strike off all service I have done
30 In most accepted pain.
 Agamemnon.   Let Diomed bear him,
And bring us Cressid hither; Calchas shall have
What he requests of us. Good Diomed,
Furnish you fairly for this interchange;
Withal, bring word if Hector will tomorrow
Be answered in his challenge: Ajax is ready.
 Diomedes. This shall I undertake, and 'tis a burden
Which I am proud to bear. [*Diomedes and Calchas go*

Enter ACHILLES *and* PATROCLUS, *before their tent*

Ulysses. Achilles stands i'th'entrance of his tent:
Please it our general pass strangely by him,
As if he were forgot; and, princes all,   40
Lay negligent and loose regard upon him.
I will come last. 'Tis like he'll question me
Why such unplausive eyes are bent on him.
If so, I have derision medicinable
To use between your strangeness and his pride,
Which his own will shall have desire to drink.
It may do good: pride hath no other glass
To show itself but pride; for supple knees
Feed arrogance and are the proud man's fees.
Agamemnon. We'll execute your purpose and put on 50
A form of strangeness as we pass along;
So do each lord, and either greet him not
Or else disdainfully, which shall shake him more
Than if not looked on. I will lead the way.
                                            [*they pass along*
Achilles. What, comes the general to speak with me?
You know my mind: I'll fight no more 'gainst Troy.
Agamemnon. What says Achilles? Would he aught
    with us?
Nestor. Would you, my lord, aught with the general?
Achilles. No.
Nestor. Nothing, my lord.   60
Agamemnon. The better. [*Agamemnon and Nestor go*
Achilles. Good day, good day.
Menelaus. How do you? how do you?   [*goes*
Achilles. What, does the cuckold scorn me?
Ajax. How now, Patroclus!
Achilles. Good morrow, Ajax.
Ajax. Ha?

Achilles. Good morrow.

Ajax. Ay, and good next day too.   [*goes*

70   *Achilles.* What mean these fellows? Know they
    not Achilles?

Patroclus. They pass by strangely. They were used
    to bend,

To send their smiles before them to Achilles,

To come as humbly as they use to creep

To holy altars.

   Achilles.   What, am I poor of late?

'Tis certain, greatness, once fallen out with fortune,

Must fall out with men too. What the declined is

He shall as soon read in the eyes of others

As feel in his own fall; for men, like butterflies,

Show not their mealy wings but to the summer,

80   And not a man, for being simply man,

Hath any honour but honour for those honours

That are without him—as place, riches, and favour,

Prizes of accident as oft as merit;

Which, when they fall, as being slippery standers,

The love that leaned on them as slippery too,

Doth one pluck down another and together

Die in the fall. But 'tis not so with me:

Fortune and I are friends; I do enjoy

At ample point all that I did possess,

90   Save these men's looks; who do, methinks, find out

Something not worth in me such rich beholding

As they have often given. Here is Ulysses;

I'll interrupt his reading.

How now, Ulysses!

   Ulysses.   Now, great Thetis' son!

   Achilles. What are you reading?

   Ulysses.   A strange fellow here

Writes me that man, how dearly ever parted,

How much in having, or without or in,
Cannot make boast to have that which he hath,
Nor feels not what he owes, but by reflection;
As when his virtues, shining upon others, 100
Heat them and they retort that heat again
To the first giver.
   Achilles.   This is not strange, Ulysses.
The beauty that is borne here in the face
The bearer knows not, but commends itself
To others' eyes; nor doth the eye itself,
That most pure spirit of sense, behold itself,
Not going from itself; but eye to eye opposed
Salutes each other with each other's form:
For speculation turns not to itself
Till it hath travelled and is mirrored there 110
Where it may see itself. This is not strange at all.
   Ulysses. I do not strain at the position—
It is familiar—but at the author's drift;
Who in his circumstance expressly proves
That no man is the lord of anything,
Though in and of him there be much consisting,
Till he communicate his parts to others;
Nor doth he of himself know them for aught
Till he behold them forméd in th'applause
Where they're extended; who, like an
     arch, reverberate 120
The voice again; or, like a gate of steel
Fronting the sun, receives and renders back
His figure and his heat. I was much rapt in this,
And apprehended here immediately
The unknown Ajax.
Heavens! what a man is there! a very horse,
That has he knows not what. Nature, what things
     there are

Most abject in regard and dear in use!
What things again most dear in the esteem
130 And poor in worth! Now shall we see tomorrow—
An act that very chance doth throw upon him—
Ajax renowned. O heavens, what some men do,
While some men leave to do!
How some men creep in skittish Fortune's hall,
Whiles others play the idiots in her eyes!
How one man eats into another's pride,
While pride is fasting in his wantonness!
To see these Grecian lords!—why, even already
They clap the lubber Ajax on the shoulder,
140 As if his foot were on brave Hector's breast
And great Troy shrinking.
  Achilles. I do believe it; for they passed by me
As misers do by beggars, neither gave to me
Good word nor look. What, are my deeds forgot?
  Ulysses. Time hath, my lord, a wallet at his back
Wherein he puts alms for oblivion,
A great-sized monster of ingratitude.
Those scraps are good deeds past, which are devoured
As fast as they are made, forgot as soon
150 As done. Perseverance, dear my lord,
Keeps honour bright: to have done, is to hang
Quite out of fashion, like a rusty mail
In monumental mockery. Take the instant way;
For honour travels in a strait so narrow
Where one but goes abreast. Keep then the path;
For emulation hath a thousand sons
That one by one pursue. If you give way,
Or hedge aside from the direct forthright,
Like to an entered tide they all rush by
160 And leave you hindmost;
Or, like a gallant horse fallen in first rank,

Lie there for pavement to the abject rear,
O'er-run and trampled on. Then what they do
    in present,
Though less than yours in past, must o'ertop yours;
For Time is like a fashionable host
That slightly shakes his parting guest by th'hand
And, with his arms outstretched as he would fly,
Grasps in the comer: welcome ever smiles,
And farewell goes out sighing. O, let not virtue seek
Remuneration for the thing it was;   170
For beauty, wit,
High birth, vigour of bone, desert in service,
Love, friendship, charity, are subject all
To envious and calumniating Time.
One touch of nature makes the whole world kin,
That all with one consent praise new-born gawds,
Though they are made and moulded of things past,
And give to dust that is a little gilt
More laud than gilt o'er-dusted.
The present eye praises the present object: 180
Then marvel not, thou great and complete man,
That all the Greeks begin to worship Ajax;
Since things in motion sooner catch the eye
Than what not stirs. The cry went once on thee,
And still it might, and yet it may again,
If thou wouldst not entomb thyself alive
And case thy reputation in thy tent,
Whose glorious deeds but in these fields of late
Made emulous missions 'mongst the gods themselves,
And drave great Mars to faction.
   Achilles.   Of this my privacy   190
I have strong reasons.
   Ulysses.   But 'gainst your privacy
The reasons are more potent and heroical.

'Tis known, Achilles, that you are in love
With one of Priam's daughters.
  Achilles.   Ha! known?
  Ulysses. Is that a wonder?
The providence that's in a watchful state
Knows almost every grain of Pluto's gold,
Finds bottom in th'uncomprehensive deeps,
Keeps place with thought and almost like the gods
200 Does thoughts unveil in their dumb cradles.
There is a mystery, with whom relation
Durst never meddle, in the soul of state,
Which hath an operation more divine
Than breath or pen can give expressure to.
All the commerce that you have had with Troy
As perfectly is ours as yours, my lord;
And better would it fit Achilles much
To throw down Hector than Polyxena.
But it must grieve young Pyrrhus now at home,
210 When fame shall in our islands sound her trump,
And all the Greekish girls shall tripping sing
'Great Hector's sister did Achilles win,
But our great Ajax bravely beat down him'.
Farewell, my lord. I as your lover speak:
The fool slides o'er the ice that you should break.
                                     [goes

  Patroclus. To this effect, Achilles, have I
      moved you.
A woman impudent and mannish grown
Is not more loathed than an effeminate man
In time of action. I stand condemned for this:
220 They think my little stomach to the war
And your great love to me restrains you thus.
Sweet, rouse yourself, and the weak wanton Cupid
Shall from your neck unloose his amorous fold

And, like a dew-drop from the lion's mane,
Be shook to air.

  Achilles.   Shall Ajax fight with Hector?

  Patroclus. Ay, and perhaps receive much honour
    by him.

  Achilles. I see my reputation is at stake;
My fame is shrewdly gored.

  Patroclus.   O, then, beware;
Those wounds heal ill that men do give themselves:
Omission to do what is necessary   230
Seals a commission to a blank of danger;
And danger, like an ague, subtly taints
Even then when we sit idly in the sun.

  Achilles. Go call Thersites hither, sweet Patroclus;
I'll send the fool to Ajax and desire him
T'invite the Trojan lords after the combat
To see us here unarmed. I have a woman's longing,
An appetite that I am sick withal,
To see great Hector in his weeds of peace,
To talk with him, and to behold his visage,   240
Even to my full of view.

Enter THERSITES

                A labour saved!

  Thersites. A wonder!

  Achilles. What?

  Thersites. Ajax goes up and down the field, asking
for himself.

  Achilles. How so?

  Thersites. He must fight singly tomorrow with Hector,
and is so prophetically proud of an heroical cudgelling
that he raves in saying nothing.

  Achilles. How can that be?   250

  Thersites. Why, 'a stalks up and down like a peacock—

a stride and a stand; ruminates like an hostess that hath
no arithmetic but her brain to set down her reckoning;
bites his lip with a politic regard, as who should say
'There were wit in this head, an 'twould out'—and so
there is; but it lies as coldly in him as fire in a flint,
which will not show without knocking. The man's
undone for ever, for if Hector break not his neck i'th'
combat, he'll break't himself in vainglory. He knows
260 not me. I said 'Good morrow, Ajax', and he replies
'Thanks, Agamemnon'. What think you of this man,
that takes me for the general? He's grown a very land-
fish, languageless, a monster. A plague of opinion!—
a man may wear it on both sides, like a leather jerkin.

    Achilles. Thou must be my ambassador to him,
Thersites.

    Thersites. Who, I? Why, he'll answer nobody. He
professes not answering. Speaking is for beggars; he
wears his tongue in's arms. I will put on his presence.
270 Let Patroclus make demands to me, you shall see the
pageant of Ajax.

    Achilles. To him, Patroclus. Tell him I humbly
desire the valiant Ajax to invite the most valorous
Hector to come unarmed to my tent, and to procure
safe-conduct for his person of the magnanimous and
most illustrious six-or-seven-times-honoured captain-
general of the Grecian army, Agamemnon, et cetera.
Do this.

    Patroclus. Jove bless great Ajax!

280   *Thersites.* Hum!

    Patroclus. I come from the worthy Achilles—

    Thersites. Ha!

    Patroclus. Who most humbly desires you to invite
Hector to his tent—

    Thersites. Hum!

Patroclus. And to procure safe-conduct from Agamemnon.

Thersites. Agamemnon?

Patroclus. Ay, my lord.

Thersites. Ha!   290

Patroclus. What say you to't?

Thersites. God bu'y you, with all my heart.

Patroclus. Your answer, sir.

Thersites. If tomorrow be a fair day, by eleven o'clock it will go one way or other. Howsoever, he shall pay for me ere he has me.

Patroclus. Your answer, sir.

Thersites. Fare you well, with all my heart.

Achilles. Why, but he is not in this tune, is he?

Thersites. No, but he's out o' tune thus. What music 300 will be in him when Hector has knocked out his brains, I know not; but, I am sure, none, unless the fiddler Apollo get his sinews to make catlings on.

Achilles. Come, thou shalt bear a letter to him straight.

Thersites. Let me carry another to his horse; for that's the more capable creature.

Achilles. My mind is troubled like a fountain stirred, And I myself see not the bottom of it.

                  [Achilles and Patroclus go in

Thersites. Would the fountain of your mind were 310 clear again, that I might water an ass at it! I had rather be a tick in a sheep than such a valiant ignorance.

                                [goes

[4. 1.]   *Troy. A street*

Enter, at one side, ÆNEAS, and Servant with a torch; at the other, PARIS, DEIPHOBUS, ANTENOR, DIOMEDES, and others, with torches

  Paris. See, ho! who is that there?
  Deiphobus. It is the Lord Æneas.
  Æneas. Is the prince there in person?
Had I so good occasion to lie long
As you, Prince Paris, nothing but heavenly business
Should rob my bed-mate of my company.
  Diomedes. That's my mind too. Good morrow,
      Lord Æneas.
  Paris. A valiant Greek, Æneas—take his hand—
Witness the process of your speech, wherein
10 You told how Diomed, a whole week by days,
Did haunt you in the field.
  Æneas. Health to you, valiant sir,
During all question of the gentle truce;
But when I meet you armed, as black defiance
As heart can think or courage execute.
  Diomedes. The one and other Diomed embraces
Our bloods are now in calm; and so long, health!
But when contention and occasion meet,
By Jove, I'll play the hunter for thy life
20 With all my force, pursuit, and policy.
  Æneas. And thou shalt hunt a lion, that will fly
With his face backward. In humane gentleness,
Welcome to Troy! now, by Anchises' life,
Welcome indeed! By Venus' hand I swear
No man alive can love in such a sort
The thing he means to kill more excellently.
  Diomedes. We sympathise. Jove, let Æneas live,

If to my sword his fate be not the glory,
A thousand complete courses of the sun!
But, in mine emulous honour, let him die   30
With every joint a wound, and that tomorrow.
  Æneas. We know each other well.
  Diomedes. We do; and long to know each other worse.
  Paris. This is the most despiteful-gentle greeting,
The noblest-hateful love, that e'er I heard of.
What business, lord, so early?
  Æneas. I was sent for to the king; but why,
    I know not.
  Paris. His purpose meets you: 'twas to bring this Greek
To Calchas' house, and there to render him,
For the enfreed Antenor, the fair Cressid.   40
Let's have your company, or, if you please,
Haste there before us. [*aside*] I constantly do think—
Or rather, call my thought a certain knowledge—
My brother Troilus lodges there tonight;
Rouse him and give him note of our approach,
With the whole quality wherefore; I fear
We shall be much unwelcome.
  (*Æneas.*   That I assure you,
Troilus had rather Troy were borne to Greece
Than Cressid borne from Troy.
  (*Paris.*   There is no help;
The bitter disposition of the time   50
Will have it so. [*aloud*] On, lord; we'll follow you.
  Æneas. Good morrow all.   [*goes, with Servant*
  Paris. And tell me, noble Diomed, faith, tell me true,
Even in the soul of sound good-fellowship,
Who, in your thoughts, merits fair Helen most,
Myself or Menelaus?
  Diomedes.   Both alike:
He merits well to have her that doth seek her,

Not making any scruple of her soilure,
With such a hell of pain and world of charge;
60 And you as well to keep her that defend her,
Not palating the taste of her dishonour,
With such a costly loss of wealth and friends.
He, like a puling cuckold, would drink up
The lees and dregs of a flat taméd piece;
You, like a lecher, out of whorish loins
Are pleased to breed out your inheritors.
Both merits poised, each weighs nor less nor more;
But he as he, the heavier for a whore.
    Paris. You are too bitter to your countrywoman.
70   *Diomedes.* She's bitter to her country. Hear me, Paris:
For every false drop in her bawdy veins
A Grecian's life hath sunk; for every scruple
Of her contaminated carrion weight
A Trojan hath been slain; since she could speak,
She hath not given so many good words breath
As for her Greeks and Trojans suffered death.
    Paris. Fair Diomed, you do as chapmen do,
Dispraise the thing that you desire to buy;
But we in silence hold this virtue well,
80 We'll but commend what we intend to sell.
Here lies our way.   [*they go*

[4. 2.] *The same. The court of Pandarus' house*

Enter *Troilus and Cressida*

    Troilus. Dear, trouble not yourself; the morn is cold.
    Cressida. Then, sweet my lord, I'll call mine
        uncle down;
He shall unbolt the gates.

Troilus.   Trouble him not;
To bed, to bed! sleep lull those pretty eyes,
And give as soft attachment to thy senses
As infants empty of all thought!
  Cressida.   Good morrow, then.
  Troilus. I prithee now, to bed!
  Cressida.   Are you aweary of me?
  Troilus. O Cressida! but that the busy day,
Waked by the lark, hath roused the ribald crows,
And dreaming night will hide our joys no longer,   10
I would not from thee.
  Cressida.   Night hath been too brief.
  Troilus. Beshrew the witch! with venomous wights
    she stays
As tediously as hell, but flies the grasps of love
With wings more momentary-swift than thought.
You will catch cold, and curse me.
  Cressida.   Prithee, tarry.
You men will never tarry.
O foolish Cressid! I might have still held off,
And then you would have tarried. Hark! there's
    one up.
  Pandarus [*within*]. What's all the doors open here?
  Troilus. It is your uncle.   20
  Cressida. A pestilence on him! now will he
    be mocking;
I shall have such a life!

Enter PANDARUS

  Pandarus. How now, how now! how go maiden-
heads? Here, you maid! where's my cousin Cressid?
  Cressida. Go hang yourself, you naughty
    mocking uncle!
You bring me to do—and then you flout me too.

Pandarus. To do what? to do what? let her say what!
What have I brought you to do?

    Cressida. Come, come, beshrew your heart! you'll
        ne'er be good,
30 Nor suffer others.

    Pandarus. Ha, ha! Alas, poor wretch! a poor
capocchia! Has't not slept tonight? Would he not,
a naughty man, let it sleep? A bugbear take him!

    Cressida. Did not I tell you? Would he were
        knocked i'th' head!   *[knocking*
Who's that at door? Good uncle, go and see.
My lord, come you again into my chamber.
You smile and mock me, as if I meant naughtily.

    Troilus. Ha, ha!

    Cressida. Come, you're deceived, I think of no
        such thing.   *[knocking*
40 How earnestly they knock! Pray you, come in;
I would not for half Troy have you seen here.

                [Troilus and Cressida go in

    Pandarus. Who's there? what's the matter? will you
beat down the door? How now! what's the matter?

Enter ÆNEAS

    Æneas. Good morrow, lord, good morrow.

    Pandarus. Who's there? my Lord Æneas! By my
troth, I knew you not. What news with you so early?

    Æneas. Is not prince Troilus here?

    Pandarus. Here! what should he do here?

    Æneas. Come, he is here, my lord. Do not
        deny him;
50 It doth import him much to speak with me.

    Pandarus. Is he here, say you? 'Tis more than I know,
I'll be sworn; for my own part, I came in late. What
should he do here?

Æneas. Ho! nay, then; come, come, you'll do him
wrong ere you're ware; you'll be so true to him, to be
false to him. Do not you know of him, but yet go fetch
him hither; go.

Re-enter TROILUS

Troilus. How now! what's the matter?

Æneas. My lord, I scarce have leisure to salute you,
My matter is so rash: there is at hand   60
Paris your brother and Deiphobus,
The Grecian Diomed, and our Antenor
Delivered to us; and for him forthwith,
Ere the first sacrifice, within this hour,
We must give up to Diomedes' hand
The Lady Cressida.

Troilus.   Is it so concluded?

Æneas. By Priam and the general state of Troy.
They are at hand and ready to effect it.

Troilus. How my achievements mock me!
I will go meet them; and, my Lord Æneas,   70
We met by chance: you did not find me here.

Æneas. Good, good, my lord; the secrets of
        neighbour Pandar
Have not more gift in taciturnity.

                              [*Troilus and Æneas go*

Pandarus. Is't possible? no sooner got but lost? The
devil take Antenor! The young prince will go mad.
A plague upon Antenor! I would they had broke's neck!

Re-enter CRESSIDA

Cressida. How now! what's the matter? who was
here?

Pandarus. Ah, ah!

Cressida. Why sigh you so profoundly? Where's my 80
lord? Gone? Tell me, sweet uncle, what's the matter?

Pandarus. Would I were as deep under the earth as
I am above!

Cressida. O the gods! What's the matter?

Pandarus. Prithee, get thee in. Would thou hadst
ne'er been born! I knew thou wouldst be his death.
O, poor gentleman! A plague upon Antenor!

Cressida. Good uncle, I beseech you, on my knees
I beseech you, what's the matter?

90 *Pandarus.* Thou must be gone, wench, thou must be
gone; thou art changed for Antenor; thou must to thy
father, and be gone from Troilus: 'twill be his death;
'twill be his bane; he cannot bear it.

Cressida. O you immortal gods! I will not go.

Pandarus. Thou must.

Cressida. I will not, uncle. I have forgot my father;
I know no touch of consanguinity;
No kin, no love, no blood, no soul so near me
As the sweet Troilus. O you gods divine!

100 Make Cressid's name the very crown of falsehood,
If ever she leave Troilus! Time, force, and death,
Do to this body what extremes you can;
But the strong base and building of my love
Is as the very centre of the earth,
Drawing all things to it. I'll go in and weep

Pandarus. Do, do.

Cressida. Tear my bright hair and scratch my
praiséd cheeks,
Crack my clear voice with sobs and break my heart
With sounding Troilus. I will not go from Troy.

[they go

[4. 3.]   *The same. A street before Pandarus' house*

Enter PARIS, TROILUS, *followed by* ÆNEAS,
DEIPHOBUS, ANTENOR, *and* DIOMEDES

Paris. It is great morning, and the hour prefixed
For her delivery to this valiant Greek
Comes fast upon us. Good my brother Troilus,
Tell you the lady what she is to do
And haste her to the purpose.
Troilus.   Walk into her house;
I'll bring her to the Grecian presently;
And to his hand when I deliver her,
Think it an altar, and thy brother Troilus
A priest, there offering to it his own heart.   [*goes*
Paris. I know what 'tis to love,   10
And would, as I shall pity, I could help!
Please you walk in, my lords.   [*they go*

[4. 4.]   *The same. Pandarus' house*

Enter PANDARUS *and* CRESSIDA

Pandarus. Be moderate, be moderate.
Cressida. Why tell you me of moderation?
The grief is fine, full, perfect, that I taste,
And violenteth in a sense as strong
As that which causeth it. How can I moderate it?
If I could temporise with my affection,
Or brew it to a weak and colder palate,
The like allayment could I give my grief.
My love admits no qualifying dross;
No more my grief, in such a precious loss.   10

Enter TROILUS

Pandarus. Here, here, here he comes. Ah sweet
ducks!

Cressida. O Troilus! Troilus!   [*embracing him*

Pandarus. What a pair of spectacles is here! Let me
embrace too. 'O heart', as the goodly saying is,

        O heart, O heavy heart,
        Why sigh'st thou without breaking?

where he answers again,

        Because thou canst not ease thy smart
20   By friendship nor by speaking.

There was never a truer rhyme. Let us cast away
nothing, for we may live to have need of such a verse.
We see it, we see it. How now, lambs!

Troilus. Cressid, I love thee in so strained a purity,
That the blest gods, as angry with my fancy,
More bright in zeal than the devotion which
Cold lips blow to their deities, take thee from me.

Cressida. Have the gods envy?

Pandarus. Ay, ay, ay, ay; 'tis too plain a case.

30 *Cressida.* And is it true that I must go from Troy?

Troilus. A hateful truth.

Cressida.   What, and from Troilus too?

Troilus. From Troy and Troilus.

Cressida.   Is it possible?

Troilus. And suddenly; where injury of chance
Puts back leave-taking, jostles roughly by
All time of pause, rudely beguiles our lips
Of all rejoindure, forcibly prevents
Our locked embraces, strangles our dear vows
Even in the birth of our own labouring breath.
We two, that with so many thousand sighs
40 Did buy each other, must poorly sell ourselves

With the rude brevity and discharge of one.
Injurious Time now with a robber's haste
Crams his rich thievery up, he knows not how:
As many farewells as be stars in heaven,
With distinct breath and consigned kisses to them,
He fumbles up into a loose adieu,
And scants us with a single famished kiss,
Distasted with the salt of broken tears.

Æneas [*within*]. My lord, is the lady ready?

Troilus. Hark! you are called. Some say the
    Genius so   50
Cries 'Come!' to him that instantly must die.
Bid them have patience; she shall come anon.

Pandarus. Where are my tears? Rain, to lay this wind,
or my heart will be blown up by th'root!   [*goes*

Cressida. I must then to the Grecians?

Troilus.   No remedy

Cressida. A woeful Cressid 'mongst the
    merry Greeks!
When shall we see again?

Troilus. Hear me, my love: be thou but true
    of heart—

Cressida. I true! how now! what wicked deem
    is this?

Troilus. Nay, we must use expostulation kindly,   60
For it is parting from us.
I speak not 'be thou true', as fearing thee,
For I will throw my glove to Death himself
That there's no maculation in thy heart;
But 'be thou true' say I, to fashion in
My sequent protestation: be thou true,
And I will see thee.

Cressida. O, you shall be exposed, my lord, to dangers
As infinite as imminent! But I'll be true.

70 *Troilus*. And I'll grow friend with danger. Wear
      this sleeve.
   Cressida. And you this glove. When shall I see you?
   Troilus. I will corrupt the Grecian sentinels,
To give thee nightly visitation.
But yet, be true.
   Cressida.   O heavens! 'Be true' again!
   Troilus. Hear why I speak it, love:
The Grecian youths are full of quality;
Their loving well composed with gifts of nature,
And flowing o'er with arts and exercise.
How novelties may move and parts with person—
80 Alas, a kind of godly jealousy,
Which, I beseech you, call a virtuous sin—
Makes me afeard.
   Cressida.   O heavens! you love me not.
   Troilus. Die I a villain then!
In this I do not call your faith in question
So mainly as my merit: I cannot sing,
Nor heel the high lavolt, nor sweeten talk,
Nor play at subtle games—fair virtues all,
To which the Grecians are most prompt
         and pregnant;
But I can tell that in each grace of these
90 There lurks a still and dumb-discoursive devil
That tempts most cunningly. But be not tempted.
   Cressida. Do you think I will?
   Troilus. No;
But something may be done that we will not,
And sometimes we are devils to ourselves,
When we will tempt the frailty of our powers,
Presuming on their changeful potency.
   Æneas [*within*]. Nay, good my lord!
   Troilus.   Come, kiss; and let us part.

Paris [*within*]. Brother Troilus!
Troilus.   Good brother, come
    you hither;
And bring Æneas and the Grecian with you.   100
    Cressida. My lord, will you be true?
    Troilus. Who, I? alas, it is my vice, my fault!
Whiles others fish with craft for great opinion,
I with great truth catch mere simplicity;
Whilst some with cunning gild their copper crowns,
With truth and plainness I do wear mine bare.
Fear not my truth: the moral of my wit
Is 'plain and true'; there's all the reach of it.

       Enter ÆNEAS, PARIS, ANTENOR, DEIPHOBUS,
                and DIOMEDES

Welcome, Sir Diomed! Here is the lady
Which for Antenor we deliver you.   110
At the port, lord, I'll give her to thy hand,
And by the way possess thee what she is.
Entreat her fair; and, by my soul, fair Greek,
If e'er thou stand at mercy of my sword,
Name Cressid, and thy life shall be as safe
As Priam is in Ilion.
    Diomedes.   Fair Lady Cressid,
So please you, save the thanks this prince expects.
The lustre in your eye, heaven in your cheek,
Pleads your fair usage; and to Diomed
You shall be mistress, and command him wholly.   120
    Troilus. Grecian, thou dost not use me courteously,
To shame the zeal of my petition to thee
In praising her. I tell thee, lord of Greece,
She is as far high-soaring o'er thy praises
As thou unworthy to be called her servant.
I charge thee use her well, even for my charge;

For, by the dreadful Pluto, if thou dost not,
Though the great bulk Achilles be thy guard,
I'll cut thy throat.
    Diomedes.   O, be not moved, Prince Troilus.
130 Let me be privileged by my place and message
To be a speaker free. When I am hence,
I'll answer to my lust; and know you, lord,
I'll nothing do on charge: to her own worth
She shall be prized; but that you say 'Be't so',
I'll speak it in my spirit and honour 'No!'
    Troilus. Come, to the port. I'll tell thee, Diomed,
This brave shall oft make thee to hide thy head.
Lady, give me your hand; and, as we walk,
To our own selves bend we our needful talk.

               [*Troilus, Cressida, and Diomedes go;*
                            trumpet sounds

140   *Paris.* Hark! Hector's trumpet.
    Æneas.   How have we spent
    this morning!
The prince must think me tardy and remiss,
That swore to ride before him to the field.
    Paris. 'Tis Troilus' fault; come, come, to field
    with him.
    Deiphobus. Let us make ready straight.
    Æneas. Yea, with a bridegroom's fresh alacrity,
Let us address to tend on Hector's heels.
The glory of our Troy doth this day lie
On his fair worth and single chivalry.   [*they go*

[4. 5.]   *The Greek camp. Lists set out*

Enter AJAX, armed; AGAMEMNON, ACHILLES, PATRO-
CLUS, MENELAUS, ULYSSES, NESTOR, and others

Agamemnon. Here art thou in appointment fresh
      and fair,
Anticipating time with starting courage.
Give with thy trumpet a loud note to Troy,
Thou dreadful Ajax, that the appalléd air
May pierce the head of the great combatant
And hale him hither.
  Ajax.   Thou trumpet, there's my purse.
Now crack thy lungs, and split thy brazen pipe;
Blow, villain, till thy spheréd bias cheek
Outswell the choller of puffed Aquilon.
Come, stretch thy chest, and let thy eyes spout blood; 10
Thou blow'st for Hector.   [*trumpet sounds*
  Ulysses. No trumpet answers.
  Achilles.   'Tis but early days.
  Agamemnon. Is not yon Diomed, with
      Calchas' daughter?
  Ulysses. 'Tis he, I ken the manner of his gait:
He rises on the toe; that spirit of his
In aspiration lifts him from the earth.

              Enter DIOMEDES, with CRESSIDA

  Agamemnon. Is this the Lady Cressid?
  Diomedes.   Even she.
  Agamemnon. Most dearly welcome to the Greeks,
      sweet lady.   [*kisses her*
  Nestor. Our general doth salute you with a kiss.
  Ulysses. Yet is the kindness but particular;   20
'Twere better she were kissed in general.

Nestor. And very courtly counsel. I'll begin.
So much for Nestor.   [*kisses her*

 Achilles. I'll take that winter from your lips,
  · fair lady.
Achilles bids you welcome.   [*kisses her*

 Menelaus. I had good argument for kissing once.

 Patroclus. But that's no argument for kissing now;
For thus popped Paris in his hardiment,
And parted thus you and your argument. [*kisses her*
30 (*Ulysses.* O deadly gall, and theme of all our scorns!
For which we lose our heads to gild his horns.

 Patroclus. The first was Menelaus' kiss; this, mine—
Patroclus kisses you.   [*kisses her again*

 Menelaus.   O, this is trim!

 Patroclus. Paris and I kiss evermore for him.

 Menelaus. I'll have my kiss, sir. Lady, by your leave.

 Cressida. In kissing, do you render or receive?

 Menelaus. Both take and give.

 Cressida.   I'll make my match
  to live,
The kiss you take is better than you give;
Therefore no kiss.

40 *Menelaus.* I'll give you boot, I'll give you three
  for one.

 Cressida. You're an odd man; give even, or
  give none.

 Menelaus. An odd man, lady! every man is odd.

 Cressida. No, Paris is not; for you know 'tis true
That you are odd, and he is even with you.

 · *Menelaus.* You fillip me o'th' head.

 Cressida.   No, I'll be sworn.

 Ulysses. It were no match, your nail against
  his horn.
May I, sweet lady, beg a kiss of you?

Cressida. You may.

Ulysses.   I do desire it.

Cressida.   Why, beg too.

Ulysses. Why then, for Venus' sake, give me a kiss

When Helen is a maid again, and his.   50

Cressida. I am your debtor; claim it when 'tis due.

Ulysses. Never's my day, and then a kiss of you.

Diomedes. Lady, a word; I'll bring you to

   your father.   [*goes, with Cressida*

Nestor. A woman of quick sense.

Ulysses.   Fie, fie upon her!

There's language in her eye, her cheek, her lip,

Nay, her foot speaks; her wanton spirits look out

At every joint and motive of her body.

O, these encounterers, so glib of tongue,

That give accosting welcome ere it comes,

And wide unclasp the tables of their thoughts   60

To every tickling reader!—set them down

For sluttish spoils of opportunity

And daughters of the game.   [*trumpet within*

  All. The Trojans' trumpet.

  Agamemnon.   Yonder comes the troop.

Flourish. Enter HECTOR, *armed;* ÆNEAS, TROILUS,
   and other Trojans, with Attendants

Æneas. Hail, all the state of Greece! What shall

   be done

To him that victory commands? Or do you purpose

A victor shall be known? Will you the knights

Shall to the edge of all extremity

Pursue each other, or shall they be divided

By any voice or order of the field?   70

Hector bade ask.

  Agamemnon.   Which way would Hector have it?

Æneas. He cares not; he'll obey conditions.

Agamemnon. 'Tis done like Hector.

Achilles.   But securely done,
A little proudly, and great deal misprizing
The knight opposed.

Æneas.   If not Achilles, sir,
What is your name?

Achilles.   If not Achilles, nothing.

Æneas. Therefore Achilles. But whate'er, know this:
In the extremity of great and little,
Valour and pride excel themselves in Hector;
80 The one almost as infinite as all,
The other blank as nothing. Weigh him well,
And that which looks like pride is courtesy.
This Ajax is half made of Hector's blood;
In love whereof, half Hector stays at home;
Half heart, half hand, half Hector comes to seek
This blended knight, half Trojan and half Greek.

Achilles. A maiden battle then? O, I perceive you.

Re-enter DIOMEDES

Agamemnon. Here is Sir Diomed. Go,
    gentle knight,
Stand by our Ajax. As you and Lord Æneas
90 Consent upon the order of their fight,
So be it; either to the uttermost,
Or else a breath. The combatants being kin
Half stints their strife before their strokes begin.
                    [*Ajax and Hector enter the lists*

Ulysses. They are opposed already.

Agamemnon. What Trojan is that same that looks
    so heavy?

Ulysses. The youngest son of Priam, a true knight;
Not yet mature, yet matchless-firm of word;

Speaking in deeds and deedless in his tongue;
Not soon provoked nor, being provoked, soon calmed;
His heart and hand both open and both free;   100
For what he has he gives, what thinks he shows;
Yet gives he not till judgement guide his bounty,
Nor dignifies an impair thought with breath;
Manly as Hector, but more dangerous;
For Hector in his blaze of wrath subscribes
To tender objects, but he in heat of action
Is more vindicative than jealous love;
They call him Troilus, and on him erect
A second hope, as fairly built as Hector:
Thus says Æneas, one that knows the youth   110
Even to his inches, and with private soul
Did in great Ilion thus translate him to me.
                    [alarum; Hector and Ajax fight

Agamemnon. They are in action.
Nestor. Now, Ajax, hold thine own!
Troilus.   Hector, thou sleep'st;
Awake thee!
Agamemnon. His blows are well disposed.
    There, Ajax!   *[trumpets cease*
Diomedes. You must no more.
Æneas.   Princes, enough, so please you.
Ajax. I am not warm yet; let us fight again.
Diomedes. As Hector pleases.
Hector.   Why, then will I no more:
Thou art, great lord, my father's sister's son,   120
A cousin-german to great Priam's seed;
The obligation of our blood forbids
A gory emulation 'twixt us twain.
Were thy commixtion Greek and Trojan so,
That thou couldst say 'This hand is Grecian all,
And this is Trojan; the sinews of this leg

All Greek, and this all Troy; my mother's blood
Runs on the dexter cheek, and this sinister
Bounds in my father's', by Jove multipotent,
130 Thou shouldst not bear from me a Greekish member
Wherein my sword had not impressure made
Of our rank feud; but the just gods gainsay
That any drop thou borrow'dst from thy mother,
My sacred aunt, should by my mortal sword
Be drainéd! Let me embrace thee, Ajax.
By him that thunders, thou hast lusty arms;
Hector would have them fall upon him thus.
Cousin, all honour to thee!
   Ajax.   I thank thee, Hector.
Thou art too gentle and too free a man.
140 I came to kill thee, cousin, and bear hence
A great addition earnéd in thy death.
   Hector. Not Neoptolemus so mirable,
On whose bright crest Fame with her loud'st oyez
Cries 'This is he', could promise to himself
A thought of added honour torn from Hector.
   Æneas. There is expectance here from both
      the sides
What further you will do.
   Hector.   We'll answer it:
The issue is embracement; Ajax, farewell.
   Ajax. If I might in entreaties find success,
150 As seld I have the chance, I would desire
My famous cousin to our Grecian tents.
   Diomedes. 'Tis Agamemnon's wish; and
      great Achilles
Doth long to see unarmed the valiant Hector.
   Hector. Æneas, call my brother Troilus to me,
And signify this loving interview
To the expecters of our Trojan part;

Desire them home. Give me thy hand, my cousin;
I will go eat with thee, and see your knights.
 Ajax. Great Agamemnon comes to meet us here.
 Hector. The worthiest of them tell me name
  by name;   160
But for Achilles, my own searching eyes
Shall find him by his large and portly size.
 Agamemnon. Worthy of arms! as welcome as to one
That would be rid of such an enemy—
But that's no welcome; understand more clear,
What's past and what's to come is strewed with husks
And formless ruin of oblivion;
But in this extant moment, faith and troth,
Strained purely from all hollow bias-drawing,
Bids thee, with most divine integrity,   170
From heart of very heart, great Hector, welcome.
 Hector. I thank thee, most imperious Agamemnon.
 Agamemnon [*to Troilus*]. My well-famed lord of
  Troy, no less to you.
 Menelaus. Let me confirm my princely
  brother's greeting;
You brace of warlike brothers, welcome hither.
 Hector. Who must we answer?
 Æneas.   The noble Menelaus.
 Hector. O, you, my lord! by Mars his
  gauntlet, thanks!
Mock not that I affect th'untraded oath;
Your quondam wife swears still by Venus' glove.
She's well, but bade me not commend her to you.   180
 Menelaus. Name her not now, sir; she's a
  deadly theme.
 Hector. O, pardon; I offend.
 Nestor. I have, thou gallant Trojan, seen thee oft,
Labouring for destiny, make cruel way

Through ranks of Greekish youth; and I have
    seen thee,
As hot as Perseus, spur thy Phrygian steed,
And seen thee scorning forfeits and subduements
When thou hast hung thy advancéd sword i'th'air,
Not letting it decline on the declined,
190 That I have said to some my standers-by
'Lo, Jupiter is yonder, dealing life!'
And I have seen thee pause and take thy breath
When that a ring of Greeks have hemmed thee in,
Like an Olympian wrestling. This have I seen,
But this thy countenance, still locked in steel,
I never saw till now. I knew thy grandsire,
And once fought with him. He was a soldier good;
But, by great Mars the captain of us all,
Never like thee. O, let an old man embrace thee;
200 And, worthy warrior, welcome to our tents.
   Æneas. 'Tis the old Nestor.
   Hector. Let me embrace thee, good old chronicle,
That hast so long walked hand in hand with time;
Most reverend Nestor, I am glad to clasp thee.
   Nestor. I would my arms could match thee
    in contention,
As they contend with thee in courtesy.
   Hector. I would they could.
   Nestor. Ha!
By this white beard, I'ld fight with thee tomorrow.
210 Well, welcome, welcome! I have seen the time.
   Ulysses. I wonder now how yonder city stands
When we have here her base and pillar by us.
   Hector. I know your favour, Lord Ulysses, well.
Ah, sir, there's many a Greek and Trojan dead,
Since first I saw yourself and Diomed
In Ilion, on your Greekish embassy.

Ulysses. Sir, I foretold you then what would ensue.
My prophecy is but half his journey yet;
For yonder walls, that pertly front your town,
Yon towers, whose wanton tops do buss the clouds,   220
Must kiss their own feet.

Hector.   I must not believe you.
There they stand yet; and modestly I think
The fall of every Phrygian stone will cost
A drop of Grecian blood. The end crowns all;
And that old common arbitrator, Time,
Will one day end it.

Ulysses.   So to him we leave it.
Most gentle and most valiant Hector, welcome.
After the general, I beseech you next
To feast with me and see me at my tent.

Achilles. I shall forestall thee, Lord Ulysses, thou!   230
Now Hector, I have fed mine eyes on thee;
I have with exact view perused thee, Hector,
And quoted joint by joint.

Hector.   Is this Achilles?

Achilles. I am Achilles.

Hector. Stand fair, I pray thee; let me look on thee.

Achilles. Behold thy fill.

Hector.   Nay, I have done already.

Achilles. Thou art too brief. I will the second time,
As I would buy thee, view thee limb by limb.

Hector. O, like a book of sport thou'lt read me o'er;
But there's more in me than thou understand'st.   240
Why dost thou so oppress me with thine eye?

Achilles. Tell me, you heavens, in which part of
     his body
Shall I destroy him?—whether there, or there,
     or there?—
That I may give the local wound a name,

And make distinct the very breach whereout
Hector's great spirit flew. Answer me, heavens!
  Hector. It would discredit the blest gods, proud man,
To answer such a question. Stand again;
Think'st thou to catch my life so pleasantly
250 As to prenominate in nice conjecture
Where thou wilt hit me dead?
  Achilles.   I tell thee yea.
  Hector. Wert thou an oracle to tell me so,
I'ld not believe thee. Henceforth guard thee well;
For I'll not kill thee there, nor there, nor there;
But, by the forge that stithied Mars his helm,
I'll kill thee everywhere, yea, o'er and o'er.
You wisest Grecians, pardon me this brag:
His insolence draws folly from my lips;
But I'll endeavour deeds to match these words,
260 Or may I never—
  Ajax.   Do not chafe thee, cousin;
And you, Achilles, let these threats alone
Till accident or purpose bring you to't.
You may have every day enough of Hector,
If you have stomach. The general state, I fear,
Can scarce entreat you to be odd with him.
  Hector. I pray you, let us see you in the field;
We have had pelting wars since you refused
The Grecians' cause.
  Achilles.   Dost thou entreat me, Hector?
Tomorrow do I meet thee, fell as death;
270 Tonight all friends.
  Hector.   Thy hand upon that match.
  Agamemnon. First, all you peers of Greece, go to
    my tent;
There in the full convive we. Afterwards,
As Hector's leisure and your bounties shall

Concur together, severally entreat him.
Beat loud the taborins, let the trumpets blow,
That this great soldier may his welcome know.

     [Flourish; all go but Troilus and Ulysses

 Troilus. My Lord Ulysses, tell me, I beseech you,
In what place of the field doth Calchas keep?

 Ulysses. At Menelaus' tent, most princely Troilus.
There Diomed doth feast with him tonight;   280
Who neither looks upon the heaven nor earth,
But gives all gaze and bent of amorous view
On the fair Cressid.

 Troilus. Shall I, sweet lord, be bound to you
  so much,
After we part from Agamemnon's tent,
To bring me thither?

 Ulysses.   You shall command me, sir.
As gentle tell me, of what honour was
This Cressida in Troy? Had she no lover there
That wails her absence?

 Troilus. O, sir, to such as boasting show their scars,   290
A mock is due. Will you walk on, my lord?
She was beloved, she loved; she is, and doth;
But still sweet love is food for fortune's tooth.

             [they go

[5. 1.]   *The same. Before Achilles' tent*

    Enter ACHILLES and PATROCLUS

 Achilles. I'll heat his blood with Greekish
  wine tonight,
Which with my scimitar I'll cool tomorrow.
Patroclus, let us feast him to the height.

 Patroclus. Here comes Thersites.

Enter THERSITES

Achilles.   How now, thou core of envy!
Thou crusty botch of nature, what's the news?

Thersites. Why, thou picture of what thou seemest,
and idol of idiot-worshippers, here's a letter for thee.

Achilles. From whence, fragment?

Thersites. Why, thou full dish of fool, from Troy.

10   *Patroclus.* Who keeps the tent now?

Thersites. The surgeon's box, or the patient's wound.

Patroclus. Well said, adversity! and what need these
tricks?

Thersites. Prithee, be silent, boy; I profit not by thy
talk; thou art thought to be Achilles' male varlet.

Patroclus. Male varlet, you rogue! what's that?

Thersites. Why, his masculine whore. Now, the rotten
diseases of the south, the guts-griping, ruptures, catarrhs,
loads o' gravel i'th'back, lethargies, cold palsies, raw
20   eyes, dirt-rotten livers, wheezing lungs, bladders full
of impostume, sciaticas, limekilns i'th'palm, incurable
bone-ache, and the rivelled fee-simple of the tetter,
take and take again such preposterous discoveries!

Patroclus. Why, thou damnable box of envy, thou;
what mean'st thou to curse thus?

Thersites. Do I curse thee?

Patroclus. Why, no, you ruinous butt; you whoreson
indistinguishable cur, no.

Thersites. No! Why art thou then exasperate, thou
30   idle immaterial skein of sleave-silk, thou green sarsenet
flap for a sore eye, thou tassel of a prodigal's purse,
thou? Ah, how the poor world is pestered with such
waterflies, diminutives of nature!

Patroclus. Out, gall!

Thersites. Finch-egg!

Achilles. My sweet Patroclus, I am thwarted quite
From my great purpose in tomorrow's battle.
Here is a letter from Queen Hecuba,
A token from her daughter, my fair love,
Both taxing me and gaging me to keep   40
An oath that I have sworn. I will not break it:
Fall Greeks; fail fame; honour or go or stay;
My major vow lies here; this I'll obey.
Come, come, Thersites, help to trim my tent;
This night in banqueting must all be spent.
Away, Patroclus!   [*Achilles and Patroclus go in*
  Thersites. With too much blood and too little brain,
these two may run mad; but if with too much brain and
too little blood they do, I'll be a curer of madmen.
Here's Agamemnon, an honest fellow enough and one 50
that loves quails, but he has not so much brain as ear-
wax; and the goodly transformation of Jupiter there,
his brother, the bull, the primitive statue and oblique
memorial of cuckolds, a thrifty shoeing-horn in a chain,
hanging at his brother's leg—to what form but that he
is, should wit larded with malice and malice forced with
wit turn him to? To an ass, were nothing: he is both ass
and ox; to an ox, were nothing: he is both ox and ass.
To be a dog, a mule, a cat, a fitchew, a toad, a lizard,
an owl, a puttock, or a herring without a roe, I would 60
not care; but to be Menelaus, I would conspire against
destiny! Ask me not what I would be, if I were not
Thersites; for I care not to be the louse of a lazar, so
I were not Menelaus. Hoy-day! spirits and fires!

Enter HECTOR, TROILUS, AJAX, AGAMEMNON,
ULYSSES, NESTOR, MENELAUS, *and* DIOMEDES, *with
lights*

  Agamemnon. We go wrong, we go wrong.

Ajax. No, yonder 'tis;
There, where we see the lights.
Hector. I trouble you.
Ajax. No, not a whit.

Re-enter ACHILLES

Ulysses. Here comes himself to guide you.
Achilles. Welcome, brave Hector; welcome,
    princes all.
Agamemnon. So now, fair Prince of Troy, I bid
    good night.
70 Ajax commands the guard to tend on you.
Hector. Thanks and good night to the
    Greeks' general.
Menelaus. Good night, my lord.
Hector. Good night, sweet Lord Menelaus.
(*Thersites.* Sweet draught: sweet, quoth 'a! sweet
sink, sweet sewer.
Achilles. Good night and welcome, both at once,
    to those
That go or tarry.
Agamemnon. Good night.
                    [*Agamemnon and Menelaus go*
Achilles. Old Nestor tarries; and you too, Diomed,
Keep Hector company an hour or two.
80 *Diomedes.* I cannot, lord; I have important business,
The tide whereof is now. Good night, great Hector.
Hector. Give me your hand.
Ulysses [*aside to Troilus*]. Follow his torch; he goes
    to Calchas' tent.
I'll keep you company.
Troilus. Sweet sir, you honour me.
Hector. And so, good night.
           [*Diomedes goes; Ulysses and Troilus following*

Achilles.   Come, come, enter my tent.

            [*Achilles, Hector, Ajax and Nestor go in*

Thersites. That same Diomed's a false-hearted rogue,
a most unjust knave; I will no more trust him when he
leers than I will a serpent when he hisses; he will spend
his mouth and promise, like Babbler the hound; but
when he performs, astronomers foretell it; it is pro- 90
digious, there will come some change; the sun borrows
of the moon when Diomed keeps his word. I will
rather leave to see Hector than not to dog him. They
say he keeps a Trojan drab and uses the traitor Calchas'
tent; I'll after. Nothing but lechery! all incontinent
varlets!   [*goes*

[5. 2.]   *The same. Before Calchas' tent*

            Enter DIOMEDES

Diomedes. What, are you up here, ho? speak.
Calchas [*within*]. Who calls?
Diomedes. Diomed. Calchas, I think. Where's your
daughter?
Calchas [*within*]. She comes to you.

      Enter TROILUS *and* ULYSSES, *at a distance;*
                after them THERSITES

Ulysses. Stand where the torch may not discover us.

            Enter CRESSIDA

Troilus. Cressid comes forth to him.
Diomedes.   How now, my charge!
Cressida. Now, my sweet guardian! Hark, a word
      with you.   [*whispers*

Troilus. Yea, so familiar!

10 *Ulysses.* She will sing any man at first sight.

Thersites. And any man may sing her, if he can take her clef; she's noted.

Diomedes. Will you remember?

Cressida. Remember? Yes.

Diomedes. Nay, but do then;
And let your mind be coupled with your words.

Troilus. What should she remember?

Ulysses. List.

Cressida. Sweet honey Greek, tempt me no more
    to folly.

20 *Thersites.* Roguery!

Diomedes. Nay, then—

Cressida. I'll tell you what—

Diomedes. Foh, foh! come, tell a pin; you are forsworn.

Cressida. In faith, I cannot. What would you have
    me do?

Thersites. A juggling trick—to be secretly open.

Diomedes. What did you swear you would bestow
    on me?

Cressida. I prithee, do not hold me to mine oath;
Bid me do anything but that, sweet Greek.

Diomedes. Good night.

30 *Troilus.* Hold, patience!

Ulysses. How now, Trojan!

Cressida. Diomed—

Diomedes. No no, good night; I'll be your fool
    no more.

Troilus. Thy better must.

Cressida. Hark, one word in your ear.

Troilus. O plague and madness!

Ulysses. You are moved, prince; let us depart,
    I pray you,

Lest your displeasure should enlarge itself
To wrathful terms. This place is dangerous;
The time right deadly; I beseech you, go. 40

Troilus. Behold, I pray you!

Ulysses.   Nay, good my lord, go off;
You flow to great distraction; come, my lord.

Troilus. I pray thee, stay.

Ulysses.   You have not patience; come.

Troilus. I pray you, stay; by hell and all
    hell's torments,
I will not speak a word.

Diomedes.   And so, good night.

Cressida. Nay, but you part in anger.

Troilus.   Doth that grieve thee?
O withered truth!

Ulysses.   Why, how now, lord!

Troilus.   By Jove,
I will be patient.

Cressida.   Guardian! Why, Greek!

Diomedes. Foh, foh! adieu; you palter.

Cressida. In faith, I do not; come hither once again. 50

Ulysses. You shake, my lord, at something; will
    you go?
You will break out.

Troilus.   She strokes his cheek!

Ulysses.   Come, come.

Troilus. Nay, stay; by Jove, I will not speak
    a word;
There is between my will and all offences
A guard of patience. Stay a little while.

Thersites. How the devil luxury, with his fat rump
and potato-finger, tickles these together! Fry, lechery,
fry!

Diomedes. But will you then?

60   *Cressida.* In faith, I will, la; never trust me else.
     Diomedes. Give me some token for the surety of it.
     Cressida. I'll fetch you one.   [*goes*
     Ulysses. You have sworn patience.
     Troilus.   Fear me not, sweet lord;
I will not be myself, nor have cognition
Of what I feel. I am all patience.

Re-enter CRESSIDA

Thersites. Now the pledge; now, now, now!
Cressida. Here, Diomed, keep this sleeve.
                              [*gives him the sleeve*
Troilus. O beauty! where is thy faith?
Ulysses.   My lord—
Troilus. I will be patient; outwardly I will.
70   *Cressida.* You look upon that sleeve; behold it well.
He loved me—O false wench!—Give't me again.
                                  [*takes it back*

Diomedes. Whose was't?
Cressida. It is no matter, now I have't again.
I will not meet with you tomorrow night.
I prithee, Diomed, visit me no more.
Thersites. Now she sharpens; well said, whetstone!
Diomedes. I shall have it.
Cressida.   What, this?
Diomedes.   Ay, that.
Cressida. O, all you gods! O pretty, pretty pledge!
Thy master now lies thinking in his bed
80 Of thee and me, and sighs, and takes my glove,
And gives memorial dainty kisses to it,
As I kiss thee. Nay, do not snatch it from me;
He that takes that doth take my heart withal.
                          [*Diomedes snatches it*
Diomedes. I had your heart before; this follows it.

Troilus. I did swear patience.

Cressida. You shall not have it, Diomed; faith, you
    shall not;

I'll give you something else.

Diomedes. I will have this. Whose was it?

Cressida.   It is no matter.

Diomedes. Come, tell me whose it was.

Cressida. 'Twas one's that loved me better than
    you will.   90

But now you have it, take it.

Diomedes.   Whose was it?

Cressida. By all Diana's waiting-women yond,

And by herself, I will not tell you whose.

Diomedes. Tomorrow will I wear it on my helm,

And grieve his spirit that dares not challenge it.

Troilus. Wert thou the devil, and wor'st it on
    thy horn,

It should be challenged.

Cressida. Well, well, 'tis done, 'tis past—and yet it
    is not;

I will not keep my word.

Diomedes.   Why then, farewell;

Thou never shalt mock Diomed again.   100

Cressida. You shall not go; one cannot speak a word,

But it straight starts you.

Diomedes.   I do not like this fooling.

Troilus. Nor I, by Pluto; but that that likes not you

Pleases me best.

Diomedes.   What, shall I come? the hour?

Cressida. Ay, come. O Jove! do come; I shall
    be plagued.

Diomedes. Farewell till then.

Cressida.   Good night; I prithee, come.

                                  [*Diomedes goes*

Troilus, farewell! One eye yet looks on thee,
But with my heart the other eye doth see.
Ah, poor our sex! this fault in us I find,
110 The error of our eye directs our mind;
What error leads must err—O, then conclude
Minds swayed by eyes are full of turpitude.   [*goes*

  Thersites. A proof of strength she could not
     publish more,
Unless she said 'My mind is now turned whore'.
  Ulysses. All's done, my lord.
  Troilus.   It is.
  Ulysses.   Why stay we then?
  Troilus. To make a recordation to my soul
Of every syllable that here was spoke.
But if I tell how these two did co-act,
Shall I not lie in publishing a truth?
120 Sith yet there is a credence in my heart,
An esperance so obstinately strong,
That doth invert th'attest of eyes and ears;
As if those organs had deceptious functions,
Created only to calumniate.
Was Cressid here?
  Ulysses.   I cannot conjure, Trojan.
  Troilus. She was not, sure.
  Ulysses.   Most sure she was.
  Troilus. Why, my negation hath no taste
    of madness.
  Ulysses. Nor mine, my lord; Cressid was here
    but now.
  Troilus. Let it not be believed for womanhood!
130 Think we had mothers. Do not give advantage
To stubborn critics, apt without a theme
For depravation, to square the general sex
By Cressid's rule; rather think this not Cressid.

Ulysses. What hath she done, prince, that can soil
    our mothers?
Troilus. Nothing at all, unless that this were she.
Thersites. Will 'a swagger himself out on's own eyes?
Troilus. This she? No; this is Diomed's Cressida.
If beauty have a soul, this is not she;
If souls guide vows, if vows be sanctimonies,
If sanctimony be the gods' delight,   140
If there be rule in unity itself,
This is not she. O madness of discourse,
That cause sets up with and against itself!
Bifold authority! where reason can revolt
Without perdition, and loss assume all reason
Without revolt. This is, and is not, Cressid!
Within my soul there doth conduce a fight
Of this strange nature, that a thing inseparate
Divides more wider than the sky and earth;
And yet the spacious breadth of this division   150
Admits no orifex for a point as subtle
As Ariachne's broken woof to enter.
Instance, O instance! strong as Pluto's gates:
Cressid is mine, tied with the bonds of heaven.
Instance, O instance! strong as heaven itself:
The bonds of heaven are slipped, dissolved
    and loosed,
And with another knot, five-finger-tied,
The fractions of her faith, orts of her love,
The fragments, scraps, the bits and greasy relics
Of her o'ereaten faith are given to Diomed.   160
  Ulysses. May worthy Troilus be but half attached
With that which here his passion doth express?
  Troilus. Ay, Greek; and that shall be divulgéd well
In characters as red as Mars his heart
Inflamed with Venus. Never did young man fancy

With so eternal and so fixed a soul.
Hark, Greek: as much as I do Cressid love,
So much by weight hate I her Diomed.
That sleeve is mine that he'll bear on his helm.
170 Were it a casque composed by Vulcan's skill,
My sword should bite it. Not the dreadful spout
Which shipmen do the hurricano call,
Constringed in mass by the almighty sun,
Shall dizzy with more clamour Neptune's ear
In his descent, than shall my prompted sword
Falling on Diomed.
    Thersites. He'll tickle it for his concupy.
    Troilus. O Cressid! O false Cressid! false,
      false, false!
Let all untruths stand by thy stainéd name,
180 And they'll seem glorious.
    Ulysses.   O, contain yourself;
Your passion draws ears hither.

Enter ÆNEAS

    Æneas. I have been seeking you this hour, my lord.
Hector by this is arming him in Troy;
Ajax your guard stays to conduct you home.
    Troilus. Have with you, prince. My courteous
      lord, adieu.
Farewell, revolted fair! and, Diomed,
Stand fast, and wear a castle on thy head!
    Ulysses. I'll bring you to the gates.
    Troilus. Accept distracted thanks.
               [Troilus, Æneas, and Ulysses go
190 *Thersites.* Would I could meet that rogue Diomed! I
would croak like a raven; I would bode, I would bode.
Patroclus will give me anything for the intelligence of
this whore; the parrot will not do more for an almond

than he for a commodious drab. Lechery, lechery!
Still wars and lechery! Nothing else holds fashion.
A burning devil take them!   *[goes*

[5. 3.]   *Troy. Before Priam's palace*

Enter HECTOR *and* ANDROMACHE

Andromache. When was my lord so much
    ungently tempered,
To stop his ears against admonishment?
Unarm, unarm, and do not fight today.
Hector. You train me to offend you; get you in.
By all the everlasting gods, I'll go!
Andromache. My dreams will sure prove ominous to
    the day.
Hector. No more, I say.

Enter CASSANDRA

Cassandra.   Where is my brother Hector?
Andromache. Here, sister; armed, and bloody
    in intent.
Consort with me in loud and dear petition;
Pursue we him on knees; for I have dreamed   10
Of bloody turbulence, and this whole night
Hath nothing been but shapes and forms of slaughter.
Cassandra. O, 'tis true.
Hector.   Ho! bid my trumpet sound!
Cassandra. No notes of sally, for the heavens,
    sweet brother.
Hector. Be gone, I say. The gods have heard
    me swear.
Cassandra. The gods are deaf to hot and peevish vows:

They are polluted offerings, more abhorred
Than spotted livers in the sacrifice.

Andromache. O, be persuaded! Do not count it holy
20 To hurt by being just; it is as lawful,
For we would give much, to use violent thefts
And rob in the behalf of charity.

Cassandra. It is the purpose that makes strong the vow;
But vows to every purpose must not hold.
Unarm, sweet Hector.

Hector.   Hold you still, I say;
Mine honour keeps the weather of my fate.
Life every man holds dear; but the dear man
Holds honour far more precious-dear than life.

Enter TROILUS

How now, young man! Mean'st thou to fight today?
30 *Andromache.* Cassandra, call my father to persuade.

                                        [*Cassandra goes*

Hector. No, faith, young Troilus; doff thy
        harness, youth;
I am today i'th'vein of chivalry.
Let grow thy sinews till their knots be strong,
And tempt not yet the brushes of the war.
Unarm thee, go; and doubt thou not, brave boy,
I'll stand today for thee and me and Troy.

Troilus. Brother, you have a vice of mercy in you,
Which better fits a lion than a man.

Hector. What vice is that? Good Troilus, chide me
        for it.
40 *Troilus.* When many times the captive Grecian falls,
Even in the fan and wind of your fair sword,
You bid them rise and live.

Hector. O, 'tis fair play.

Troilus.   Fool's play, by heaven, Hector.

Hector. How now! how now!

Troilus. For th'love of all the gods,
Let's leave the hermit pity with our mother;
And when we have our armours buckled on,
The venomed vengeance ride upon our swords,
Spur them to ruthful work, rein them from ruth!

Hector. Fie, savage, fie!

Troilus. Hector, then 'tis wars.

Hector. Troilus, I would not have you fight today. 50

Troilus. Who should withhold me?
Not fate, obedience, nor the hand of Mars
Beckoning with fiery truncheon my retire;
Not Priamus and Hecuba on knees,
Their eyes o'ergallèd with recourse of tears;
Nor you, my brother, with your true sword drawn,
Opposed to hinder me, should stop my way,
But by my ruin.

Re-enter CASSANDRA, with PRIAM

Cassandra. Lay hold upon him, Priam, hold him fast;
He is thy crutch; now if thou lose thy stay, 60
Thou on him leaning, and all Troy on thee,
Fall all together.

Priam. Come, Hector, come, go back.
Thy wife hath dreamed; thy mother hath had visions;
Cassandra doth foresee; and I myself
Am like a prophet suddenly enrapt,
To tell thee that this day is ominous;
Therefore, come back.

Hector. Æneas is afield;
And I do stand engaged to many Greeks,
Even in the faith of valour, to appear
This morning to them.

Priam. Ay, but thou shalt not go. 70

Hector. I must not break my faith.
You know me dutiful; therefore, dear sir,
Let me not shame respect, but give me leave
To take that course by your consent and voice
Which you do here forbid me, royal Priam.
　Cassandra. O Priam, yield not to him!
　Andromache.　　　　　　　　Do not, dear father.
　Hector. Andromache, I am offended with you;
Upon the love you bear me, get you in.　　*[she goes*
　Troilus. This foolish, dreaming, superstitious girl
80 Makes all these bodements.
　Cassandra.　　　　　O, farewell, dear Hector!
Look how thou diest! look how thy eye turns pale!
Look how thy wounds do bleed at many vents!
Hark how Troy roars! how Hecuba cries out!
How poor Andromache shrills her dolours forth!
Behold, distraction, frenzy, and amazement,
Like witless antics, one another meet,
And all cry 'Hector! Hector's dead! O Hector!'
　Troilus. Away! away!
　Cassandra. Farewell—yet soft! Hector, I take
　　my leave;
90 Thou dost thyself and all our Troy deceive.　　*[goes*
　Hector. You are amazed, my liege, at her exclaims.
Go in and cheer the town; we'll forth and fight,
Do deeds worth praise and tell you them at night.
　Priam. Farewell. The gods with safety stand
　　about thee!
　　　　　　[Priam and Hector go severally; alarum
　Troilus. They are at it, hark! Proud Diomed, believe,
I come to lose my arm, or win my sleeve.

　　　　　　　Enter PANDARUS

Pandarus. Do you hear, my lord? do you hear?

Troilus. What now?

Pandarus. Here's a letter come from yon poor girl.

Troilus. Let me read.   100

Pandarus. A whoreson tisick, a whoreson rascally
tisick so troubles me, and the foolish fortune of this
girl; and what one thing, what another, that I shall
leave you one o'these days. And I have a rheum in
mine eyes too, and such an ache in my bones that,
unless a man were cursed, I cannot tell what to think
on't. What says she there?

 Troilus. Words, words, mere words; no matter
     from the heart;
Th'effect doth operate another way. [*tearing the letter*
Go, wind, to wind! there turn and change together.   110
My love with words and errors still she feeds,
But edifies another with her deeds.   [*they go severally*

[5. 4.]   *The field between Troy and the Greek camp*

Alarums. Excursions. Enter THERSITES

 Thersites. Now they are clapper-clawing one another;
I'll go look on. That dissembling abominable varlet,
Diomed, has got that same scurvy doting foolish young
knave's sleeve of Troy there in his helm. I would fain
see them meet; that that same young Trojan ass, that
loves the whore there, might send that Greekish whore-
masterly villain with the sleeve back to the dissembling
luxurious drab of a sleeveless errand. O't'other side,
the policy of those crafty-swearing rascals, that stale old
mouse-eaten dry cheese, Nestor, and that same dog-fox, 10
Ulysses, is proved not worth a blackberry. They set me
up in policy that mongrel cur, Ajax, against that dog of

as bad a kind, Achilles; and now is the cur Ajax prouder
than the cur Achilles, and will not arm today; whereupon the Grecians begin to proclaim barbarism, and
policy grows into an ill opinion. Soft! here comes sleeve,
and t'other.

Enter DIOMEDES, TROILUS *following*

Troilus. Fly not; for shouldst thou take the river Styx,
I would swim after.
Diomedes.   Thou dost miscall retire;
20 I do not fly; but advantageous care
Withdrew me from the odds of multitude.
Have at thee!
Thersites. Hold thy whore, Grecian! Now for thy
whore, Trojan! Now the sleeve, now the sleeve!
                    [*Troilus and Diomedes go off fighting*

Enter HECTOR

Hector. What art thou, Greek? Art thou for
      Hector's match?
Art thou of blood and honour?
Thersites. No, no; I am a rascal; a scurvy railing
knave; a very filthy rogue.
Hector. I do believe thee. Live.   [*goes*
30 *Thersites.* God-a-mercy, that thou wilt believe me;
but a plague break thy neck for frighting me! What's
become of the wenching rogues? I think they have
swallowed one another. I would laugh at that miracle;
yet in a sort lechery eats itself. I'll seek them.   [*goes*

[5. 5.]   *Another part of the field*

Enter DIOMEDES and Servant

Diomedes. Go, go, my servant, take thou
        Troilus' horse;
Present the fair steed to my lady Cressid.
Fellow, commend my service to her beauty;
Tell her I have chastised the amorous Trojan,
And am her knight by proof.
    Servant.   I go, my lord.   [*goes*

Enter AGAMEMNON

Agamemnon. Renew, renew! The fierce Polydamas
Hath beat down Menon; bastard Margarelon
Hath Doreus prisoner,
And stands colossus-wise, waving his beam,
Upon the pashéd corpses of the kings   10
Epistrophus and Cedius; Polyxenes is slain;
Amphimachus and Thoas deadly hurt;
Patroclus ta'en or slain; and Palamedes
Sore hurt and bruised; the dreadful sagittary
Appals our numbers; haste we, Diomed,
To reinforcement, or we perish all.   [*goes*

Enter NESTOR and other Greeks

Nestor. Go, bear Patroclus' body to Achilles,
And bid the snail-paced Ajax arm for shame. [*some go*
There is a thousand Hectors in the field:
Now here he fights on Galathe his horse,   20
And there lacks work; anon he's there afoot,
And there they fly or die, like scaléd sculls
Before the belching whale; then is he yonder,
And there the strawy Greeks, ripe for his edge,

Fall down before him, like a mower's swath;
Here, there and everywhere he leaves and takes,
Dexterity so obeying appetite
That what he will he does, and does so much
That proof is called impossibility.

Enter ULYSSES

30   *Ulysses.* O, courage, courage, princes!
     great Achilles
Is arming, weeping, cursing, vowing vengeance;
Patroclus' wounds have roused his drowsy blood,
Together with his mangled Myrmidons,
That noseless, handless, hacked and chipped, come
     to him,
Crying on Hector. Ajax hath lost a friend,
And foams at mouth, and he is armed and at it,
Roaring for Troilus; who hath done today
Mad and fantastic execution,
Engaging and redeeming of himself
40 With such a careless force and forceless care
As if that luck, in very spite of cunning,
Bade him win all.

Enter AJAX

  Ajax. Troilus! thou coward Troilus!   *[goes*
  Diomedes.   Ay, there, there *[follows*
  Nestor. So, so, we draw together.

Enter ACHILLES

  Achilles.   Where is this Hector?
Come, come, thou boy-queller, show me thy face;
Know what it is to meet Achilles angry;
Hector! where's Hector? I will none but Hector.
                                 [they go

[5. 6.]   *Another part of the field*

Enter AJAX

Ajax. Troilus, thou coward Troilus, show
 thy head!

Enter DIOMEDES

Diomedes. Troilus, I say! where's Troilus?
Ajax.   What wouldst thou?
Diomedes. I would correct him.
Ajax. Were I the general, thou shouldst have
 my office
Ere that correction. Troilus, I say! what, Troilus!

Enter TROILUS

Troilus. O traitor Diomed! Turn thy false face,
 thou traitor,
And pay the life thou ow'st me for my horse.
Diomedes. Ha! art thou there?
Ajax. I'll fight with him alone; stand, Diomed.
Diomedes. He is my prize; I will not look upon.   10
Troilus. Come both you cogging Greeks; have at
 you both!   [*they go, fighting*
Enter HECTOR

Hector. Yea, Troilus? O, well fought, my
 youngest brother!

Enter ACHILLES

Achilles. Now do I see thee; ha! have at
 thee, Hector!   [*they fight*
Hector. Pause, if thou wilt.
Achilles. I do disdain thy courtesy, proud Trojan.
Be happy that my arms are out of use;

My rest and negligence befriends thee now,
But thou anon shalt hear of me again;
Till when, go seek thy fortune.   [goes
  Hector.   Fare thee well.
20 I would have been much more a fresher man,
Had I expected thee.

Re-enter TROILUS

      How now, my brother!
  Troilus. Ajax hath ta'en Æneas. Shall it be?
No, by the flame of yonder glorious heaven,
He shall not carry him; I'll be ta'en too,
Or bring him off. Fate, hear me what I say!
I reck not though thou end my life today.   [goes

Enter one in sumptuous armour

  Hector. Stand, stand, thou Greek; thou art a
    goodly mark.
No? wilt thou not? I like thy armour well;
I'll frush it and unlock the rivets all,
30 But I'll be master of it. [*the Greek flees*] Wilt thou
    not, beast, abide?
Why then, fly on; I'll hunt thee for thy hide.
                   [goes after

[5. 7.]   *Another part of the field*

Enter ACHILLES, *with Myrmidons*

  Achilles. Come here about me, you my Myrmidons;
Mark what I say. Attend me where I wheel;
Strike not a stroke, but keep yourselves in breath,
And when I have the bloody Hector found
Empale him with your weapons round about;

In fellest manner execute your arms.
Follow me, sirs, and my proceedings eye;
It is decreed Hector the great must die.   [*they go*

Enter MENELAUS *and* PARIS, *fighting;*
then THERSITES

Thersites. The cuckold and the cuckold-maker are at
it. Now, bull! now, dog! 'Loo, Paris, 'loo! now, my 10
double-horned Spartan! 'loo, Paris, 'loo! The bull has
the game. Ware horns, ho!   [*Paris and Menelaus go*

Enter MARGARELON

Margarelon. Turn, slave, and fight.
Thersites. What art thou?
Margarelon. A bastard son of Priam's.
Thersites. I am a bastard too; I love bastards. I am
a bastard begot, bastard instructed, bastard in mind,
bastard in valour, in everything illegitimate. One bear
will not bite another, and wherefore should one
bastard? Take heed; the quarrel's most ominous to us; 20
if the son of a whore fight for a whore, he tempts
judgement. Farewell, bastard.   [*goes*
Margarelon. The devil take thee, coward!   [*goes*

[5. 8.]   *Another part of the field*

Enter HECTOR

Hector. Most putrefiéd core, so fair without,
Thy goodly armour thus hath cost thy life.
Now is my day's work done. I'll take good breath.
Rest, sword; thou hast thy fill of blood and death.
                                                [*disarms*

Enter ACHILLES *and Myrmidons*

Achilles. Look, Hector, how the sun begins to set,
How ugly night comes breathing at his heels;
Even with the vail and darking of the sun,
To close the day up, Hector's life is done.
  Hector. I am unarmed; forego this vantage, Greek.
10 *Achilles.* Strike, fellows, strike; this is the man
      I seek.   [*Hector falls*
So, Ilion, fall thou next! now, Troy, sink down!
Here lies thy heart, thy sinews, and thy bone.
On, Myrmidons, and cry you all amain
'Achilles hath the mighty Hector slain'.
                           [*retreat sounded*
Hark! a retire upon our Grecian part.
  Myrmidon. The Trojan trumpets sound the like,
    my lord.
  Achilles. The dragon wing of night o'erspreads
    the earth,
And stickler-like the armies separates.
My half-supped sword that frankly would have fed,
20 Pleased with this dainty bait, thus goes to bed.
                        [*sheathes his sword*
Come, tie his body to my horse's tail;
Along the field I will the Trojan trail.
                  [*they go; retreat sounded*

[5. 9.]   *Another part of the field*

  Enter AGAMEMNON, AJAX, MENELAUS, NESTOR,
DIOMEDES, *and the rest, marching. Shouts within.*

Agamemnon. Hark! hark! what shout is that?
Nestor. Peace, drums!

Soldiers [*within*]. Achilles! Achilles! Hector's
    slain! Achilles!
Diomedes. The bruit is Hector's slain, and
    by Achilles.
Ajax. If it be so, yet bragless let it be;
Great Hector was as good a man as he.
Agamemnon. March patiently along. Let one be sent
To pray Achilles see us at our tent.
If in his death the gods have us befriended,
Great Troy is ours, and our sharp wars are ended.   10
                               [*they march off*

[5. 10.]   *Another part of the field*

   Enter ÆNEAS, PARIS, ANTENOR, *and* DEIPHOBUS

Æneas. Stand, ho! yet are we masters of the field.
Never go home; here starve we out the night.

               Enter TROILUS

Troilus. Hector is slain.
All.   Hector! The gods forbid!
Troilus. He's dead; and at the murderer's horse's tail
In beastly sort dragged through the shameful field.
Frown on, you heavens, effect your rage with speed!
Sit, gods, upon your thrones and smite at Troy!
I say, at once let your brief plagues be mercy,
And linger not our sure destructions on!
Æneas. My lord, you do discomfort all the host.   10
Troilus. You understand me not that tell me so;
I do not speak of flight, of fear, of death,
But dare all imminence that gods and men
Address their dangers in. Hector is gone:
Who shall tell Priam so, or Hecuba?

Let him that will a screech-owl aye be called:
Go in to Troy and say there 'Hector's dead',
There is a word will Priam turn to stone,
Make wells and Niobes of the maids and wives,
20 Cold statues of the youth, and, in a word,
Scare Troy out of itself. But march away.
Hector is dead; there is no more to say.
Stay yet. You vile abominable tents,
Thus proudly pight upon our Phrygian plains
Let Titan rise as early as he dare,
I'll through and through you! and thou
    great-sized coward,
No space of earth shall sunder our two hates;
I'll haunt thee like a wicked conscience still,
That mouldeth goblins swift as frenzy's thoughts.
30 Strike a free march to Troy! with comfort go:
Hope of revenge shall hide our inward woe.

                      [Æneas and Trojans go

Enter PANDARUS

  Pandarus. But hear you, hear you!
  Troilus. Hence, broker-lackey! ignomy and shame
Pursue thy life, and live aye with thy name!   *[goes*
  Pandarus. A goodly medicine for my aching bones!
O world! world! world! thus is the poor agent despised!
O traders and bawds, how earnestly are you set a-work,
and how ill requited! Why should our endeavour be so
desired and the performance so loathed? What verse
40 for it? what instance for it? Let me see:

      Full merrily the humble-bee doth sing
      Till he hath lost his honey and his sting;
      And being once subdued in arméd tail,
      Sweet honey and sweet notes together fail.

Good traders in the flesh, set this in your painted cloths:
As many as be here of Pandar's hall,
Your eyes, half out, weep out at Pandar's fall;
Or if you cannot weep, yet give some groans,
Though not for me, yet for your aching bones.
Brethren and sisters of the hold-door trade, 50
Some two months hence my will shall here be made.
It should be now, but that my fear is this,
Some galléd goose of Winchester would hiss.
Till then I'll sweat and seek about for eases,
And at that time bequeath you my diseases. [goes

THE COPY FOR
TROILUS AND CRESSIDA
1609 AND 1623

We have two good texts of this play: the quarto of 1609 (Q.), printed by George Eld for Richard Bonian and Henry Walley,[1] and the First Folio text of 1623 (F.).

Editors of today are fortunate, since much bibliographical work has recently been done on both texts and many problems concerning their transmission have consequently been laid to rest. As regards F., it has been shown that its position in the Folio was determined by convenience: Jaggard's first intention was that it should follow *Romeo and Juliet* among the Tragedies; but after three Folio pages (the beginning of the play proper) had been printed, work on *Troilus* was broken off and it was not resumed until after the rest of the collection (including the colophon and preliminaries) was ready. The completed text was therefore inserted between the Histories and Tragedies.[2]

Jaggard's delay in completing this text is thought to have been due to difficulties over copyright[3] and had printing proceeded in accordance with the original plan

---

[1] Cf. Introduction, p. ix.

[2] For an account of the stages by which these conclusions were reached see Greg, 'The Printing of Shakespeare's *Troilus and Cressida* in the First Folio' (in *Papers of the Bibliographical Society of America*, XLV (1951), pp. 273–82); see also Greg, *The Shakespeare First Folio* (1955), pp. 445–9.

[3] See Greg, as above, n. 2.

we should have had in F. merely a reprint of Q.[1] The first three F. pages to be printed (the text of 1. 1. 1–1. 2. 235 above)[2] are, in fact, derivative, the variants representing merely compositors' errors, conjectural emendations, and the usual Folio sophistications. But from the point where printing was resumed, the F. text takes on a very different character.[3] The Prologue (absent from Q.) was recovered, many words, lines and short passages omitted in Q. were restored, and F.'s many corrections of Q. errors plainly rested on the use of an authoritative manuscript.

From the appearance in F. of duplicated matter,[4] best explained as due to afterthoughts in the course of composition, it would seem that this authority was foul papers, though F. was not set up from this manuscript direct but from a hand-corrected example of Q. which had been collated with it. That the copy for F. was of this character was argued by Alexander in 1928[5] and confirmed by Williams in 1950.[6]

As regards Q., it seems to be generally agreed that

[1] See A. Walker, 'The textual problem of *Troilus and Cressida*' (in *Modern Language Review*, XLV (1950), pp. 459–64).

[2] See note to 1. 2. 235.

[3] When printing was resumed, the first of the three pages in print had to be re-set; for a facsimile of the original setting see E. E. Willoughby, *The Printing of the First Folio of Shakespeare* (Bibliographical Society, 1932), Plate 4. The second setting was, however, a mere reprint of the first.

[4] See notes to 4. 5. 96 and 5. 3. 112 +.

[5] See Peter Alexander, '*Troilus and Cressida*, 1609' (in *Library*, IX (1929), pp. 267–86).

[6] See Philip Williams, 'Shakespeare's *Troilus and Cressida*: the Relationship of Quarto and Folio' (in *Studies in Bibliography*, University of Virginia, III (1950–1), pp. 131–43).

the manuscript behind it was a transcript. This is evident from its many errors in speech prefixes, pointing to the copyist's having followed the by no means uncommon practice of transcribing the dialogue first and adding the speakers' names later, with the result that the latter were sometimes misalined, mis-assigned, omitted and interpolated;[1] and, as it would appear from the preface to Q. that the play was published without the consent of its 'grand possessors', it is thought that what Bonian and Walley had acquired was a private transcript, made perhaps with a view to securing the play's approval by the authorities responsible for some private performance.[2] This hypothesis would plausi¹·¹ᵥ explain the provisional entry to Roberts in 1603[3] as aₙ attempt to preclude publication without the consent of the players.[4]

So far these inferences seem either certain or the most reasonable that can be drawn from the available evidence and, if the transmission of the two texts was as straightforward as this, an editor could accept Q. as the authoritative text for 1. 1. 1–1. 2. 235 and F. as the higher authority elsewhere for the substance of what Shakespeare wrote. Unfortunately, the problem is not quite so simple, inasmuch as Alexander[5] also argued that the manuscript from which Q. was printed was a fair copy of the play made by Shakespeare himself. Critical opinion has since inclined to this view[6] and to the corollary that this manuscript might therefore

[1] See A. Walker in *M.L.R.* (as above, p. 123 n. 1), p. 461, and *Textual Problems of the First Folio* (1953), pp. 77–8.

[2] See Greg, *Shakespeare First Folio*, p. 347.

[3] Cf. Introduction, p. ix.

[4] See Greg, *London Publishing* (1956), pp. 114 ff.

[5] In *Library* (as above, p. 123 n. 5).

[6] E. K. Chambers was the notable exception.

have contained authoritative revision. If this were the case, then F.'s authority would be inferior to Q.'s throughout.[1]

Alexander's belief that the Q. manuscript was autograph rested on spellings, misreadings and peculiarities in punctuation explicable in the light of *Sir Thomas More* D and paralleled in other Shakespearian texts printed from foul papers. This was challenged by Chambers[2] on the grounds that a naive transcript might have preserved such peculiarities—if indeed they were the monopoly of Shakespeare; and we are not much better equipped than we were about 1930 for pursuing the question along these lines since a comprehensive study of spelling in this period has not yet been made. It is even not yet known what features of Q. are foreign to the usual habits of Eld's compositors.[3] Fortunately, what seriously matters is not whether the Q. manuscript was autograph[4] but whether it did, in fact, contain authoritative revision, and for an examination of this

[1] It should be remembered that, because F. was set up from an example of Q. (and not from MS.), Q. is necessarily closer to autograph in respect of accidentals—i.e. punctuation and spelling, which the F. compositors sophisticated and altered according to their fancy, thereby removing the text, in this respect, one stage further from the original. But Q.'s closer link with the original in accidentals does not mean that it was necessarily closer in substance to what Shakespeare intended; see Greg, 'The Rationale of Copy-Text' (in *Studies in Bibliography*, III (1950–1), pp. 19–36).

[2] See E. K. Chambers, *William Shakespeare* (1930), I, p. 441.

[3] An American, George Hummer, is now, however, working on Eld's compositors.

[4] For even if it was autograph, we should still not know whether the variants were accidentally or deliberately introduced.

problem we have all the material we are ever likely to possess in the variants themselves.

One thing is immediately apparent from a consideration of the variants as a whole, and this is that, if there was revision, it was of so trivial a character that its importance is negligible. Of the 500 odd variants in the text for which we have rival authorities by far the majority amount to no more than the difference of a word or a letter and there is nowhere so much as a line which differs wholly from its counterpart. The most substantial variant occurs at 4. 5. 275, where Q. reads

<blockquote>
afterwards
As Hectors leisure, and your bounties shall
Concurre together, seuerally entreate him
To taste your bounties, let the trumpets blowe,
That this great souldier may his welcome know.
</blockquote>

For the words I italicize F. reads (terminating the previous line with a period) 'Beate lowd the Taborins'. Here editors[1] prefer F., presumably because of the awkward repetition of 'bounties', though the Q. phrase might certainly have been written by Shakespeare since its like occurs twice in *Timon of Athens*.[2] Here, assuming revision, the verdict of editors suggests that, if it was in Q., Shakespeare's second thoughts were less happy than his first. On the evidence of this reading, an equally strong case could be made for revision in F.,[3] which, indeed, some critics have argued. Once revision subsequent to Shakespeare's first writing of the play is postulated to explain the variants, the position is, in

---

[1] Including Rowe, Johnson, Capell, Malone, the old Cambridge editors, Kittredge, Alexander, Sisson.

[2] 'And taste Lord Timon's bounty' (1. 1. 277); 'Having often of your open bounty tasted' (5. 1. 57).

[3] Cf. the preference of editors for F. at 1. 3. 92; 2. 3. 129, 130.

fact, one of stalemate, for neither text is consistently better than the other.

The belief that the Q. manuscript was autograph stands, I believe, on very slippery foundations, and the corollary that Q. represented an authoritatively revised version of the matter is supported neither by the evidence of Q.'s variants as a whole nor by the practice of recent editors who hold this opinion. The textual consequences of this hypothesis, if put into practice, are all the more dangerous because the Q. manuscript had passed out of the hands of Shakespeare's company and may therefore have been conjecturally tinkered with between the time when it was transcribed (presumably *c.* 1602) and its reaching the printer. Q. certainly reveals some bodging. A simple instance occurs at 4. 4. 53–4:

Where are my teares[1] raine to lay this winde, or my heart wilbe blowne vp *by my throate*.

For the words I italicize F. substituted 'by the root' and manifestly what happened to the Q. text is that 'th'roote' (possibly written as one word) was misinterpreted as 'throat' and 'my' was supplied to complete the sense. Another example occurs at 3. 3. 197. Here, F.'s line

Knowes almost euery graine of Plutoes gold

appears in Q. as

Knowes almost euery thing

—a similarly unhappy effort to tie in a broken thread.[2] Bodging of this kind need not have been extensive, and

[1] A question mark is, of course, wanted after 'teares'.

[2] Greg, however, defends Q. (*Shakespeare First Folio*, p. 346), but the reading is too inept to be anything but a random shot at completing the sense because 'graine of Plutoes gold' had proved illegible; cf. 3. 3. 197 n.

there is certainly no evidence that it was, but it inevitably arouses the suspicion that it may have been more insidious than we can detect and it provides a warning against accepting Q. as the higher authority when the merits of substantive readings seem evenly matched.

Broadly, Chambers's conclusion seems to me to square best with the evidence of the variants—that they were due to printing-house errors, Folio sophistication, and the difficulty experienced (especially by the scribe of the Q. manuscript) in deciphering the foul papers. Given the fair certainty that Shakespeare made some alterations in these *currente calamo*, their occasional illegibility and compositors' errors adequately explains why the dialogue of the two texts differs so frequently and yet, for the most part, in so very trivial a way.

The belief that either Q. or F. represented a revised text has been encouraged, I suspect, by the assumption that proof was read with copy, and therefore, that the divergencies between them had at least the authority of the copy from which they were printed behind them. Though we still do not know what Jaggard's proof-reading of *Troilus* amounted to, Williams recorded that he had collated ten copies of F. and found no evidence of systematic proofing;[1] and so far as Q. is concerned, we can be quite certain that no proper care was taken to eliminate compositors' errors. Fourteen out of fifteen located copies of Q. were collated by Hillebrand, who found only trivial variants,[2] and though most of the formes are invariant we can be certain that Eld took no pains over the accuracy of his text from one type of error very prevalent in Q.—its frequent

[1] See *Troilus and Cressida*, New Variorum ed. (1953), p. 347.

[2] *Ibid.* pp. 321–3. The variants occur on E(o), F(o) and K(i).

loss of a word. This proves to have been a marked failing of the first of Eld's two compositors (Eld *A*), for out of thirty-four (single) words which the old Cambridge editors, Kittredge, Alexander and Sisson agree in accepting as Q. losses made good in F. thirty-one of these losses occur in his stints. For this feature of Q. the compositor, and not his manuscript, must have been to blame and, had proof been read with copy, most of these omissions could have been made good.

That two compositors were engaged on Q. was first shown by Williams, who communicated his analysis of the presswork to Baldwin.[1] The two hands can be identified from their spelling habits[2] as well as from the frequency of colons for periods in the stints of Eld *A* and from his inability to punctuate intelligibly.[3] When the stints of Eld's compositors are related to Williams's presswork analysis, the picture is as follows:

Press	Sheet	Skeleton	Compositor	
1	A	X	E *A* A 2–4	1. 1. 1–1. 2. 286
2	B	Y	E *A* B 1–2	
1	C	X	E *B* B 3–4	1. 2. 287–1. 3. 295
			E *B* C 1–2	
2	D	Y	E *A* C 3–4	1. 3. 296–2. 2. 103
			E *A* D 1–2	
1	E	X	E *B* D 3–4	2. 2. 104–2. 3. 204
			E *B* E 1–2	

[1] *Ibid.* p. 346.

[2] These are:

Eld *A*	Eld *B*
Cressid, Cressida	Cresseid, Cresseida
Hellen	Helen
shalbe, wilbe	shall be, will be
ritch	rich
els	else

[3] For an instance, see Q.'s reading at 4. 4. 53–4 (cited above, p. 127 and cf. below, p. 139).

Press	Sheet	Skeleton	Compositor	
			E A	E 3–4⎫
2	F	Z	E A	F 1–4⎬ 2. 3. 205–4. 1. 46
1	G	Y	E A	G 1–4⎭
2	H	X	E B	H 1–2　4. 1. 47–4. 3. 3
			E A	H 3–4⎫
1	I	Y	E A	I 1–2⎬ 4. 3. 4 –4. 5. 136
			E B	I 3–4　4. 5. 137–4. 5. 289
2	K	Z	E A	K 1–3　4. 5. 290–5. 2. 122
			E B	K 4^r　5. 2. 123–5. 2. 159
			E A	K 4^v　5. 2. 160–5. 2. 196
1	L ⎫	X+Y	E B	L 1–2　5. 3. 1–5. 4. 24
	⎬		E A	L 3–4⎫
2	M ⎭		E A	M 1 ⎬ 5. 4. 24–end

On this analysis, E A set fifty-nine pages and E B
(the more skilled workman) set only twenty-nine, and
the reason for this unequal distribution would appear to
be that the two compositors combined could set sheets
faster than two presses could print them off. This is
a fair inference from the fact that a third skeleton forme
was constructed for sheet F, and it would account for
the temporary withdrawal of E B, whose participation
in sheets H and I seems again to have put composition
ahead of printing. From this it would appear that the
Q. manuscript presented no obstacles to rapid composition and, therefore, that the troubles that led to bodging
at 3. 3. 197 and 4. 4. 53–4 were encountered when the
manuscript was copied from the foul papers.[1] That the
foul papers were sometimes confused is to be inferred
from the tangles in some of F.'s recoveries[2] and difficulty
in deciphering them may explain some of Q.'s more

[1] This seems to me to point away from Shakespeare as
the transcriber, for even if he could not recover what
Johnson called the 'elegant line' at 3. 3. 197 already cited
(p. 127), he could presumably have supplied something less
trite than Q.'s reading. It also constitutes the best evidence
we have that Q. was a transcript of foul papers and not of a
prompt book.

[2] See notes to 1. 3. 354–6, 3. 3. 161–3, 5. 3. 20–2.

extensive lacunae; for the omission of phrases, lines and longer passages is as common in the work of E *B* as E *A* and it seems unlikely that a compositor who had lost only three words[1] would have been guilty of eleven more considerable omissions. Miscalculation in casting off copy might explain some losses of this kind, but the distribution of Q.'s longer omissions does not suggest that this is a plausible explanation and the likelihood would seem to be that these passages were for the most part missing from the Q. manuscript.

I have described elsewhere some of the shortcomings of the Folio text,[2] which is certainly not the reliable check on Q.'s readings that it should have been— possibly owing to its belated addition to the volume. But unreliable as it manifestly is, it is the text to whose substantive variants an editor must defer whenever they are inexplicable as collator's[3] or compositors'[4] blunders,

---

[1] See notes to 2. 3. 152, 4. 1. 54, 5. 4. 3.

[2] See *Textual Problems of the First Folio* (as above), pp. 86–93.

[3] Collator's misreadings are unusually numerous in this F. text, partly no doubt because the manuscript was not always legible and partly, perhaps, because his work was hurried.

[4] The first three F. pages to be printed were set by Jaggard *B* and the first of these was re-set by *A* when printing was resumed. From the point where F. has independent status (the Prologue and the text from 1. 2. 235) the stints were as follows: *B* set the Prologue and 1. 2. 235 to 2. 2. 188 and 4. 5. 173 to the end of 5. 1. *A* set the rest. I accept Philip Williams's conclusion that *A* set the lower portion of col. 2 on ¶¶ 4v, but am doubtful about Hinman's attribution of the second and third (derivative) F. pages to compositor *E* (see 'The Prentice Hand in the Tragedies of the Shakespeare First Folio: Compositor *E*', in *Studies in Bibliography*, IX (1957), pp. 3–20, especially p. 7 n. 8).

for we can at least be certain that the manuscript used in preparing the copy for F. had remained in the custody of the players. This does not mean that F. is the better text in the sense that it contains fewer perversions than Q., for the accuracy with which compositors reproduced copy in no way affects the authority of their copy. What it means is that, when misreadings and printing-house errors have been weeded out, F. seems the safer guide to what Shakespeare wrote.

The present text is, therefore, eclectic, like the Old Cambridge text (with a bias towards F.) and the more recent texts of Kittredge, Alexander and Sisson (all with a bias towards Q.). But whatever their bias, they concur in rejecting about 80 per cent of the variants and in my choice of readings I have been guided by what these rejected readings imply about the shortcomings of Q. and F. By far the majority of the variants unanimously rejected look to me like printing-house blunders which careful proof-reading would have eliminated. When it is remembered that there are about 500 verbal variants, of which editors reject about 200 from Q. and another 200 from F., and that of the remaining 100 or so variants about half amount to no more than the difference between 'a' and 'he', 'an' and 'if', or differences in concord, it will be evident that, whatever an editor's bias, comparatively few readings present a serious problem. The choice is seldom, indeed, a genuinely substantive one.

Where the present text differs most from recent editions is in the following respects:

(1) In the dialogue of 1. 1. 1–1. 2. 235, since it is now recognized that we have here only the authority of Q., I have emended more freely than is usual. There is manifestly something wrong in the implication of recent editions that Q. was here so much more reliable than in the text of 1. 2. 235, etc. The difference is simply

that we have F.'s assistance in the detection of errors from this point and that Eld *A*, responsible for the Q. text to this point, is likely to have made the kind of mistake he habitually made later. Contrary to custom, I have therefore emended readings at 1. 1. 24, 1. 2. 23, 29, 96, 188, 215.

(2) In the conviction that F. was printed from a corrected example of Q., I have emended, in the rest of the play, far more freely than my predecessors what I take to be common errors—i.e. Q. errors which F. failed to correct through oversight. Substantive emendations[1] of this kind occur as follows, an asterisk indicating that the emendation is not made in any of the four editions already cited or in Deighton's Arden edition (one of the more enlightened in this respect):

1. 3. *51, 54, 63, *220, 386–7
2. 1. *42–3, 104, *110, 113
2. 2. *38
2. 3. *78
3. 1. *34
3. 2. 21, *23, 67, 131, *159, 207
3. 3. *3, 4, 43, *73, 110, *147, 168, *173, 178
4. 1. 80
4. 2. *4, *54
4. 3. *3
4. 4. *15, *37, 122
4. 5. *9, *48, 59
5. 1. *5, *89
5. 2. 60, 161, 167
5. 3. *91
5. 4. *11, 15
5. 5. *45

[1] The list does not, therefore, include emendations of an insignificant kind made for metre or normalizations of spelling and grammar.

5. 6. *7
5. 7. 11
5. 10. 7
5. 10. 37

(3) Contrary to custom, I have also emended readings peculiar to F. in Prol. 25 and 1. 3. 355; and (4), in view of the many common errors in speech prefixes, I have emended at 2. 1. 41, 4. 5. 73 and 5. 2. 103, as well as making the usual emendations of this kind elsewhere.

ACCIDENTALS

Spelling has been silently modernized and variants of this kind are recorded only if the sense intended is in doubt. Where the present text differs most from its immediate predecessors is in the emendation of common errors for the sake of the metre—for compositors no more reproduced their copy literatim in accidentals than in substantive readings. For punctuation, see below (p. 139).

SPELLING

The spelling of the text is that of the relevant *O.E.D.* main entry except in a few cases where a distinctive traditional spelling has obvious advantages: e.g. *breese* = gadfly (*O.E.D.* 'breeze'), *empale* = surround (*O.E.D.* 'impale').

NOTES

I have recorded as a rule three kinds of variants: (1) verbal variants in the dialogue, (2) variants in speech prefixes, and (3) variants in stage directions. To have recorded all the variants would have occupied a disproportionate amount of space and I have therefore disregarded all readings (whether in Q. or F.) where a combination of letters fails to make a word. Errors due to foul case and the omission and transposition of letters are particularly rife in Q., especially in the work of Eld *A.* Further, since the pointing of Q. so often shows little comprehension of the matter (see below), I have recorded the punctuation of Q. and F. only when an emendation usually made seems questionable. I have also, as a rule, excluded notes on lineation, etc. My aim, in short, has been to give, within the physical limits of this edition, a picture of the substantive differences between the texts. Readings common to Q. and F. are cited from Q. (regardless of differences in spelling and punctuation). The first and second settings of the first F. page (1. 1. 1–94) are distinguished as F^a and F^b. For Q. readings I have relied on the Shakespeare Association Facsimile (1952) and for F. readings on the Oxford Facsimile, using Willoughby's facsimile (cf. p. 123 n. 3) for F^a.

I have modernized matter cited from Caxton, whose old spelling would be even more troublesome to readers than that of Shakespearian texts.

The following is a list of abridged titles, etc.:

Abbott=*A Shakespearian Grammar*, by E. A. Abbott (2nd ed. 1870).
Al.=ed. of Sh. by Peter Alexander, 1951.

Camb.=*The Cambridge Sh.* (3rd ed. 1891–3).

Cap.=ed. of Sh. by Edward Capell, 1768.

Caxton=*The Recuyell of the Historyes of Troye*, trans. by William Caxton, ed. H. Oskar Sommer, 1894. (2 vols., pagination continuous: Vol. 1, pp. 1–320; Vol. 2, pp. 321 ff.)

Collier ii=ed. of Sh. by J. P. Collier (2nd ed. 1858).

Cooper=*Thesaurus Linguae Romanae et Britannicae* by Thomas Cooper (4th ed. 1584).

Deighton=ed. by K. Deighton (Arden Sh.), 1906.

Delius=ed. by Nicholas Delius (2nd ed. 1864).

Dyce=ed. of Sh. by Alexander Dyce (5th ed. 1886).

G.=Glossary.

Greg, *Sh. F. F.*=*The Shakespeare First Folio*, by W. W. Greg, 1955.

Grey=*Critical Notes on Shakespeare*, by Zachary Grey, 1754.

Hanmer=ed. of Sh. by Thomas Hanmer, 1743–4.

J.=ed. of Sh. by Samuel Johnson, 1765.

Kellner=*Restoring Shakespeare*, by Leon Kellner, 1925.

Kit.=ed. of Sh. by G. L. Kittredge, 1936.

Kökeritz=*Shakespeare's Pronunciation*, by Helge Kökeritz, 1953.

Linthicum=*Costume in the Drama of Shakespeare and his Contemporaries*, by M. C. Linthicum, 1936.

Lydgate=*Troy Book*, by John Lydgate, ed. Henry Bergen (E.E.T.S.), 1906.

Mal.=ed. of Sh. by Edmund Malone, 1790.

N.V.S.=The New Variorum ed. of *Troilus and Cressida*, by H. N. Hillebrand and T. W. Baldwin, 1953.

Noble=*Shakespeare's Biblical Knowledge*, by Richmond Noble, 1935.

O.E.D.=*The Oxford English Dictionary.*

On.=*A Shakespeare Glossary*, by C. T. Onions (2nd ed. 1919).

Pope = ed. of Sh. by Alexander Pope, 1723–5 (2nd ed. 1728).

Rann = ed. of Sh. by Joseph Rann, 1786–94.

Ritson = *Remarks on the Text and Notes of the Last Edition of Shakespeare*, by Joseph Ritson, 1783.

Rowe = ed. of Sh. by Nicholas Rowe, 1709 (2nd ed. 1709; 3rd ed. 1714).

S.D. = Stage Direction.

S.N. = Speaker's Name.

Schmidt = *Shakespeare-Lexicon*, by Alexander Schmidt, 1874.

Sh. Eng. = *Shakespeare's England*, 2 vols. 1916.

Singer = ed. of Sh. by S. W. Singer (2nd ed. 1856).

Sisson = ed. of Sh. by C. J. Sisson, 1954.

Sisson *N.R.* = *New Readings in Shakespeare*, by C. J. Sisson, 1956.

Staunton = ed. of Sh. by Howard Staunton, 1858–60.

Steev. = ed. of J.'s Sh. by George Steevens, 1773, 1778, 1785.

Tannenbaum[1] = 'Notes on *Troilus and Cressida*' by S. A. Tannenbaum (in *Sh. Assoc. Bull.* VII (1932)).

Tannenbaum[2] = 'A Critique of the Text of *Troilus and Cressida*' (in *Sh. Assoc. Bull.* IX (1934)).

Theob. = ed. of Sh. by Lewis Theobald, 1733 (2nd ed. 1740).

Tyrwhitt = *Observations and Conjectures upon some Passages of Shakespeare*, by Thomas Tyrwhitt 1766.

Var. '03 = Variorum ed. of J. and Steev., ed. Reed, 1803.

Var. '21 = Variorum, ed. Boswell, 1821.

S. Walker = *A Critical Examination of the text of Shakespeare*, by William Sidney Walker, 1860.

Warb. = ed. of Sh. by William Warburton, 1747.

White ii = ed. of Sh. by R. G. White (Riverside ed., 2nd ed. 1883).

Names of the Characters. An incomplete list of Dramatis Personae was first given by Rowe. The list preceding the present text is substantially Malone's, though I have added the Prologue and question whether we are right in accepting 'Margarelon' as the name of the bastard son of Priam. The name occurs once only in Q. F. (at 5. 5. 7) and it was probably a common error, due to misreading, for 'Margareton', Benoît's name for this son (*Roman de Troie*, 15768), which all his medieval successors apparently preserved.

There are no variations in the nomenclature of characters with personal names apart from the alternation of 'Cressida' and 'Cressid', 'Diomedes' and 'Diomed', 'Pandarus' and 'Pandar', and 'Priamus' and 'Priam'; 'Helena' for 'Helen' occurs once in F. (3. 1. 43 S.D.) and 'Nell' is twice used by Paris (3. 1. 53, 138). Variations of this kind are partly Shakespearian and partly due to F.'s usual tendency to normalize. The designations of servants and other minor characters are more variable. Q. and F. agree in describing Troilus' servant as 'Boy' in 1. 2. 272–6 and 'Man' at the beginning of 3. 2, but Paris' servant at the opening of 3. 1 is 'Man' in Q. and 'Servant' in F. The same variants occur again at 5. 5. 5. The only other variant occurs in the speech prefix at 5. 8. 16, where Q. has 'One' but F. an abbreviation for 'Greek'. It is impossible to assign responsibility for such variants with any certainty. They might have originated in the book-keeper's clarifications in the foul papers or in Jaggard's printing house (cf. F.'s substitution of 'Servant' for 'Man' in *Rich. II*, 3. 4, and of 'Page' for 'Boy' in the second setting of *Rom.* 5. 3. 281).

Acts and Scenes. There are no divisions in Q. and F. For convenience of reference, I follow the now customary divisions, which are satisfactory up to and including 5. 4. The traditional act divisions and many of the scene divisions to this point were made by Rowe, though Theobald's scene divisions were the first to correspond in all respects with those now in vogue. The scene divisions beginning at 5. 5 go back to Capell and they have probably contributed a good deal to the impression that the battle scenes were scrappy work, since their fidgety changes from one part of the field to another slow down the action. Editors before Capell had here far fewer scene divisions. Capell (following Pope) also marked a new scene at 5. 7. 8.

Localities. The only serious puzzle is what (if anything) Shakespeare intended the audience to infer about the Pandarus-Cressida ménage (see 3. 2. *Loc.* n.), but the question is of no great importance except in so far as it may have some bearing on the reading at 4. 2. 72 (see note).

Punctuation. The punctuation of Eld *A* suggests that the Q. manuscript was very lightly punctuated indeed and that he often supplied stops at random without having understood the sense of what he was setting. In view of the prevalence of foul case in Q., it is only reasonable to suppose that this affected stops as well as letters, but this does not explain all Eld *A*'s blunders. Eld *B*, like Jaggard *A* and *B*, had a far better understanding of the matter, though a fair number of Q.'s errors were reproduced in F. Since Q.'s point is so often manifestly contrary to common sense, I have accepted all the usual emendations of the pointing of both texts without comment, unless the change merits discussion.

Stage Directions. Q.'s (so far as they go) suggest foul papers as their basis, though they are unusually scrappy. F.'s are fuller, though they are not such as to suggest that the foul papers had been prepared for use as prompt copy, since they are sometimes vague (see, for instance, 4. 4. 108 S.D. and note) and at other times misleading—

suggesting additions casually made without adequate
thought about the action (see, for instance, 4. 4. 48
S.D. n. and 101 n). I record all significant substantive
variants of this kind. A feature of Q. is a tendency to
abbreviate names with a following colon, and as this
appears in the work of both of Eld's compositors
(though it is commoner in the work of Eld *A* than in
that of Eld *B*), it may derive from their manuscript.
F. sets the names in full and, although such changes
were normally made by the F. compositors on their own
account, I have recorded all variants of this kind unless
there was only one way of expanding the Q. abbreviation (thus recording 'Diomed' or 'Diomedes' for
'Diom:' but not 'Agamemnon' for 'Agam:').

Verse Lining. For the most part I have tried to keep
in step with that of the 1891–3 Cambridge edition. The
verse lining of longer passages is usually good, but in
shorter speeches both texts tend to print prose as verse
or verse as prose as well as to economize space by
printing a line and a half of verse as a single line. Both
texts were set from cast-off copy and this may sometimes
have encouraged crowding. The repulsive appearance
of some pages of Q. was fairly certainly due to miscalculation in casting off.

Prologue

Material. Caxton (pp. 545–6) describes the assembly at
the 'port of Athens' of sixty-nine 'kings and dukes' and
their arrival, after many delays, at Tenedos. The names of
the six gates of Troy correspond more closely with the forms
given by Caxton (p. 507) than with other known accounts
(see N.V.S. note to Prol. 17). Lydgate uses the word 'haven'
for 'port' and does not mention the number 'sixty-nine'.

S.D. *Entry* (after Collier ii) F. 'The Prologue.'
Q. omits (omitting the Prologue entirely).
1. S.N. F. omits.

2. *orgulous* The inversion (cf. 'crownets regal', l. 6) and choice of word (cf. 'immures', l. 8, 'Dardan', l. 13, and 'pavilions', l. 15) contribute to the deliberately elevated style, intended as a significant contrast to the unheroic temper of the play.

12. *barks* (F2) F. '*Barke*'.

17. *Antenorides* (Theob.) F. 'Antenonidus'.

18. *corresponsive and fulfilling bolts* i.e. corresponding bolts fitting tightly. O.E.D. and On. gloss 'fulfilling' as 'complementary', but the original meaning of 'fulfil' (=to fill to the full) makes the meaning more weighty.

19. *Sperr* (Theob.) F. '*Stirre*'.

23. *A Prologue armed* An allusion to Jonson's *Poetaster* (1601), where the Prologue was armed in 'well erected confidence' against the author's detractors. The usual dress for the speaker of a prologue was a black cloak.

25. *condition* (A.W.) F. '*conditions*'. The sense requires the singular: the character ('condition') of the subject is martial.

28. *Beginning...away* In view of the rhyme, an alexandrine is unexpected and Theob.'s ''Ginning i'th' middle...' may be right.

in the middle According to 1. 3. 12, 'after seven years' siege'.

30–1. *are...war* A perfect rhyme in Shakespeare's day.

31. S.D. F. omits.

I. I

Head Title Q. 'The history of *Troylus* and *Cresseida*.' F. 'The Tragedie of Troylus and Cressida.'

Material. See note to l. 83.

S.D. *Loc*. (Cap.) *Entry* (after Cap.) Q. F. '*Enter* Pandarus *and* Troylus.'

7–8. *to...to...to* Generally taken as = 'in addition to', though Abbott (§ 187) took as = 'in proportion to'.

14. *meddle nor make* A common alliterative phrase; see G. 'make'.

15. *tarry* (Q.) F. 'needes tarrie'. The interpolated word has nothing to recommend it and the repeated 'must tarry' (ll. 18, 21) tells against it.

24. *there's* (A.W.) Q. F. 'heares' (possibly in anticipation of 'hereafter').

24–5. *the word* The word is 'tarry' (Delius), though some take it to be 'hereafter': after waiting for the leavening there is still ('yet') after this ('hereafter') more waiting—i.e. for the kneading, etc.

26. *of the oven* (F.ᵇ) Q.F.ᵃ 'the ouen'. The previous phrase makes omission in Q. fairly certain.

27. *you may* (F.) Q. 'yea may'.
to burn (F.) Q. 'burne'. F.'s idiom is in accordance with Shakespearian usage.

30. *Doth lesser...I do* i.e. Patience herself is not more patient than Troilus. The construction is confused.

33. *When...thence?* (Rowe iii) Q. F. 'then she comes when she is thence'. The emendation has common sense in its favour: Troilus breaks off to accuse himself of treachery for implying that Cressida could ever be out of mind.

38. *perceive* Probably = 'observe' (O.E.D. 1). Schmidt and On. gloss as 'see through', but all the relevant O.E.D. examples (s.v. 5) imply seeing through some subterfuge, whereas the point here is that Troilus' patently glum looks would attract attention.

39. *a storm* (Rowe) Q. 'a scorne'; F. 'a-scorne'. The triteness of the emendation, to which N.V.S. cites Keats's objection, is, in fact, a recommendation. The simplicity of the two other similes in this speech precludes the idea that any subtlety was intended.

45. *she is* (Q. F.) A.W. conj. 'for she is' (as giving a smoother sequence of thought).

46. *praise her* (Q.) F. 'praise it'.

56–7. *voice;...discourse—* (Theob.) Q.'s punctuation ('voice,...discourse:') is too haphazard to have any weight (see p. 139) and Theob.'s aposiopesis is in accordance with Troilus' style. Cf. *Tit.* 3. 2. 29, 'O, handle not the theme, to talk of hands'.

57. *that her hand* i.e. that hand of hers.

60. *spirit of sense* i.e. the spirit of the sense of touch. 'Spirits' were supposed to be subtle vapours generated by the blood and the intermediaries between the body and soul.

62. *As* (Q. F.) S. Walker conj. 'And'. The emphatic 'And' improves the sense and 'As' might have been picked up from the previous line.

68. *in't* (F.) Q. 'in it'. F. accords with Pandarus' colloquial style.

70. *has...hands* i.e. 'she can find her own remedy', with, Warb. and J. thought, allusion to cosmetics.

71. *Good Pandarus...* In expostulation against his decision to wash his hands of the business.

73. *on of you* (F.) Q. 'of you'.

77. *not kin* (F.ᵇ) Q. F.ᵃ 'kin'.

78. *as fair... Sunday* i.e. as fair in fast-day dress as Helen in her best; hence, fairer than Helen.

o'...o' (A.W.) Q. 'a...on'; F. 'on...on'.

78–9. *what care* (F.) Q. 'what'.

82. S.N. (Q. F.ᵃ) F.ᵇ 'Troy.'

83. *behind her father* According to Caxton (pp. 550–1), Calchas had joined the Greeks at 'the yle of delphe'. He had been sent there by Priam to consult the oracle about the outcome of the quarrel and the oracle advised him not to return to Troy because the Trojans would be defeated, but to join Achilles, who had been sent there from Athens before the Greeks

sailed, on the same mission. Calchas therefore returned to Athens with Achilles. Cf. note to 3. 3. 15.

90. S.D. Q. F. '*Exit. Sound alarum.*'

96. *do you* (Q. F.) A.W. conj. 'you do'.

103. *Ilium* The name 'Ylion' was used by Benoît and his successors for Priam's palace and 'Troy' for the city. Shakespeare preserves the distinction. The Latin form occurs again at 1. 2. 44, 47, but it may be merely the Q. compositor's error. At 1. 2. 180, where Q. has 'Ilion', the F. compositor normalized to 'Illium', but thereafter on the five occasions when the word occurs the compositors of both texts agree on the -ion ending and this may have been the reading of the original manuscript throughout.

113. *a scar to scorn* i.e. a wound (see G. 'scar') for mockery, since (as N.V.S. explains) Paris was gored by the cuckold's horn he gave Menelaus; cf. 1. 2. 215–17.

116. *Better...may* i.e. amorous sport would be more to his liking.

117–18. *thither...together* The rhyme was a perfect one in Shakespeare's day and Q. F. provide an eye rhyme by reading 'togither'.

I. 2

S.D. *Loc.* (Cap. after Theob.) *Entry* (after Theob.) Q. F. '*Enter* Cressid *and her man.*'

1 etc. S.N. Alexander. (Mal.) Q. F. '*Man.*'

5. *as a virtue fixed* Patience was one of the four cardinal virtues and the stoic virtue; 'fixed'=steadfast.

6. *chid* (Q.) F. 'chides'.

7. *husbandry* The conceit of the husbandman is continued in the two senses of 'field' in l. 9; cf. Introduction, p. xii.

15–16. *They...alone* As verse (Cap.) Q. F. as one line (...and...).

16. *stands alone* Cressida's following quibble turns on the two senses (1) is unique, and (2) stands up without support.

17. *they* (F.)　Q. 'the'.

23. *forced* (A.W. after Theob. conj.)　Q. F. 'sauced'. The emendation better maintains the paradoxical balance between Ajax's folly and wisdom.

29. *or a*　　(A.W. after Hanmer)　Q. F. 'or'. Omission seems certain in view of 'a gouty Briareus'.

purblind (Q.)　F. 'purblinded'.

37. S.D. As in Dyce F. after l. 35; Q. omits.

47. *you* (Theob. ii)　Q. F. 'yea'.

64. *knew him* For the quibble, see G. 'know'.

65. *Troilus is Troilus* Cf. *Ant.* 3. 2. 13, 'Would you praise Caesar, say 'Caesar': go no further'. The quibbling reply turns on this sense (=perfection in himself) and the usual one (=himself and no one else).

68. *nor* (Q.)　F. 'not'.

74. *Condition* Pandarus continues the speech interrupted by Cressida: he would go barefoot to India to restore Troilus to himself; see G. 'condition'.

81. *Excuse me* The first O.E.D. example of this phrase as an apology for a contradiction.

86. *wit* (Rowe)　Q. F. 'will'.

93–4. *a brown favour* Dark complexions (see G. 'favour') were not admired.

95. *but*=merely.

96. *the truth* (A.W.)　Q. F. 'truth'. Cressida's mocking reply suggests that 'the' was omitted here; 'to say the truth' was, in any case, the more usual idiom.

107. *copper nose* See G. 'copper'. Lodge, prescribing 'remedies for the infirmities of the face, the extreame rednes thereof, pimples and fierie speckles' says that this infirmity 'is in scorne called coppernose, and is an excessive rednes of the face, either in the nose

or other parts thereof' (*The poore Mans Talentt*, Hunterian Club ed., 1881, p. 11).

110. *merry Greek* Another common expression; see G. 'Greek'.

114. *a tapster's arithmetic* i.e. the most elementary kind of reckoning.

118. *he so* (Q.) F. 'he is so'.

lifter Generally taken as=thief (a conycatching term), but a 'limb-lifter' was a fornicator and this may be the point of the quibble here; 'old'=experienced.

130. *the* (F2) Q. F. 'thee'.

134–5. *addle...idle* A common, and possibly stale, pun; Kökeritz (p. 68) cites two parallels in Lyly, and cf. Lodge, *Euphues Shadow*, Hunterian Club ed., 1883, p. 39.

145. *With millstones* Proverbial (cf. *R. III*, 1.3.353, 'Your eyes drop millstones, when fools' eyes fall tears'), implying (like ll. 147–8, 150) that the mirth seems excessive.

147. *a more* (Q.) F. 'more'.

153. *a green hair* The kind to be expected of a greenhorn.

158–9. *two and fifty* According to Homeric tradition, Priam had fifty sons (cf. *Tit.* 1.1.79–80); since the white hair is Priam and Paris a forked hair, the number serves for the jest.

168. *passed* For the point of the quibble in l. 170, see G. 'pass'.

169. *it has* (Q.) F. 'is has'.

171. *a thing* i.e. a certain thing; see Abbott, § 81.

173. *do* (Q.) F. 'does'.

177. S.D. Q. F. '*Sound a retreate.*' (after l. 175).

180. *Ilion* (Q.) F. 'Illium'.

185. S.D. (after Rowe) Q. F. '*Enter Æneas.*' (after l. 184).

187. *tell* (Q.) F. omits.

188. *see Troilus* (A.W.) Q. F. 'see'. Troilus is surely the cynosure; cf. ll. 193–4, 218.

S.D. (after Rowe) Q. F. '*Enter Antenor.*' (after l. 189).

191. *a man* (F.) Q. 'man'.

192. *judgements* (Q.) F. 'iudgement'.

194. *him* (Q.) F. 'him him'.

197. *You shall see* See G. 'nod'. Since O.E.D. cites two instances of 'nod'=noddy, Deighton's conj. 'Ay, you shall see', putting the joke more plainly (cf. *Gent.* 1. 1. 110), seems unnecessary.

198. *the rich...more* i.e. you will be more of a fool than you are.

S.D. (after Rowe) Q. F. '*Enter Hector.*'

203. *a brave* (Q.) F. 'braue'.

204. *man's* (F.) Q. 'man'.

206–7. *there's laying* (Q.) F. 'laying'.

207. *take't off who will* A catch phrase='and no mistake' (lit. 'notches such as no smith or armourer could obliterate'). O.E.D. (s.v. 'lay' vb.¹ 55*e*) cites Cotgrave: '*Cocher sur la grosse taille*, (as wee say) to lay it on, (take it off who as will;) to spend or borrow, exceeding much'. *will* (Q.) F. 'ill'.

209. *Be* Often used in questions for 'are'; see Abbott, § 299 and cf. § 300.

213. S.D. (after Rowe) Q. F. '*Enter Paris.*' (after l. 209).

215. *home hurt* (A.W. after Rowe) Q. F. 'hurt home'.

218. *see* (Q.) F. omits.

S.D. (after Rowe) Q. F. '*Enter Helenus:*' (after l. 219).

227. S.D. (after Rowe) Q. F. '*Enter Troylus.*'

232. *note* (Q.) F. 'not'.

235. *how he* The third of the F. pages representing a mere reprint of Q. ends here (catchword 'lookes,').

236. *ne'er* (F.) Q. 'neuer'.

240. *an eye* (Q.) F. 'money'.

S.D. (after Cap.) F. '*Enter common Souldiers.*' Q. omits.

241. *come* (F.) Q. 'comes'.

243–4. *i'th'eyes* (F.) Q. 'in the eyes'. Something of the love symbolism of exchanging eyes colours the meaning here, which is not so much 'in the sight of Troilus' as 'for the love of Troilus'.

248. *among* (F.) Q. 'amongst'.

255. *such like* (Q.) F. 'so forth'.

256. *season* (Q.) F. 'seasons'.

257. *minced* With obvious allusion to pies and the inventory of Pandarus' praise, but perhaps in the further sense of 'deprived of some essential part, mutilated', of which the first O.E.D. example is of 1609.

258. *date is* (Q.) F. 'dates'.

date is out See G. 'out', but also, as Deighton thought, with indecent implication.

259. *such another* (F.) Q. 'such a'. I follow F. doubtfully because, although 'such another' is fairly well authenticated (=such a), I doubt if it is as appropriate here as Q.'s reading, since it detracts from the climax of this dialogue in l. 272 ('You are such another').

a man (Q.) F. 'one'.

262. *wiles* (Q. F.) J. conj. 'will'.

263. *honesty* What Cressida is concerned to keep is not, of course, her chastity but her reputation for it.

mask 'These masks were oblong pieces of velvet or other silk, lined with soft skin or silk, having holes for eyes, and were used to protect a lady's complexion from the sun, or to shield her from public gaze' (Linthicum, p. 272).

264. *at a* (Q.) F. 'at, at a'.

272. S.D. (Cap.) Q.F. '*Enter Boy:*' (F. after l. 271).

275. *there...him* (Q.) F. omits.

276. S.D. (after Cap.) Q. F. omit.

279. *I'll be* (F.) Q. 'I wilbe'.

280. *To bring* The words seem to have had intensive force when 'be with' (see G. 'with') implied a threat. The origin of the expression and its precise significance are obscure. Pandarus ignores the quibble.

282. S.D. (after F.) Q. omits.

283 ff. *Words, vows*...With these trite couplets in which Cressida reveals that she is a Daphne who enjoys the chase (cf. 1. 1. 100), cf. her valedictory couplets, 5. 2. 107–12.

287. *wooing* i.e. when being wooed.

288. *Things...doing* i.e. her value is never higher than when she is beyond reach; cf. l. 290.

lies (Q. F.) Seymour conj. in Camb. 'lives' (very plausibly).

290. *Men...is* A significant line, which Q. distinguished (like l. 288) by placing it in inverted commas. The marking of *sententiae* by inverted commas or italics was not a feature of playhouse MSS. but was very fashionable about now in presentation MSS., the work of academic authors, edited texts, and certain printing houses (among them Eld's); see G. K. Hunter, 'The Marking of *Sententiae* in Elizabethan Printed Plays, Poems, and Romances' (in *Library*, 5 Ser. VI (1951), pp. 171–88). Q. marks *sententiae* again at l. 294, 1. 3. 117 and 5. 2. 112.

293. *out of love* = 'taught by love' (Deighton).

295. *Then...content* (Q.) F. 'That...Contents'.

296. S.D. (after Cap.) Q. F. '*Exit*.' Cressida's attendant appears to have been a mute onlooker for the latter part of the scene and editors perforce supply '*Exeunt*' here. His presence is last acknowledged in Cressida's off hand 'So he says here' in l. 53. Mr George Rylands tells me that, in Marlowe Society productions, Pandarus waves Alexander off at this point.

I. 3

Material. Homer (*Iliad*, VII) describes how Hector challenged any Greek to single combat and how Ajax drew the lot to fight against him. The idea of rigging the lottery seems to be Shakespeare's own. Ovid (*Met.* XIII. 87–80, 275–7) refers to the lottery and the choice of Ajax. Caxton's material is less relevant, for there (pp. 602–3), during the truce which saw the return of Cressida to her father, Hector visited Achilles' tent and challenged him to single combat, which neither Greeks nor Trojans would sanction as a means of settling the quarrel.

S.D. *Loc.* (after Rowe) *Entry* (after Cap.) Q. F. '...Vlisses, Diomedes...' (Q. omitting '*Sennet*').

2. *this* (Cap.) Q. 'these'; F. 'the'. Though 'jaundice' (Q. F. 'Iaundies') was apprehended as a plural, it seems not to have been so construed. The choice therefore lies between 'this' and F.'s 'the', which may be right.

on (F.) Q. 'ore' (unnaturally, and suggestive of a misreading).

8. *Infect* (F.) Q. 'Infects'.

divert (Rowe) Q. F. 'diuerts'.

13–17. *Sith...shape* i.e. history shows that set-backs and misfortunes in projects such as this are usual.

13. *every* (F.) Q. 'euer'.

19. *call...shames* (Q.) F. 'thinke...shame'.

22–30. *The fineness...unmingléd* The trials are biblical: for the metal image, cf. Job. xxiii. 10, Zech. xiii. 9; and for the winnowing of the wheat from the chaff, cf. Luke xxii. 31 (all cited N.V.S.).

27. *broad* (Q.) F. 'lowd'.

30. *unmingléd* The metre requires the pronunciation 'unmingeléd'.

31. *thy* (F.) Q. 'the'.

godlike (Q) F. 'godly'.

32. *apply* A word commonly used for the expounding of texts.

33–4. *In the reproof...men* i.e. men's real qualities are seen in the way they respond to misfortune. Difficulty has been found here, but as this is the proposition of the speech it must accord with the conclusion in ll. 51–4.

36. *patient* (F.) Q. 'ancient'.

39. *Thetis* See G.

42. *Perseus' horse* According to a tradition going back to classical times, Perseus (not Bellerophon) was the owner of Pegasus, the winged horse. N.V.S. has a long and interesting note on this association.

51. *flee* (A.W. after Cap.) Q. F. 'fled'. I assume a misreading in Q. carried over into F. through oversight—a simpler explanation of the awkward construction than the ellipsis ('being fled') supposed by Abbott, § 377.

54. *Retorts* (Dyce) Q. F. 'Retires'. Pope's emendation 'Returns' lacks the musical associations of 'retorts': 'retorted' meant that notes were re-sung twice as fast (see O.E.D. 'retorted', 1) and hence that the man of worth was more than a match for misfortune.

55. *nerve* (F.) Q. 'nerues'.

56. *spirit* (F.) Q. 'spright'.

58. *shut up* i.e. (fig.) included, embodied. As the heart and soul of Greece, Agamemnon should embody all their moods and thoughts.

59. *th'* (Q.) F. 'the'.

60, 61. S.Ds. (Rowe) Q. F. omit.

61. *thy* (F.) Q. 'the'.

stretched-out life Perhaps an echo of Ovid (*Met.* XII. 186, 'spatiosa senectus').

63. *all the hands* (A.W. after Orger conj.+ Deighton) Q. F. 'and the hand'. The end of l. 63 should correspond with the end of l. 67. Ulysses praises

Agamemnon for a weighty speech, worthy of commemoration in brass (with allusion to the engraving of laws and public records in brass), and Nestor for a persuasive speech, worthy to be hatched (=engraved) in silver (silver being emblematic of sweetness). Hence, since the ears of every Greek will be captivated by the sweetness of Nestor's speech, so the hands of every Greek should be moved to uphold the weightiness of Agamemnon's. Orger's emendation presupposes Q.'s perversion of 'all' (either through assimilation to 'hand' or in anticipation of 'and' in l. 64) and singular for plural—both common types of error.

65. *hatched in silver* To suppose that the phrase is merely a conceited allusion to Nestor's white hair robs the connection between brass and silver of proper significance.

66. *a bond of air* The idea of speech (see G. 'air') captivating the hearers was a renaissance commonplace, illustrated (as N.V.S. points out) in Alciati's *Emblems* (no. 180).

the axletree Possibly an error for 'th'axtree' (the latter a cognate word with the same meaning). According to pre-Copernican astronomy, the heavens wheeled in their spheres round the earth; see *Sh. Eng.* I, 444–5.

67. *On...ears* (Q.) F. 'In which the Heauens ride, knit all Greekes eares' (a typical compositor *B* perversion).

68. *his* (Q. F.) Confusion of this kind was very common after a parenthesis; Orger conj.+Deighton 'thy'.

70–4. (F.) Q. omits the speech. It would seem natural for Ulysses to wait for permission to proceed, but the compliment paid to him is so cumbersome that this may explain Q.'s omission.

70. *be't...expect* i.e. it is less likely that Ulysses will

say anything unnecessary or useless than that Thersites will utter something worth listening to.

73. *mastic* The meaning is uncertain: 'mastiff', 'mastix' (a scourge), 'masticating' and 'mastic' (a gum used for filling teeth) have all been proposed in explanation. If the text is correct, the last offers least difficulty and, if 'divide thy lips' implies clarity, 'gummy' provides an appropriate antithesis; cf. the 'ruinous butt' and 'indistinguishable cur' of 5. 1. 27–8.

75. *basis* (F.) Q. 'bases'.

77–137. *But for…strength* Commentators have found parallels to this speech in Plato's *Republic* (Bk. VIII), Elyot's *Governor* (Chs. I–II), the *Homilies* ('Of Obedience'), *The Faerie Queene* (Bk. V), Hooker's *Ecclesiastical Polity* (Bk. I, iii), and elsewhere. Extracts are cited by N.V.S. (pp. 389 ff.), which remarks that 'the speech…follows a familiar pattern.…The pattern, repeated in the various political treatises of the age, presents a picture of orderly government based on a supreme head and on the harmonious relations of parts …followed by one of the chaos which results from sedition and a democratic disruption of order.…Order among men is always presented as a part of the law of nature, corresponding to order among the heavenly bodies and the elements.…It is not necessary, or wise, therefore to suppose, without a more compelling parallel than we have yet found, that the speech of Ulysses is indebted to any one treatise.…We may be sure that Shakespeare was familiar with some of the standard works on government, and with the rather stereotyped order and details of presentation. He follows the pattern, but the embroidery we may suppose to be his own' (pp. 396–7).

80. *Hollow upon* (Q. F.) Hanmer 'Upon', perhaps rightly, for the tents are only too much occupied by the factious Greeks. It is the factions which are 'hollow'

(=empty, useless), because (as the bee parallel explains) they produce nothing for the common good.

81. *the general* J.'s interpretation is usually accepted: '*when the general is not* to the army *like the hive* to the bees, the repository of the stock of every individual'.

83–4. *Degree...mask* The 'specialty of rule' (see G. 'specialty') is the contract to *observe* authority, which is here expressed in the metaphor of masked identity. If all men are masked, the worst seems as good as the best and authority is disregarded (cf. *Tim.* 4. 1). From now on, 'degree' (see G.) is the symbol of order and the key-word, in a variety of technical senses, to the imagery of this speech. It is as essential to society (civic, academic, commercial) as it is to cosmic order or harmony in music, and when order is not observed there is universal chaos and the law of the jungle prevails.

87. *Insisture* See G. The word is not known to occur elsewhere. Baldwin (N.V.S.), like Hudson, explains as 'the apparent stopping when a planet appears to become stationary at either end of its course', but so technical a meaning seems alien to the otherwise general terms in which this analogy is presented.

91. *other*=others; see Abbott, § 12.

92. *influence...planets* (Q.) F. 'ill Aspects of Planets euill'. I see no point in F.'s inversion of the last two words and contrary to custom accept Q.'s 'influence' (defended by Greg, *Sh. F. F.*, p. 346 n. 20): 'ill' suggests interpolation in anticipation of 'evil', leading to the perhaps unconscious substitution of 'aspects' for 'influence'. The popular use of 'aspect' (strictly=the way in which the planets looked upon *each other*) in the sense of 'influence' (see G.) perhaps encouraged the error.

93. *posts* What 'posts' (see G.) is the sun's eye. The sun itself could not post to good and bad without causing even greater disorder than the failure of the other

planets to pursue their appointed courses. The argument is that leadership is necessary (cf. ll. 89–91, 'And therefore...other') and beneficial (its radiant eye transmitting health to all) provided that *all* recognize their obligations.

like...king The Elizabethan postal system was designed for Government service and was the fastest means of travel (*Sh. Eng.* 1, 201). Cf. 'the eyes of the Lord run to and fro' (2 Chron. xvi. 9, Zech. iv. 10).

94–5. *Sans...bad* Punctuated as in Q. (+Camb.). F.'s comma after 'check' (+most edd.) makes 'sans check' (=without sudden stoppage) qualify 'posts' to the detriment of the sense.

95. *mixture* i.e. failing to observe 'degree, priority, and place'. The opening of *The Faerie Queene*, Bk. v illustrates how even gradual planetary deviation was thought to affect the earth.

to disorder i.e. leading to disorder ('to' expressing motion towards).

102. *of* (Q.) F. 'to'. The ladder is not the means by which 'high designs' are achieved but the symbol of them: great enterprises depend on the subordination of the parts to the whole and there must be 'line of order' as in a ladder or the grand design of the universe.

105. *dividable* See G., but the context makes it likely that the word refers to degrees of latitude and longitude (i.e. 'charted' shores).

106. *primogenitive* (F.) Q. 'primogenitie'. The usual word was 'primogeniture' and as a coinage F. seems the more explicable since 'prerogative' in the next line may have suggested it. Cf. 'protractive' and 'persistive' (both new words) in ll. 20–1.

110. *meets* (F.) Q. 'melts'. F. is more forceful.

114. *Strength...imbecility* i.e. the strong would dominate the weak.

116–18. *Force...too* i.e. if physical force (which is

wrong) became right, the distinction between right
and wrong would be destroyed and so too would
Justice (one of the cardinal virtues); cf. *The Faerie
Queene*, v, 4 and v, 10.

118. *their* (Q.) F. 'her'.

119. *includes* (F.) Q. 'include'. Schmidt glossed
as 'terminate', On. as 'resolve itself into', but the idea
is perhaps that of embodiment (cf. 'shut up', l. 58)
into something progressively more dangerous. The
general sense is that when Justice no longer prevails,
everything becomes confined to physical strength, then
to self-seeking ('will') and then to self-indulgence
('appetite'), to the destruction of all.

124. *eat up himself* Cf. 5. 4. 32–4.

127. *it is* (Q.) F. 'is it'.

128. *with* (Q.) F. 'in'.

134. *pale* A conventional characteristic of Envy
(N. V. S.).

137. *stands* (Q.) F. 'liues'.

143. *sinew and the forehand* i.e. the foremost in
strength.

149. *awkward* (F). Q. 'sillie'.

153–4. *whose conceit...hamstring* i.e. whose understanding is in his hams.

159. *unsquared* (F.) Q. 'vnsquare'.

161. *seem* (Q.) F. 'seemes'.

fusty (Q. F.) That the reading is an error for
'fustian' has very naturally been suspected, but 'fusty'
='stale', 'old fashioned', seems adequate for the sense.

164. *right* (Q.) F. 'iust'. Since Achilles 'still cries
"Excellent! 'tis Nestor right!"' (ll. 169–70), it seems
very probable that Q. is correct here and that 'just' was
the F. compositor's substitution; cf. the same F. change
in *R.II*, 1. 3. 55.

165. *hem* (Q.) F. 'hum'.

168. *his wife* i.e. Venus.

175. *And at* (Q. F.) Pope 'At' (very attractively since 'and' occurs earlier in the line).

176. *Sir Valour* With this contemptuous use of 'sir' + an abstract noun, cf. *Tp.* 2. 1. 283, 'Sir Prudence'.

180. *of grace exact* = of consummate merit. The phrase qualifies 'severals and generals'. What Ulysses resents is that their individual and general excellencies, against which no exception can be taken, should be held up for ridicule.

188–9. *bears...rein* i.e. bridles.

190. *broad* On. glosses as 'arrogant', but the allusion is to Achilles' well-known size; Caxton speaks of his 'broad shoulders' (p. 541).

keeps (Q.) F. 'and keepes'.

·195. *and* (F.) Q. 'our'.

197. *They tax...* With this speech, cf. Ovid, *Met.* XIII. 360–9.

199. *Forestall* Schmidt glosses as 'regard with prejudice' and On. as 'discount or condemn by anticipation', but neither sense is well authenticated and the common meaning 'hinder', 'obstruct' (O.E.D.4) seems the likelier one.

202. *calls* (Q.) F. 'call'.

203. *enemy's* (Delius conj.) Q. F. 'enemies'. Editors have usually interpreted this as possessive plural, but the singular seems more idiomatic.

206–10. *So that...execution* i.e. they rate the battering ram higher than the man who devised it or those whose intelligence directs its use.

209. *fineness* (F.) Q. 'finesse'.

211–12. *Let...sons* i.e. if this were so, Achilles' horse would be many times more valuable than Achilles.

212. S.D. (F.) Q. omits.

214. S.D. (F.) Q. omits.

219. *eyes* (Q.) F. 'eares'. F. suggests rationalization and Q. has support from ll. 223–5.

220. *arms* (A.W.) Q. F. 'arme'. The arms of Achilles were proverbial as the surest protection (Erasmus, *Adagia*, Auxilium, 'arma Achillea').

221. *heads* (Q. F.) Kinnear conj. in Camb. 'host'. The emendation is very attractive. There are quite a number of errors of anticipation in Q. and there is something very absurd in all the Greek heads calling Agamemnon head with one voice.

224. *A stranger...looks* Greeks and Trojans were thought of as fighting in beavers (see G.), which concealed everything but the eyes; cf. 1. 3. 296, 4. 5. 195–6, and the introductions which are necessary when Greeks and Trojans meet in the latter scene.

228. *bid* (Q.) F. 'on'.

238. *Jove's* (F.) Q. 'great *Ioues*'. There is not much interpolation in Q., but 'great' is unnecessary here for both sense and metre.

Jove's accord An asseveration, often used, as here, in ironic apology for boasting speech (see Erasmus. *Adagia*, Fides et Gravitas, 'Iovis suffragium'); cf. 'God's will'—the English equivalent.

239. *Nothing...heart* i.e. unmatched for courage.

241–2. *The worthiness...forth* A commonplace; Noble compares Prov. xxvii. 2.

242. *that the* (Q.) F. 'that he'.

245. *Sir you of Troy* = Sir Trojan.

247. *affair* (F.) Q. 'affaires'.

250. *whisper* (F.) Q. 'whisper with'. The transitive use was common.

252. *sense...the* (F.) Q. 'seat...that'. The former word is clearly a misreading in the one text or the other; I accept F. doubtfully, as it seems very flat from Æneas.

256. *loud* (F.) Q. 'alowd'.

259. S.D. Q. 'Sound trumpet.'; F. 'The Trumpets sound.'

262. this (F.) Q. 'his'.

263. resty (Q.) F. 'rusty'. Q.'s reading (=restive) seems more in accordance with what Hector says about the challenge at the close of 2. 2.

265. among (Q.) F. 'among'st' (probably assimilated to 'fair'st').

267. That seeks (F.) Q. 'And feeds'.

269–70. That loves...loves i.e. who will show his love in deeds and not merely in idle vows and protestations to his mistress. The imagery is devotional, and 'arms' is used quibblingly—in fighting, not in embraces.

275–6. He...arms The terms of this challenge belong to the conventions of the tiltyard or late chivalric romances. For the former, see E. K. Chambers, Sir Henry Lee (1936), p. 269, where 'A Cartell for a Challenge' employs much the same formula: 'of more virtue & greater beawtie then all the Amorous Dames that be at this daye in the world'; for the latter, cf. Lodge's Euphues Shadow, Hunterian Club ed., p. 33.

276. couple (Q.) F. 'compasse'. F. suggests merely embraces, which is not the main idea. The allusion is to the chivalric convention of a knight's displaying some symbol of his mistress about his armour (a fashion ridiculed in Don Quixote, 1, xviii). According to O.E.D. ('coupled' 1), the word had heraldic associations (=conjoined).

282. sunburnt Sunburn was accounted a blemish.

288. means not, hath not i.e. means not to be, hath not been.

289. If...be Similarly elliptical.
hath, or (F.) Q. 'hath a'.

290. I am (Q.) F. 'Ile be'.

293. host (Q.) F. 'mould'. The variants are difficult to account for, but 'host' has the merit of recalling that

the challenge relates to the Greeks in arms before Troy; 'mould', if='cast', 'form', generalizes too widely and, if used with particular reference to the matrix, would not include a seasoned fighter like Achilles.

294. *One...one* (F.) Q. 'A...no'. Editors have preferred F. I suspect sophistication and, although Q. seems to say the opposite of what was intended, it may be right.

297. *this...brawn* (F.) Q. 'my...braunes'.

298. *will* (F.) Q. omits.

300. *youth in flood*, i.e. in the flush of youth.

301. *prove* (Q.) F. 'pawne'.
truth (F.) Q. 'troth'.

302. *forfend* (Q.) F. 'forbid'. I suspect F. of having substituted the commoner word.
youth (F.) Q. 'men' (possibly assimilated to 'amen').

303–4. Ulysses...*Fair* (F.) Q. '*Vlis*. Amen: faire'.

305. *first* (F.) Q. 'sir' (somewhat redundantly, since Agamemnon has already addressed Æneas in this speech).

309. S.D. F. '*Exeunt. Manet Vlysses, and Nestor.*'; Q. omits.

315. *This 'tis:* (F.) Q. omits.

316. *Blunt wedges...knots* Proverbial (Erasmus, *Adagia*, Similitudo, 'malo nodo malus quaerendus cuneus').

317. *blown up*=expanded, swelled; a common figurative use in connexion with pride, which On.'s gloss 'blossom' loses.

324. *True: the...as* (Q.) F. 'The...euen as' (a typical Compositor *B* perversion).

324–5. *substance...sum up* Quibbling on (1) that which gives a thing its character, and (2) wealth. The purpose (=substance) of the challenge is as clear as if its sum total was arithmetically computed.

329. *dry* A dry brain signified a dull wit; see *A.Y.L.* G. 'dry brain'.

333. *Why* (Q.) F. 'Yes' (probably Compositor *B*'s substitution).

334. *his honour* (F.) Q. 'those honours'. F. (=emerge victorious) gives better sense.

336. *this* (F.) Q. 'the'.

340. *wild* (F.) Q. 'vilde'. The sense of 'wild' (=irresponsible) seems better than 'vile' (=paltry).

340-6. *for...at large* i.e. the result of the single combat will be interpreted as a foretaste of the fortunes of all the Greeks.

352. *receives from hence* (Q.) F. 'from hence receyues'. I give Q. the benefit of the doubt because transposition is commoner in F.

a conquering part (Q.) F. 'the...'. Q. is wanted for the sense: 'part' here='portion', 'share', and there were as many parts as there were Greeks. The word picks up the metaphor of 'a scantling' (=a small portion, sample) in l. 341; in what follows Nestor develops the idea of the one for the many and the part for the whole, and Ulysses reverts to it in ll. 366-7, quibbling with the two senses of 'share' =(1) 'cut off', and (2) 'divide or apportion in shares'.

353. *steel* To be associated with 'swords and bows' (both made of steel) in l. 355.

354-6. *Which...limbs* (F.) Q. omits. The sense is involved, but the lines are essential to the argument. Nestor is developing the idea of 'a scantling of good or bad' (ll. 341-2), arguing that Achilles is their best representative because (1) if the Greek representative fails, every Greek will be disheartened (this being the point of the rhetorical question in ll. 351-3 and a scantling of the bad), whereas (2) if he is victorious (a scantling of the good), every Greek will be encouraged just as if the victorious arms were his own. F.'s recovered lines are a prolonged metonymy of the part for the whole: Achilles is the one for the many; hence, his limbs are those of every Greek; consequently, what these limbs (the agents or·instruments of every Greek) achieve with weapons ('swords and bows') is just as encouraging as if every Greek had wielded the weapons himself. Ulysses takes up Nestor's two points at once in his reference to 'honour'=(2) above, and 'shame' =(1) above, and he develops the consequences of both in ll. 366–73, arguing that, if Achilles is successful, they will not be allowed to share in his victory: it will simply encourage his personal pride and they will get only scorn and therefore discouragement either way.

354. *Which entertained* 'Which'='a conquering part' (l. 352) and 'entertained' (see G.) is synonymous with 'receive' (l. 352). The contruction is absolute.

are his (F2) F. 'are in his' (presumably with interpolation from the next line).

his='heart' in l. 352, and (as 'heart' is the part for the whole Greek) is equivalent to 'every Greek's'.

355. *E'en* (A.W.) F. 'In'. The F. error is a common one; cf. *Ant.* p. 124.

E'en no less working=even no less (i.e. just as) operative (i.e. effective).

357–60. *Give...exceed* (lining as in Q.) F. divides after 'speech', 'Hector', 'wares', 'not' and 'show'. The F. version of the lines (see following notes) looks very much like a typical piece of muddling on the part of Compositor *B*, due to his having fouled the metre at the beginning of the speech after dividing the first line.

359. *First...wares* (Q.) F. 'shew our fowlest Wares'.

360. *shall exceed* (Q.) F. 'yet to shew'.

361. *By...first* (Q.) F. 'Shall shew the better'.

367. *share* (Q.) F. 'weare'. Either reading might have been due to accidental repetition, but so much

emphasis is laid on the sharing of honours that Q. seems more likely to be right; see G.

369. *we were* (F.) Q. 'it were'. The personal note is more appropriate.

372. *did* (F.) Q. 'do'.

375. *'mong* (A.W. after Pope) Q. F. 'among'.

376. *as* (F.) Q. 'for' (possibly an error of anticipation).

better (Q.) F. 'worthier'. F. seems less apt (cf. ll. 373, 383) and the substitution was well within the range of the compositor.

378. *broils* One of many food metaphors (=basks).

379. *crest* 'A high crest was one of the distinguishing beauties of the horse...and lowering the crest was a sign of inferiority and submission' (*Sh. Eng.* 11, 415); cf. the imagery of ll. 188–90.

prouder...bends i.e. Achilles' pride, like the rainbow, arches ('bends' like a bow) to the heavens, for which 'blue' was a conventional epithet.

381. *dress...voices* Deighton compares *Meas.* 1. 1. 19.

386–7. *Ulysses, Now* (Pope) Q. F. 'Now *Vlisses*'. Pope's transposition is wanted, as Ulysses is stressed on the second syllable.

388. *thereof* (Q.) F. 'of it' (a sophistication).

391. *tarre* (F.) Q. 'arre'.

their (F.) Q. 'a'.

2. 1

S.D. *Loc.* (Rowe)

6. *then* (Q.) F. omits.

8. *would* (Q.) F. 'there would'. Q. seems more idiomatic.

11. S.D. (F.) Q. omits.

12. *The plague of Greece* I doubt whether this imprecation refers to a particular plague, such as that

mentioned in *Iliad* 1 or by Caxton shortly before the death of Hector (p. 610).

13. *mongrel* Ajax was supposed to be half Trojan and half Greek; see note to 4. 5. 119 ff.

beef-witted i.e. 'with the brains of an ox' ('beef' sg.=ox), 'bovine', rather than with allusion to the eating of beef, said to impair the wits in *Tw. N.* 1. 3. 87–8.

14. *thou* (Q.) F. 'you'.

vinewed'st (F. 'whinid'st') Q. 'vnsalted'. Q.'s variant may have been a guess at a word not understood or a first shot, replaced by the more vivid word; see G. 'vinewed'.

leaven Cf. 1 Cor. v. 8, 'the leaven of malice and wickedness'.

15. *handsomeness* See G., but perhaps too with allusion to Thersites' deformity.

17. *oration* (F.) Q. 'oration without booke'.

18. *a prayer* (F.) Q. 'praier'.

19. *red* See G. According to Schmidt, red, yellow and black were three kinds of plague sores mentioned by physicians of this time.

o'thy (F 3) Q. 'ath thy'; F. 'o'th thy'. For this common type of error, cf. *All's*, 1. 3. 174, 'Confess it 'ton tooth to th'other'.

20. *Toadstool* (Q.) F. 'Toads stoole'.

learn me =ascertain for me (Deighton). Schmidt and On. explain as='tell', 'inform', but when the phrase is used again at l. 90 ('go learn me') it clearly supports Deighton's interpretation.

24. *a fool* (F.) Q. 'foole'.

25. *fingers itch* A common idiom (see G. 'itch'), to which Thersites answers quibblingly.

27. *of thee* (F.) Q. 'of the'.

28–9. *When...another.* (Q.) F. omits.

35. *Mistress Thersites* Commentators explain as a

gibe at Thersites' cowardice, but whether we associate
'mistress' with cowardice or a railing tongue, the abuse
seems too oblique from Ajax and the reading is probably
corrupt.

36–42. Thersites. *Thou…do, do, thou* (speeches
attributed as in F., with the exception noted below).
Q., in which the dialogue is here confused, prints as
follows:

> *Ther.* Thou shouldst strike him. *Aiax Coblofe,*
> Hee would punne…………………………as a sayler
> breakes a bisket, you horson curre. Do? do?
> *Aiax:* Thou stoole for a witch:
> *Ther.* I Do? do? thou…

40, 51 S.Ds. (Kit. after Rowe) Q. F. omit.

41. After correctly attributing 'Do? do?' in the
third line of the above extract to Thersites, F. wrongly
followed the Q. speech prefixes for the fourth and fifth
lines. As it seems beyond belief that this slanging match
should omit the familiar pun on Ajax and 'a jakes'
(=a privy), and as 'stool' was commonly used for
'privy', I assume that Thersites (more appropriately)
hurled this abuse at Ajax and that Q. (followed by F.)
here interpolated a speech prefix; cf. 3. 1. 85 n. and
5. 2. 82–3 n.

42–3. *in thy head* (A.W. after Cap. conj.) Q. F.
omit. Omission of phrases is so common in Q. that
omission here seems fairly certain, for something is
wanted to balance the following 'in mine elbows'.

44. *Thou* (F.) Q. 'you'.
45. *thrash* (Q.) F. 'thresh'.
bought and sold='treated as a mere chattel' (Deighton). The more specialized meaning of 'betrayed'
(cf. *R. III*, 5. 3. 305) is less relevant here.

53. S.D. (F.) Q. omits.
54. *you* (F.) Q. 'yee'.
thus (Q.) F. 'this'.

61. *so I do* (Q.) F. 'I do so'.

63. *whosoever* (F3) Q. F. 'who some euer'.

69. *I will* (F.) Q. 'It will'.

72-3. *who wears...head* Burton (*Anatomy of Melancholy*, 'Democritus Junior to the Reader') has the same expression ('To see a man wear his brains in his belly, his guts in his head'), citing Cornelius Agrippa (*Ep.* 28. 1. 7) as his source ('quorum cerebrum est in ventre, ingenium in patinis'); cf. Terence, *Eun.* 4. 7. 46.

73. *I'll* (F.) Q. 'I'.

75. S.D. (after Rowe) Q. F. omit.

85. *set...fool's* N.V.S. compares Prov. xxvi. 4.

86. *for* (F.) Q. omits.
the (Q.) F. 'a'.

88. *Good words* A familiar tag from Terence ('bona verba quaeso'), used as an appeal for moderation (not for approval); see Baldwin, *Small Latine* (1944), 1, 747-8, who cites Udall's gloss, 'Yet gyue vs fayre language I beseche you hartely'.

90. *the vile* (Q.) F. 'thee vile'.

100. *an* (Q. 'and') F. 'if'.
'a (Camb. conj.) F. 'he'; Q. omits.
out (F.) Q. 'at'.
'a were (Q.) F. 'he were'.

102. *too* (F2) Q. F. 'to'.

104. *your* (Theob.) Q. F. 'their'.
on their toes (F.) Q. omits.

106. *wars* (Q.) F. 'warre'.

108. *to* As Dyce noted, Thersites is urging the supposed oxen to their tasks.

110. *wit* (A.W. after Cap.) Q. F. omit. There is no sense in the Q. F. reading. Thersites cannot mean that, were his tongue cut out, Ajax would be silent too, but must mean that, without tongue, he could speak as much sense as Ajax (i.e. none).

112. *peace!* (Q.) F. omits.

113. *brach* (Rowe) Q. F. 'brooch'. Rowe's emendation implies a simple misreading and is far more in keeping with Thersites. Cf. Face's abusive 'brach' of Dol Common (Jonson, *Alchemist*, 1. 1. 111), and see also 5. 1. 15–17.

118. S.D. Q. F. '*Exit.*'

121. *fifth* (F.) Q. 'first'. It is broad day when the exchange of Cressida for Antenor takes place (4. 3. 1, 'great morning') and Thersites gives 11 o'clock as the time of the fight at 3. 3. 294.

129. *I'll* (Pope) Q. F. 'I will'.
S.D. F. '*Exit.*' Q. omits.

2. 2

Material. The scene broadly follows Caxton's account (going back to Dares) of a Trojan family council, called by Priam to determine how they can take vengeance on the Greeks for their refusal to return Hesione. In accounts from Dares to Caxton (pp. 517 ff.) the sons speak in order of seniority. Hector advises prudence (cf. 2. 2. 8 n.); Paris, fired by the promise made to him by Venus on Mt. Ida, proposes an expedition to Greece, and is supported by Deiphobus; Helenus prophesies disaster and is snubbed by Troilus (cf. 2. 2. 37 n.), who, like Paris, advocates action. The next day, Priam puts the majority verdict to all his citizens, of whom the majority support Paris' project. See also 2. 2. 100 n.

S.D. *Loc.* (after Rowe).

2. *says Nestor* According to Caxton, the important embassies to Priam were undertaken by Ulysses and Diomedes. Only one of these is described at length— the one alluded to at 4. 5. 215–16 (see note) and this took place shortly after the Greeks arrived at Tenedos.

8–17. *Though no man...worst* Hector similarly explains in Caxton's debate that it is prudence and not cowardice which makes him hesitate: an attempt to revenge themselves on the Greeks may end in disaster (pp. 519–20).

9. *toucheth* (Q.) F. 'touches'.

14–15. *surety, Surety* (F.) Q. 'surely Surely'.

19–20. *Every...Helen* 'The meaning seems to be not that every tenth soul *only*, but every soul *that has been taken as a tithe by war* is as dear as Helen, and of such tithes there have been many thousands' (Deighton).

19. *tithe-soul* (Hyphen J. D. W.).

27. *father* (F.) Q. 'fathers'.

33. *bite so sharp at reasons* i.e. snap at reasons; some see a pun on 'reasons' and 'raisins', as in *Ado*, 5. 1. 201–2.

at (F.). Q. 'of'.

35. *reasons* (F.) Q. 'reason'.

36. *tells* (F.) Q. 'tell'.

37–50. *You are...deject* In Caxton (p. 524), Troilus similarly derides Helenus as 'a coward priest', since it is the custom of all priests to fear battle and gorge themselves in eating and drinking. If Helenus is afraid, he says, 'let him go into the temple and sing the divine service'.

38. *fur your gloves* With reference to fur lining rather than mere trimming.

with reasons (A. W. after Rowe iii) Q. F. 'with reason'. The sense is not that Helenus is sensible to fur his gloves but that he gets great comfort from reasons because they provide an excuse for cowardice.

41. *the...harm* = the sight of everything harmful.

45–6. As in Q. F. transposes the lines.

46. *a star disorbed* = a shooting star (N.V.S.).

47. *Let's* (F.) Q. 'Sets'.

48. *hare* (Q.) F. 'hard'.

50. *Make...deject* i.e. lead to cowardice and despondency; see G. 'liver', and cf. 2 *H. IV*, 4. 3. 101–3.

Make (Q.) F. 'Makes'.

52. *keeping* (Q.) F. 'holding'. Q.'s variant is the keyword of the argument (cf. ll. 80–1, 93); F.'s can at best be a first shot.

What's...valued? Dramatically a significant question; cf. Introduction, pp. xii–xiii.

53–6. *But...prizer* i.e. value does not depend on what the individual chooses to make it ('will' is here, as in l. 65, contrasted with judgement); to merit the value set upon it, an object must have intrinsic worth as well as recognition of that worth by others. The latter point is Ulysses' theme in 3. 3. 114 ff., when he approaches the question of values from the standpoint of the 'prized' (Achilles). Hector's emphasis here is on the 'prizer'.

57. *To...god* i.e. to pay tribute in excess of what is due (to make the mistake of overestimating what one values).

58–60. *And...merit* i.e. it is madness to pay tribute to an object whose value merely consists of something it has 'caught' from the mad idolater: 'attributive' carries on the idea of 'service' in l. 57, and the idea of madness leads on to disease imagery in 'infectiously itself affects'. In the following line, 'affected' is to be associated with 'affection' and not 'infection' as in l. 59. Idolatry is one of the leading themes of the play: cf. 1. 3. 169; 3. 3. 71–4; 5. 1. 7.

58. *attributive* (Q.) F. 'inclineable'. F. might represent a first shot or a guess at a word that was partly illegible. The sense is much the same (Q.=prepared to pay tribute to, F.=prepared to bow down to), but Q. is more cogent.

60. *Without...merit* i.e. if the thing prized has no value to show for itself.

61–8. *I take...honour* The analogy between Troilus' choosing a wife and the rape of Helen as an act of revenge is, of course, a very false one.

64. *shores* (F.) Q. 'shore'.

67. *chose* (F.) Q. 'choose'.

70. *soiled* (Q.) F. 'spoyl'd'.

71. *sieve* (Q.) F. 'same'. The paradoxical 'un-respective sieve' seems fairly certainly correct and F.'s error suggests a misreading. That 'sieves' (=baskets) were used for refuse is not, however, well established and 'in unrespective sieve' may simply be a concrete metaphor='indiscriminately'; 'sieve' then='riddle' and (fig.) 'discrimination'.

74. *of* (F.) Q. 'with'; 'breath of full consent' =fully consenting breath (see G. 'breath').

77. *an old aunt* i.e. Hesione, Priam's sister, who was held captive by Telamon, king of Salamis. According to Dares (and Caxton), revenge for this disgrace was the cause of the Trojan war, and in Caxton this council was held to determine how they could recover her, since Antenor's efforts to negotiate for her peaceful return had failed.

79. *pale* (Q.) F. 'stale' (? an error of assimilation). I accept Q., though a little doubtfully, partly because it is more euphonious and partly because the mention of Apollo suggests that 'the morning' refers not to the early hours but to the rosy Aurora, goddess of the dawn.

81. *a pearl* Cf. Introduction, p. xxi.

82. *above...ships* According to Caxton (p. 546), I, 224; cf. Marlowe, *Faustus*, 5. 1. 107, *Aen.* II. 198 and Ovid, *Met.* XII. 7.

86. *worthy* (Q.) F. 'Noble'. Q. seems more closely related to l. 81 and ll. 91–2, as well as to the general theme of values. F.'s substitution was well within the compositor's range.

90. *do...did* i.e. prove more inconstant than Fortune.

Fortune never (F.) Q. 'neuer fortune'.

94. *But* Emphatic (=moreover).

95–6. *That…place* i.e. who, on Greek soil, inflicted a disgrace which, in our own country, we are afraid to justify.

that disgrace We fear to warrant 'The relative is frequently omitted, especially where the antecedent clause is emphatic and evidently incomplete' (Abbott, §244).

97, 99. S.Ds. (Theob.) Q. F. omit.

100. S.D. Q. '*Enter Cassandra rauing*' (after l. 96); F. '*Enter Cassandra with her haire about her eares*' (after l. 96). In Caxton's account of the council, Cassandra prophesies the destruction of Troy after the council is over and after Priam had consulted his citizens. 'Shakespeare has given a more dramatic turn by plunging her into the conference, at the same time strengthening the impression that the Trojans are stubbornly bent on their own destruction' (N.V.S.). Cassandra appears at the end of what is probably the corresponding scene in the Admiral's Company plot and towards the end of the corresponding scene in Heywood's *Iron Age*.

104. *eld* (Theob. conj.) Q. 'elders' ; F. 'old'.

105. *canst* (Q.) F. 'can'.

106. *clamours* (Q.) F. 'clamour'.

110. *Our firebrand brother* As Steevens noted, Vergil alludes to the story (*Aen.* x. 704–5). Cooper (s.v. Paris) also relates how Hecuba 'being with child dreamed that she was delivered of a firebrand: which thing the soothsayers interpreted, that the child she went with should be the confusion of Troy'.

112. S.D. Q. F. '*Exit.*'

123–5. *the goodness…gracious* What this amounts to is that the righteousness of the quarrel is established by the fact that they are in honour committed to it.

145. *So*=in such a way.

156. *on our party*=on our side (the usual idiom).

165–7. *not much…philosophy* N.V.S. shows that

this *caveat* (*Nicomachean Ethics*, 1. 3) was very well known, as well as the reason for it to which Hector alludes—that their headstrong passions make them deaf to reason.

172. *more deaf than adders* Proverbial; cf. Ps. lviii. 4.

178. *that* A redundant conjunction; Abbott § 285.

178–9. *of...same* i.e. through inclination to gratify their insensate personal desires; 'partial indulgence' must mean 'personal indulgence', though the last example of 'partial' = 'individual', 'personal' (O.E.D. 2 *c*) is of 1578.

185. *nations* (Q.) F. 'Nation'.

196. *the performance...spleens* = 'the execution of spite and resentment' (J.)

210. *strike* (F.) Q. 'shrike'.

2. 3

Material. Suggested either by *Iliad* IX or Caxton (pp. 630–1), who tells how, after Achilles refused to take any further part in the war (cf. 3. 3. 193–4 n.), Agamemnon sent Nestor, Ulysses and Diomedes to reason with him. A little later (Caxton, p. 634), Agamemnon himself, accompanied by Nestor, was graciously received by Achilles, who, on this occasion, for love of Agamemnon, agreed to allow his Myrmidons to assist the Greeks. Neither story is close to this scene.

S.D. *Loc.* (after Rowe and Theob.)

6. *I'll* (Q. F.) A.W. conj. 'I'. The sense requires that 'but' = unless.

10–13. *O thou...have!* i.e. if Jove's thunder or Mercury's cunning cannot deprive them of the mighty little intelligence they have, the gods are useless.

12. *serpentine craft* See G. 'Mercury'. Mercury was associated with cunning, because as a mere child he contrived to steal the oxen of Apollo.

ye (Q.) F. 'thou'.

14. *short-armed*=inadequate in reach (of under-standing); i.e. an ignoramus would grasp the stupidity of Ajax and Achilles.

15–17. *it will not...web*='they use no means but those of violence' (J.), using their weapons instead of their wits.

16. *their* (Q.) F. 'the'.

18. *Neapolitan* (Q.) F. omits.

19. *dependent* (F.) Q. 'depending'.

20–1. *devil Envy say 'Amen'* Envy was one of the Seven Deadly Sins; the words have the ring of an allusion, though the closest seems to be the Epilogue (of uncertain date) to the 1610 edition of *Mucedorus*.

22. S.D. (A.W. after Anon. conj. in Camb.) F. '*Enter Patroclus.*' (after l. 21); Q. omits. It seems unlikely that Patroclus should enter, listen silently to Thersites' imprecations, and then ask (at l. 34) 'art thou devout? Wast thou in prayer?'. Cf. l. 32 S.D. and, for the same kind of error in F., see note to 4. 4. 48.

24. *a'* (Q.) F. 'haue'.

24–5. *gilt...slipped* With a pun on 'slip' (=a counterfeit coin), as in *Rom.* 2. 4. 46–8.

25. *wouldst* (F.) Q. 'couldst'

26. *thyself upon thyself* i.e. 'I can invoke no worse curse than this' (Deighton).

31. *art* (F.) Q. 'art not'.

32. S.D. (A.W. after Anon. conj. in Camb.) Q. F. omit; cf. l. 22 n.

34. *in* (Q.) F. 'in a'.

37. Patroclus. *Amen.* (Q.) F. omits.

38. S.D. (A.W.) Q. F. omit.

39. S.D. Q. F. after l. 37. Since Achilles will speak only with the chosen few, it seems unlikely that he would enter before he knew it was Thersites.

40. *Where...where?* Possibly a tag from a song. *O where?* (Q.) F. omits.

41. *my cheese, my digestion* Cheese was thought to be an aid to digestion.

42. *in to* (Cap.) Q. F. 'into'.

so many meals = for so many meals; see Abbott, § 202.

47. *thyself* (F.) Q. '*Thersites*' (caught from earlier in the speech).

50. *mayst* (F.) Q. 'must'.

52. *decline* See G. Thersites leads Achilles and Patroclus to suppose that he will decline the matter in the grammatical sense, but in the end he refuses to give a reason why Patroclus is a fool other than that he was born a fool.

55–9. Patroclus. *You...a fool.* (F.) Q. omits.

62–3. *of Agamemnon* (F.) Q. omits.

64. *Patroclus* (F.) Q. 'this *Patroclus*'.

fool positive i.e. the rest are fools in the respects mentioned, but Patroclus is a fool in all respects.

66. *of* (Q.) F. 'to'.

the (Q. F.) Rowe ii 'thy'.

Creator (F.) Q. 'Prouer'. The reason for the variants is obscure unless there was (quite exceptionally) expurgation in Q. or a misguided attempt to make the argument more logical.

68. *Patroclus* (F.) Q. 'Come *Patroclus*' (with interpolation in anticipation of 'Come' later in the speech).

69. S.D. F. '*Exit*.' Q. omits.

71–2. *a whore and a cuckold* (Q.) F. 'a Cuckold and a Whore'. I give Q. the benefit of the doubt because inversion is commoner in F.

72. *emulous* (Q.) F. 'emulations,' (an assimilation).

73–4. *Now...all!* (F.) Q. omits.

74. S.D.[1] (after Theob.) Q. F. omit.

S.D.[2] (Cap. and Dyce) Q. F. '...*Diomed, Aiax & Calcas*.' (F. '... *Diomedes*...'); Q. after l. 67, F. after l. 65.

78. *We sent* (A. W. after Theob. conj.) Q. 'He
sate'; F. 'He sent'. The customary emendation ('He
shent') lacks support from the sources and is out of
character, for Achilles is evasive rather than violent.
Sisson reads 'fobbed' (supposing in *N.R.* a MS. spelling
'fobd'), but this is an undignified word and not in
keeping with Agamemnon. I am inclined to think that
the trouble lies in the pronoun and that the error
originated in Q.'s having assimilated it to the preceding
'here'.

79. *appertainments* (F.) Q. 'appertainings' (possibly assimilated to the following 'visiting').

80. *so, lest* (Q.) F. 'of, so' ('of' interpolated
from l. 79, and a word omitted).

82. *I shall*='I'se'. 'The extra-metrical 'shall'
warrants the assumption that writers intended it to be
contracted' (Tannenbaum[1], p. 73).

say so (Q.) F. 'so say'.

S.D. (after Rowe ii) Q. F. omit.

85. *lion-sick* The lion was symbolic of pride;
hence='sick of proud heart'.

86–7. *melancholy...pride* i.e. not a 'humour' but a
deadly sin.

86. *you will* (Q.) F. 'will'.

87. *'tis* (Q.) F. 'it is'.

88. *the cause* (F.) Q. 'a cause'.

A...lord. (F.) Q. omits.

S.D. (after Rowe) Q. F. omit.

95–6. *he is...Achilles.* As Grey (cited N.V.S.)
noted, with allusion to the saying '*argumentum Achil-
leum*' (=an insuperable argument); see Erasmus,
Adagia, Audacia, 'Alter Hercules'. Thus, Ajax will
never lack matter because an Achillean dispute is
interminable.

98. *composure* (Q.) F. 'counsell that'. I give Q. the
benefit of the doubt over 'that', since interpolation is

fairly common in F. The other variant is more difficult
to account for, but it may have been due to the F. compositor, whose work in this play is unusually careless.

101. S.D. F. 'Enter Patroclus.' Q. omits.

104–5. The...flexure As prose (Mal.) Q. F. as
verse, dividing after 'courtesy'. The belief that the
elephant could not flex the knees was widespread, but
the source was probably Erasmus (Adagia, Arrogantia,
'Homo genibus elephantinis'), where the application is
the same.

105. legs are (Q.) F. 'legge are'.

flexure (Q.) F. 'flight'. Cf. note to l. 98.

110. digestion's sake Q. F. 'disgestion sake'.
Although the omission of possessive final 's' was
fairly common (as in 'heaven sake', 'goodness sake'),
I normalize, as it was not invariably observed (cf.
'request's sake', l. 167).

113–14. evasion...apprehensions The metaphor is
of a fugitive avoiding arrest: they will not be shaken off
by Achilles' subterfuge.

117. Not...beheld i.e. 'not regarded by himself as
it becomes a virtuous man, but with pride and arrogance' (Schmidt, s.v. 'behold').

on (Q.) F. 'of'.

119. Yea, (Q.) F. 'Yea, and'.

121. come (Q.) F. 'came'.

you shall=(metrically) 'you'se'; cf. note to l. 82.

124. note of judgement Probably with allusion to the
legal sense of 'note' (see G.): Achilles arrogates more
to himself than he is entitled to.

125. tend (Q.) F. 'tends'.

128. predominance O.E.D. notes that the word was
especially associated with the preponderance of some
humour.

129. pettish lunes (Hanmer) F. 'pettish lines';
Q. 'course, and time'. I accept Hanmer's emendation

very doubtfully because planetary influence is not represented elsewhere in the play as accountable for Achilles'
'humour', and 'lines' in the established sense of 'course
of action or conduct' (O.E.D. line sb.² 27), with the
qualifying 'pettish' (=ill-humoured), adequately describes Achilles' behaviour. Q.'s 'time' could, of course,
be a misreading of either 'lunes' or 'lines' (assuming
the loss, through negligence, of the final 's'). As
emended by Pope and Theob. to 'course and times',
Q. would not in itself incur suspicion, but I do not
think that F. can be rejected; for Compositor *A*, though
careless in this play, was not apt to indulge in the sort of
substitution that 'pettish' for 'course, and' would
suggest. The variants seem more likely to have been
due to first and second shots in the foul papers or
editing in Q (suggesting MS. 'lines').

and (Q.) F. 'his' (possibly due to repetition).

as if (F.) Q. 'and if' (clearly due to repetition).

130. *carriage of this action* (F.) Q. 'streame of his
commencement'. F.'s reading has the approval of
recent editors, though with the emendation of 'his' to
'this' and 'commencement' to 'commercement'
(=business), Q. is adequate in sense.

138. S.D. (after Rowe) Q. F. omit.

140. *enter you* (F.) Q. 'entertaine'.

S.D. F. '*Exit Vlisses.*' Q. omits.

151. *pride is* (Q.) F. 'it is'.

152. *Ajax* (F.) Q. omits.

157. *do hate the* (Q.) F. 'hate the'.

159. S.D.¹ Aside after Cap. Q. F. omit.

And yet (Q.) F. 'Yet'.

is it (A.W. after Cap.) Q. F. 'ist'.

S.D.² Q. F. '*Enter* Vlisses.' (after l. 156).

164. *In will...self-admission* i.e. self-willed and
self-satisfied.

166. *th'* (Q.) F. 'the'.

167. *for...only* i.e. simply because they are requested of him (=out of sheer contrariness).

168. *possessed...greatness* i.e. possessed by the devil Pride.

169–70. *And speaks...self-breath* i.e. is not only at war with everyone else but with himself.

170. *worth* (Q.) F. 'wroth'.

172. *mental...parts* i.e. mind and body.

173. *Kingdomed* See G. and cf. *J.C.* 2. 1. 67–9.

174. *down himself* (Q.) F. 'gainst it selfe'. F.'s pronoun certainly suggests rationalization, but there is not much to choose between Q.'s 'down' and F.'s 'gainst', and I follow Q. with some hesitation.

175. *plaguey...death-tokens* See G. 'death-tokens'.

178. *led* (F.) Q. 'lead'.

185. *doth* (Q.) F. 'doe'.

189. *Must* (F.) Q. 'Shall'.

191. *titled* (F.) Q. 'liked'.

198, 199. S.Ds. Asides first in J.

199. *this* (F.) Q. 'his'.

201. *pash* (F.) Q. 'push'.

203. *'a* (F.) Q. 'he'.

207–20. Asides first in Cap.

210. *let...humour's blood* (F. '...humours...') Q. 'tell...humorous bloud'. Editors have mostly taken 'let blood' as transitive, but Hudson's interpretation of F.'s 'humours' as possessive singular seems to me better.

213. *o'* (Rowe iii) F. 'a'; Q. 'of'.

215. *eat swords* To 'eat swords' seems to be well authenticated as='to be stabbed' (O.E.D. eat 2 *d*) and violent measures are certainly what Ajax intends as a cure for Achilles' pride (cf. ll. 200–1). For the same expression, cf. 2 *H. VI*, 4. 10. 27–9 ('eat iron') and (quibblingly) *Ado*, 4. 1. 273–4.

218. S.N. (F.) Q. '*Aiax*.'

ten shares i.e. all.

219. S.N. (F.) Q. cont. to Ajax.
I'll...I'll (A.W.) Q. F. 'I will...Ile'.

219–21. *I'll knead...dry* Ajax uses 'knead' in a
transferred sense (='let me get my hands on him') and
Nestor takes up the literal sense with metaphors from
baking.

220. S.N. (Theob.) Cont. to Ajax (Q. F.)
Force (Theob.) Q. F. '*Nest.* Force'. See G. 'force'.
praises (F.) Q. 'praiers'.

221. *pour in, pour in* (F.) Q. 'poure in, poure'.

222. S.D. (Cap.) Q. F. omit.

225. *does* (Q.) F. 'doth'.

230–1. As verse (Pope) Q. F. as prose.

230. *thus with us* (F.) Q. 'with vs thus'. F.'s
stresses fall on the significant words.

238. *Praise...suck* Possibly, as Warb. (in Theob.)
suggested, an echo of Ovid, *Met.* IV. 322–6, but since
the latter part of this speech seems to echo Job xli. 12 on
Leviathan ('I will not conceal his parts, nor his power,
nor his comely proportion'), the echo may be biblical
here too, as Steev. suggested (cf. Luke, xi. 27).

239. *Famed* (Q.) F. 'Fame'.
parts of nature i.e. innate gifts.

240. *beyond, beyond all* (F.) Q. 'beyond all thy'
('thy' caught from l. 239). Ajax is intended to suppose
that his natural gifts (of mind) far surpass anything he
can possibly learn. F.'s ironical 'all erudition' is
certainly correct.

241. *thine* (Q.) F. 'thy'.

246. *bourn* (F.) Q. 'boord'.

247. *Thy* (F.) Q. 'This'.

252. *eminence of him* i.e. superiority over him; see
Abbott, § 165.

254. S.N. Nestor. (Q.) F. '*Vlis.*'

256. *great* (Q.) F. omits.

261. *cull* (F.) Q. 'call'.

263. *sail...hulks* (Q.) F. 'may saile...bulkes'.

S.D. Q. '*Exeunt.*' F. '*Exeunt. Musicke sounds within.*' (see note to 3. 1. 17).

3. 1

S.D. *Loc.* (after Theob.) *Entry* (F.) Q. '*Enter Pandarus.*'

1. *you not* (Q.) F. 'not you'.

3. etc. S.N. (F.) Q. '*Man.*'

5. *upon the Lord* As Delius noted, quibbling on 'lord' (=master) and 'Lord' (=God).

6. *noble* (F.) Q. 'notable'. F. seems more in accordance with the quibbling on rank.

10. *superficially* Quibblingly; see G.

11–15. *know...grace* Quibblingly, though the servant is not, I think (as Tannenbaum[1] suggested), asking for a tip, for there is nothing in the dialogue that clearly implies this. The sense is, rather, as Mal. explained, that Pandarus uses 'better' as='better acquainted', the servant replies with the meaning 'a better man', and, when Pandarus expresses the desire to be known 'better', he is in a state of grace, which Pandarus takes to refer to rank and not hope of salvation.

17. *titles* (Q.) F. 'title'.

S.D. (Cap.) F. '*Musicke sounds within.*' (after '*Exeunt.*' at 2. 3. 263); Q. omits.

26. *Command* For the quibble, see G. 'pleasure'.
friend (F.) Q. omits.

29. *art* (F.) Q. omits.

32. *who is* (Q.) F. 'who's'.

34. *indivisible* (A.W. after Daniel conj. in Camb.) Q. F. 'inuisible'. There seems no point in 'invisible'. The sense is that Helen is the embodiment of all love and beauty.

36. *you not* (F.) Q. 'not you'.

38. *that* (F.) Q. omits.

39. *Cressida* (F.) Q. '*Cressid*', perhaps rightly.

40–1. *complimental assault* In anticipation of the fusillade of compliments in ll. 44–50.

42. Aside (A.W.) Q. F. omit.

43. S.D. (Theob.) Q. '*Enter Paris and Hellen.*' (F. '*...Helena.*').

50. *broken music* See G. 'broken'. In '*Troilus and Cressida*. Music for the Play' (*English Institute Essays*, Columbia University Press, 1952), F. W. Sternfeld has some interesting comments on this scene, pointing out that a 'broken' consort played courtly and sophisticated music, especially 'fancies' and dances.

58. *in fits* See G. The text may be corrupt.

59. *I have business...* From now on, Pandarus is torn between the need to give Troilus' message privately to Paris and the importunate Helen. The latter hears nothing of Pandarus' business with Paris.

61. *hedge...out* Possibly = 'fob off' rather than 'shut out' (the usual gloss); cf. 'bob...out', l. 69.

84. *My cousin* i.e. Cressida. Rattled by Helen, Pandarus lets the cat out of the bag.

85. *You must* (Cap.) Q. F. '*Hel.* You must'.

87. *I'll...life,* (Q.) F. omits.

disposer As Cressida has ordained that Paris shall not know of Troilus' whereabouts and 'disposer' normally meant 'arranger', 'manager', this is probably the sense here or (as Delius suggested) 'mistress'.

90. *make's* (Q. 'makes') F. 'make'.

92. *poor* (F.) Q. omits.

93. *I spy* With allusion to the children's game.

94–5. *Come...instrument* The order is to an attendant, not, of course, Helen.

97–8. *My niece...have* By drawing Helen into the conversation, Pandarus is trying to extricate himself from his blunder in ll. 84–6.

97. *horribly* (Q.) F. 'horrible'.

107. *lord* (F.) Q. 'lad'.

110. *this...all* N.V.S. cites Verity's suggestion that this is a catch from a song.

113. *good now*=please; on the appellative 'good', see Abbott, § 13.

114. *In...so.* (F.) Q. omits.

S.D. (Dyce after Cap.) Q. F. omit.

115. *still love,* (Q.) F. omits.

118. *shaft confounds* (F.) Q. '*shafts confound*'.

118–19. *counfounds Not that* i.e. 'does not confound what...' The sense is clearer with ll. 118–19 printed as one line (as in Q. F.).

121, 123. *Oh, oh* Q. F. 'oh ho'.

122. *the wound to kill* i.e. the killing wound.

123. *Doth...he* i.e. turns sighs to mirth.

125, 126. *Oh! oh!* Q. F. 'O ho'.

127. *Heigh-ho!* As prose (Ritson conj.) Q. F. as part of the song.

134. *generation of vipers* Noble compares Matt. iii. 7, xii. 34, xxiii. 33 and Luke iii. 7.

148. S.D.[1] (after Rowe) Q. F. omit.

S.D.[2] (Cap.) Q. F. '*Sound a retreat?*'

149. *th'field* (Q. 'the field') F. 'fielde'.

152. *these* (F.) Q. 'this'.

155. *the island kings* i.e. the Greeks; cf. Prol. 1.

160. S.N. (Q.) F. omits.

thee (F.) Q. 'her'.

3.2

S.D. *Loc.* (Hanmer after Theob.) *Entry* (Dyce) Q. '*Enter. Pandarus Troylus, man.*'; F. '*Enter Pandarus and Troylus Man.*'

Loc. I adopt the customary description of the house as Pandarus', but references to it are puzzling unless we assume that his house adjoined Cressida's. Troilus

is unarming at Pandarus' house in 1. 2. 275 and when
Pandarus leaves for *his* house he promises to visit
Cressida soon; Troilus is here waiting for convoy to
Cressida's house; the house is Calchas' at 4. 1. 39, but
'her house' at 4. 3. 5 (but see note there).

3. S.N. (Dyce) Q. F. '*Man*.'

he (F.) Q. omits.

4. S.D. (F., after l. 3) Q. omits.

6. *walk off* i.e. withdraw.

S.D. (after Cap.) Q. F. omit.

9. *Like* (F.) Q. 'Like to'.

11. *those* (F.) Q. 'these'.

12. *lily beds* N.V.S. compares the imagery of the
Song of Solomon, ii. 16, iv. 5, vi. 1–2, vii. 2.

13. *Pandar* (Q.) F. '*Pandarus*'.

17. S.D. F. '*Exit Pandarus*.' Q. omits.

21. *palate tastes* (Hanmer) Q. F. 'pallats taste'.
Troilus is thinking of his own appetite.

22. *repuréd* (Q.) F. 'reputed'.

Swooning (Pope) Q. F. 'Sounding' (a common
Elizabethan spelling).

23. *distraction* (A. W. after Orger conj. in Camb.)
Q. F. 'distruction'. The sense is not, I think, 'death'
but 'insensibility'; cf. Q.'s errors at 5. 2. 42, 5. 3. 85.

24. *tuned* (Q.) F. 'and'.

29. S.D. F. '*Enter Pandarus*.' Q. omits.

31. *be witty*=be in full possession of your wits.

33. *sprite* (F.) Q. 'spirite'.

villain See G. Images from falconry in ll. 43, 51–2,
give the double meaning some support.

34. *as short* (Q.) F. 'so short'.

S.D. F. '*Exit Pand*.' Q. omits.

38. *unawares* (F.) Q. 'vnwares'.

39. S.D. Q. '*Enter pandar and Cressid*.'; F. '*Enter
Pandarus and Cressida*.'

43. *watched* Quibblingly, with allusion to the taming

of hawks by keeping them awake; see G. and cf. *Shr.*
4. 1. 185.

46–7. *draw...picture* Cressida is veiled; cf. *Tw. N.*
1. 5. 237.

51–2. *the falcon...river* Q. F. print as a new sen-
tence, but this makes the syntax and sense unnecessarily
obscure.

55. *o'th'* (F.) Q. 'ath''.

58. S.D. (after F 2) Q. F. omit.

60. *Cressida* (F.) Q. '*Cressed*'.

65. *curious* Schmidt glossed as 'requiring care',
'embarrassing' and Deighton and On. as 'causing
care', but Cressida's reply 'more dregs than water'
suggests a quantitative sense, 'minute'. This explains
the somewhat unusual use of the singular, 'dreg': for
Troilus, any suspicion of impurity is infinitesimal.

67. *fears* (Rowe ii) Q. F. 'teares'.

71. *safer* (Q.) F. 'safe'.

72. *worse* (Q. F.) Hanmer 'worst'.

73–4. *in all...monster* Interpreted as a reference to
Fear as an allegorical character in moralities or masques,
but Troilus is not speaking literally (any more than
when he speaks of the 'fountain' of their love). All he
means is that there is nothing to be afraid of in love
and its only 'monstrosity' is a lover's hyperboles.

75. *Nor* (Q.) F. '*Not*'.

79. *is* (F.) Q. omits.

87. *lions...hares* Proverbially juxtaposed, as in
Erasmus (*Adagia*, Inconstantia, 'Leo prius, nunc
leporem agit'). Troilus takes up Erasmus' application in
his reply that he will make no extravagant undertakings
and that the proof of his love shall be his constancy.

91. *crown...perfection* (F.) Q. 'louer part no
affection'.

95–6. *as what...his truth* i.e. 'even malice shall
not be able to impeach his truth, or attack him in any

other way, except by ridiculing him for his constancy'
(Mal.).

98. S.D. (after F. '*Enter...*') Q. omits.

109. *are wooed* (F.) Q. 'bee woed'.

119. *not, till now* (F.) Q. 'till now not'.

121. *grown* (Q. 'grone') F. 'grow'.

131. *Cunning* (Pope) Q. F. 'Comming'. The
emendation is essential: 'coming' misses the point that
Cressida supposes that Troilus is as calculating as she is:
his silence is, she argues, mere strategy to encourage her
to talk too much.

132. *My...counsel* (Q.) F. 'My soule of counsell
from me'.

133. S.D. (after Rowe) Q. F. omit.

147–9. *I have...fool* i.e. Cressida is in two minds—
torn between desire and her policy of holding off. She
is in the same predicament in 5. 2. 107–8, with one
eye on Troilus and the other on Diomedes.

149–50. *I would...wit?* (Q.) F. 'Where is my
wit? I would be gone:'. Although transposition is
commoner in F. than in Q., I follow the customary
Q. reading with misgivings because the two half lines
are divided in Q. between the recto and verso of a
leaf.

150. *I know...speak* (Q.) F. 'I speake I know not
what'.

151. *that speak* (Q.) F. 'that speakes'.

154–6. *but you...above* As Mal. noted, with allusion
to the saying of Publilius Syrus 'Amare et sapere vix
deo conceditur'. Troilus' cunning silence argues wisdom
and so, argues Cressida, he cannot love. The use of 'Or
else' is very loose, but the sense is clear and confirmed
by Troilus' reply that nothing would encourage him
more than to know that Cressida's constancy in love
would match his own, because he has only constant
love and simplicity (i.e. no wisdom) to offer.

159. *aye* (F.) Q. 'age'.

flame (A.W. after Tannenbaum[2] conj.) Q. F. 'flames'.

160. *in plight and youth* (Q. F.) Explained as a zeugma, but possibly a case of transposition = 'and plight in youth'.

161. *beauties* (Q. F.) Recent editors (except Kittredge) interpret as possessive singular and 'outward' as a noun. This seems unnecessarily indirect.

162. *blood* In the material sense: the distinction is between integrity of mind, which can be preserved, and external beauty, which cannot.

173. *truths* (F.) Q. 'trueth'. F. is more idiomatic. The plural of abstract nouns was common when referring to more than one person.

175. *Want* (F 2) Q. F. 'Wants'.

tired with iteration i.e. wearied with stock comparisons (like 'as true as steel').

176. *plantage to the moon* (Q. F.) Taken as a reference to the popular belief that the waxing of the moon promoted the growth of plants, but the neologism 'plantage' takes the simile out of the common run of proverbial sayings and the reading is probably corrupt.

179. *Yet* (F.) Q. omits.

184. *and* (F.) Q. 'or'.

190. *they've* (F. 'they'aue') Q. 'th'haue'.

191. *wind or* (Q.) F. 'as Winde, as'.

192. *or wolf* (Q.) F. 'as Wolfe'.

199. *pains* (F.) Q. 'paine'.

207. *with a bed* (Hanmer) Q. F. omit.

208. S.D. Q. '*Exeunt.*' F. omits.

209. *maidens* See G.

210. *pandar* (Q. 'Pander') F. 'and Pander'

S.D. Q. '*Exit.*' F. '*Exeunt.*'

3. 3

Material. See notes to ll. 4, 15, 18–9, 22–5, 153, 193–4.

S.D. *Loc.* (Rowe) *Entry* Ajax (added Theob.)
Q. '*Enter Vlisses, Diomed, Nestor, Agamem, Chalcas.*';
F. '*Enter Vlysses, Diomedes, Nestor, Agamemnon, Menelaus and Chalcas. Florish.*'

1. *done* (Q.) F. 'done you'.

3. *your* (F.) Q. omits.

minds (A.W.) Q. F. 'mind'.

4. *come* (F4) Q. F. 'loue'. The emendation has the
support of Caxton who uses the phrase of the fore-
knowledge of Helenus, who knew 'things future and
to come' (p. 523), of a Trojan philosopher, who knew
'the science of things to come' (p. 526), and of
Cassandra, who 'knew much of things to come' (p. 544).
Lydgate's translation uses 'future'.

15. *registered in promise* According to Caxton, after
Calchas had returned to Athens with Achilles (cf. note
to 1. 1. 83), he was warmly received by the Greeks, who
promised 'to reward him well and do him good' (p. 552).

18–19. *a Trojan...took* According to Caxton,
Antenor was taken prisoner in the fifth battle (p. 600)
and exchanged for Thoas (cf. 5. 5 *Material*) during the
following truce (p. 601). During the same truce,
Calchas 'prayed to king Agamemnon and to the other
princes that they would require the king Priam to send
Breseyda to him' (p. 601) and although the Trojans
were angry with Calchas and called him a 'false
traitor' (cf. l. 6), Priam sent Cressida back to the Greeks
(pp. 601–2). Lydgate, but not Caxton, represents
Calchas as suggesting the exchange of Antenor for
Cressida (III, 3706–11).

22–5. *this Antenor...manage* Caxton describes
Antenor (p. 544) as 'discreet and of great industry' and
'a right wise man'.

23. *a wrest* See G.; 'that upon which the harmonious ordering of their affairs depends' (Clarke, cited Deighton).

30. *In...pain* = 'in hardships to which I have most cheerfully submitted' (Deighton).

Diomed (Hanmer) Q. F. '*Diomedes*'.

37. S.D.[1] (after Cap.) Q. F. '*Exit*,'.

S.D.[2] (Theob.) F. '*Enter...in their Tent.*'; Q. 'Achilles *and* Patro *stand in their tent*.'

39. *pass* (Q.) F. 'to passe'. Both constructions are used by Shakespeare but Q. is preferable metrically.

43. *bent on him* (Pope) Q. F. 'bent? why turnd on him'. 'Why turnd' looks like a gloss in the Q. MS. which escaped deletion in F. Cf. 3. 3. 158 n.

44. *derision medicinable* As N.V.S. explains, the aloofness of the princes is the derision and Ulysses' interpretation of it to Achilles is what is salutary. According to Ulysses (in 1. 3.), it is adulation which has turned Achilles' head and scorn might therefore be expected to restore him to his senses.

47. *pride...glass* N.V.S. compares *The Faerie Queene*, 1. 4. 10.

54. S.D. (A.W. after Cap. '*they pass forward*') Q. F. omit.

61, 63. S.Ds. (after Cap.) Q. F. omit.

68. *Good morrow* Steevens was probably right in suspecting the omission of a word or words in this speech, for 'Good morrow, Ajax' (one of his suggested emendations) would regularize the metre of these short speeches and ll. 58–69 would then form five regular decasyllabic lines.

69. S.D. (after Cap.) Q. F. '*Exeunt.*'

73. *use* (S. Walker conj.) Q. F. ''vs'd' (either a misreading or an echo of 'used' in l. 71). Though the Greeks no longer worship at the altar of Achilles, they presumably still reverence holy altars.

81. *but honour* (Q.) F. 'but honour'd'.

84–7. *Which...fall* i.e. rank, wealth, etc. are precarious and the love founded on them, being therefore unstable, declines and dies with them.

95. *A strange fellow* Various candidates for this distinction have been proposed, among them Plato (*Alcibiades* 1) and Cicero (*Tusc. Disp.*), but the dialogue between Ulysses and Achilles clearly draws on renaissance commonplaces in much the same way as Ulysses' speech on Degree; see N.V.S., pp. 411–15.

96. *how...parted* = however richly endowed.

97. *or without or in* i.e. extrinsically or intrinsically.

99. *Nor...reflection* Cf. *J.C.* 1. 2. 67–70.

100. *shining* (F.) Q. 'ayming'. F. seems better to accord with the idea of reflected heat.

102. *giver* (F.) Q. 'giuers'.

104. *but* = but it (i.e. unless it).

105–6. *To...behold itself* (Q.) F. omits.

109. *speculation* See G.

110. *mirrored* (Singer) Q. F. 'married'. The emendation is necessary to the sense: the mirror reflects the image so that the eye sees itself.

112. *at* (Q.) F. 'it at'.

115–23. *That no man...heat* Cf. *Meas.* 1. 1. 29–40, especially ll. 33–5, 'for if our virtues Did not go forth of us, 'twere all alike As if we had them not'. The idea had perhaps been popularized by Erasmus (*Adagia*, Occulta, 'Occultae musices nullus respectus'), who explains the proverb in words fairly close to Shakespeare's: 'cujus sensus est, quamvis egregias ingenii dotes, si non proferas, perinde esse quasi non habeas', citing too the well-known line of Persius, 'Scire tuum nihil est, nisi te scire hoc sciat alter'.

115. *man* (Q.) F. 'may'.

116. *be* (Q.) F. 'is'.

119. *th'* (F.) Q. 'the'.

120. *Where...extended* i.e. of those they reach.

they're (F 3) Q. 'th'are'; F. 'they are'.

125–7. *The unknown...are* F.'s lining is not entirely satisfactory since the alexandrine comes so closely on the heels of a short line; Q. divides after 'there' and 'what'.

125. *The* (F.) Q. 'Th''.

128. *abject* (F.) Q. 'obiect'.

134–5. *How...eyes* i.e. there are those who are suitors for Fortune's favour (=Ajax) while others, who enjoy it, play the fool (=Achilles); cf. note to 1. 2. 243–4.

137. *fasting* (Q.) F. 'feasting'. Q. has the right antithesis between Ajax' willingness to seize an opportunity and Achilles' wilful neglect of his fame.

140. *on* (F.) Q. 'one'.

141. *shrinking* (F.) Q. 'shriking'. It seems more appropriate that greatness should shrink.

143. *neither* Monosyllabic; cf 'whether' = 'whe'r' (4. 5. 243).

145. *a wallet at his back* The wallet idea was a commonplace (see N.V.S.), emblematic, when on the back, of forgetfulness.

146. *alms for oblivion* i.e. the beggar Achilles (cf. l. 143), 'poor of late' (l. 74), cannot expect any charity from Time because his past good deeds are forgotten; 'for oblivion' = to be forgotten.

147. *A great...ingratitude* i.e. Time (not 'oblivion'). Time is monstrously ungrateful because (as ll. 165–74 explain more fully) his interest is in the newcomer. To take 'oblivion' as the monster makes nonsense of the symbolism of the wallet on the back of *Time*. Cf. Introduction, p. xlv.

ingratitude (A.W. after Hanmer) Q. F. 'ingratitudes'. The singular was usual in this kind of qualifying phrase; cf. Jonson's alteration of 'an ingratitude wretch' to monster of ingratitude' in the revised version of *Every Man in His Humour*, 3. 3. 57.

148. *Those scraps* i.e. the 'alms' of l. 146.

devoured i.e. (as Shakespeare himself explains) forgotten.

153. *monumental mockery* = mocking commemoration.

Take the instant way... The speech recalls Ulysses' persuasions in Caxton (pp. 630–1) on the occasion when he was sent with Nestor and Diomedes to induce Achilles to assist the Greeks (cf. 2. 3. *Material*). He exhorted him, now that he had got with such great labour such 'great worship and so good renown', not to lose it but to maintain his fame. But Achilles refused to hazard his life any longer, preferring to lose his reputation 'for in the end there is no prowess that is not forgotten'.

the instant (Q. F.) S. Walker conj. 'th'instant'.

155. *one* (F.) Q. 'on'.

one but goes abreast As N.V.S. notes, the idea is of single file, though it is loosely expressed. For the word order, see Abbott, § 129.

158. *hedge* (F.) Q. 'turne'. Q. suggests a gloss or a makeshift of some sort. F. rightly implies 'skulking'.

160. *hindmost* (F.) Q. 'him, most'.

161–3. *Or...trampled on* (F.) Q. omits. I think it very likely that this recovery was intended for cancellation. It not only disturbs the metre but is also somewhat irrelevant to the main thought, for the gallant horse has fallen in the course of duty—unlike Achilles, who is reproached for neglect of it.

162. *Lie* i.e. [you] lie.

the abject rear i.e. the rag-tag and bobtail of the army.

abject rear (Hanmer) F. 'abiect, neere'.

164. *past* (F.) Q. 'passe'.

168. *welcome* (Pope + Camb.) Q. F. 'the welcome'. The restoration of the article by recent editors
spoils the personification.

169. *farewell* (Q.) F. 'farewels'.

O, (F.) Q. omits.

173. *subject* (A.W.) Q. F. 'subiects'. The adjective
seems necessary to the sense.

175–6. *One touch...gawds* i.e. all men have one
trait in common—love of novelties.

178. *give* (Thirlby conj., Theob.) Q. F. 'goe'.

183. *sooner* (Q.) F. 'begin to' (caught from l. 182).

184. *Than* (F.) Q. 'That'.

not stirs (F.) Q. 'stirs not'.

once (Q.) F. 'out'.

188–90. *Whose...faction* Seemingly an allusion to
an episode in *Iliad* v, where Mars intervenes on behalf
of the Trojans. No intermediate source for it has been
found.

188. *but...late* i.e. but of late (=only recently)
in these fields; see Abbott, § 129.

190. *Of*=For; see Abbott, § 174.

193–4. *'Tis...daughters* i.e. Polyxena. According
to Caxton (pp. 620–5), Achilles first saw Polyxena on
the anniversary of Hector's death. There was a truce
and Achilles went into Troy to see his sepulchre in the
temple of Apollo. He there saw Polyxena and fell in
love, and a few days later secretly sent a messenger to
Hecuba, asking for Polyxena's hand in marriage, undertaking, in return, to persuade the Greeks to abandon
the siege. Priam and Paris agreed, and it was when the
Greeks refused to accept Achilles' advice to leave Troy
that he withdrew his aid and that of his Myrmidons.
That Lydgate used the medieval form of Polyxena
('Pol(l)ycene'), against Caxton's 'Polixena', seems to
me of no account, since the name in its classical form
must have been well known from Ovid (*Met.* xiii).

194. A defective line, presumably owing to an omission.

197. *every...gold* (F.) Q. 'euery thing'. See p. 127.

Pluto's (F. 'Plutoes'). Steev. conj. 'Plutus''. It seems best not to emend, as some editors do, following Steevens. The idea uppermost is that nothing, however deep in earth or ocean, escapes the divinely omniscient eye of those responsible for state affairs, and, though Plutus was the god of wealth, the thing concealed is here less important than the place of concealment—to be associated with Pluto, god of the Underworld. Plutus and Pluto were, in any event, confused (as N.V.S. shows) from classical times on.

198. *th'* (F.) Q. 'the'.

deeps (F.) Q. 'depth'. F. is better poetic idiom.

199–200. *Keeps...cradles* i.e. is not merely abreast of what is thought but has a godlike prescience in anticipating it before it can be spoken. On.'s gloss 'in agreement with' for 'keeps place' loses the point.

200. *Does* (F2) Q. F. 'Do'. The line is metrically defective.

201–2. *mystery...state* Not, I think, with reference to anything so narrow as the Elizabethan secret service (as N.V.S. suggests), for 'mystery' is clearly used in a theological sense for the kind of revelation of the truth of which no account ('relation') can be given; 'state' (=the state as an agent, Government) is personified, as at l. 196.

210. *our islands* (Q.) F. 'her Iland'.

214–15. *speak...break* A perfect rhyme in Shakespeare's day.

215. *The fool...break* Taken (unnecessarily) as an allusion to an anecdote in Armin's *Nest of Ninnies*, but the point is merely that Achilles should take the plunge (or lead) and prevent Ajax from taking foolish risks. The proverb 'to break the ice' meant the same as now;

see Erasmus (*Adagia*, Ab initio ad finem, 'scindere glaciem'), who explains it as meaning 'in incipiundo negocio priorem esse'. Cf. also *Adagia*, Inanis Opera, 'fidere unius noctis glaciei', where to be on thin ice is associated with folly (='inconsulte et temere ignoto homini et peregrino confidere').

S.D. (after Pope) Q. F. omit.

224. *a* (F.) Q. omits.

225. *air* (Q.) F. 'ayrie ayre'. The extra-metrical word is not necessary for the sense, which is simply 'shaken off'.

233. *we* (F.) Q. 'they'. The personal application seems more appropriate.

241. *to my full of view* = 'to the fullest satisfaction of my eyes' (Deighton).

S.D. As in White ii and Kit. Q. after l. 241; F. after l. 239.

251. *'a* (Q.) F. 'he'.

255. *this* (Q.) F. 'his'.

263–4. *A plague...jerkin* See G. 'jerkin'. Thersites implies that the reversal in Ajax' fortunes leaves the man just the same. Dressing him up in voices (1. 3. 381) has not improved him.

263. *of opinion* i.e. on opinion; see Abbott, § 175.

265. *to him* (F.) Q. omits.

270. *demands* (Q.) F. 'his demands' (caught from l. 269).

273. *most* (F.) Q. omits.

277. *Grecian* (F.) Q. omits.

et cetera (F. '&c.') Q. omits.

294. *o'clock* (F. 'a clocke') Q. 'of the clock'.

298. *you* (F.) Q. 'yee'.

300. *he's* (F.) Q. omits.

o'tune (F. 'a tune') Q. 'of tune'.

306. *carry* (F.) Q. 'beare' (caught from l. 304).

309, 312. S.Ds. (after Cap.) Q. F. omit.

4. 1

Material. See note to ll. 10–11.

S.D. *Loc.* (after Theob.) *Entry* (after Cap.) Q.
'*Enter at one doore Æneas, at another Paris, Deiphobus,
Autemor, Diomed the Grecian with torches.*' (F.
'...*Æneas with a Torch,...Anthenor...*').

5. *you* (F.) Q. 'your'.

9. *wherein* (Q.) F. 'within'.

10–11. *You...field* According to Caxton (p. 561),
the enmity between Æneas and Diomedes began in the
first embassy of Ulysses and Diomedes to Troy, shortly
after the Greeks arrived at Tenedos (see note to
4. 5. 215–16).

10. *a* (Q.) F. 'in a' (from l. 9).

a whole week by days='every day of a whole week'
(Schmidt).

13. *question...truce*='conversation while the gentle
truce lasts' (Mal.).

18. *But...meet*='but when the time is opportune
to conflict' (Deighton); 'contention'=armed combat.
Diomedes takes up the challenge in l. 14.

But (F.) Q. 'Lul'd'.

meet (Q.) F. 'meetes'.

23–4. *by Anchises'...hand* 'He swears first by the
life of his father, and then by the hand of his mother'
(Blakeway, cited Var. '21).

34. *despiteful* (Q.) F. 'despightful'st' (assimilated
to 'noblest').

34–5. Hyphens S. Walker conj.

37. *I was* As Tannenbaum[1] suggested, the unstressed
form ('I'se') is wanted for the metre.

38. *'twas* (Q.) F. 'it was'.

39. Q. '*Calcho's*'; F. '*Calcha's*'.

42. S.D. Aside (A.W.) Q. F. omit. The inter-

change between Paris and Æneas cannot have been intended for the ears of Diomedes; cf. 4. 2. 71.

do think (F.) Q. 'beleeue'. F.'s reading is wanted as a link with 'thought'.

46. *wherefore* (Q.) F. 'whereof' (caught from l. 45).

52. S.D. (after Dyce) F. '*Exit Æneas*'. Q. omits.

54. *the* (F.) Q. omits.

55. *merits...most* (F.) Q. 'deserues...best'. The keyword is 'merits', for Diomedes' reply presupposes 'merits' and l. 67 (summarizing the matter) corroborates it.

58. *soilure* (F.) Q. 'soyle'.

67–8. *Both...whore* i.e. each is bad and each is the worse on Helen's account; 'heavier' = heavier in weight and heavier in guilt.

67. *nor...nor* (Q.) F. 'no...nor'.

68. *the heavier* (Q.) F. 'which heauier'. Heath conj. 'each heavier' is very attractive.

78. *you* (F.) Q. 'they'.

80. *but* (A.W. after Jackson conj. in Camb.+ Deighton) Q. F. 'not'. The sense seems to be that Paris has no need to enlarge on Helen's worth because she is not for barter.

4. 2

Material. See note to l. 107.
S.D. *Loc.* (Cap.)

4. *lull* (A.W. after Lettsom conj.) Q. F. 'kill' (a misreading). 'Lull' is wanted as a link with the simile of sleeping infants in the next two lines.

5. *attachment...senses* = oblivion.

10. *joys* (Q.) F. 'eyes' (presumably a misreading or a recollection of l. 4).

12–13. *with...hell* The sense is presumably that the night hangs heavily when one is in distasteful company. It can hardly mean that those intent on mischief find it long because it might well seem to them as short as for a lover.

13. *tediously* (Q.) F. 'hidiously'.

19. S.D. within (F.) Q. omits.
What's = Why is (= are).

22. S.D. F. after l. 20; Q. omits.

26. *do*—Often used absolutely for sexual intercourse, as Schmidt ('do' 5) noted.

32. *capocchia* (Theob.) Q. F. '*chipochia*'.
Has't (A.W. after Tannenbaum[1] conj.) Q. F. 'hast'.

34. S.D. As in Cap. Q. F. '*One knocks*' (Q. after l. 35, F. after l. 33).

37. *as if* (Q. F.) Steevens conj. 'as'.

39. *you're* (A.W. after Cap.) Q. F. 'you are'.
S.D. As in Cap. Q. F. '*Knock.*' (after l. 40).

41. S.D. (after Cap.) Q. F. '*Exeunt.*'

43. S.D. (Rowe) Q. F. omit.

51. *'Tis* (F.) Q. 'its'.

54. *Ho!* (A.W. after Tannenbaum[1] conj.) Q. F. 'Who'.

55. *you're* (F. 'y'are') Q. 'you are'.

57. S.D. (after F.) Q. omits.

63. *us...him* (F.) Q. 'him, and'.

65. *Diomedes'* (Q.) F. '*Diomeds*'.

66. *so concluded* (Q.) F. 'concluded so'.

72. *neighbour Pandar* (Q.) F. 'nature'. I take this to allude to Pandarus' efforts to conceal Troilus' presence and, possibly, to the implication that Calchas' house and Pandar's were adjoining (see note to 3. 2. S.D. *Loc.*). F.'s 'nature' and Q.'s 'neighbor' were clearly readings of the same word (possibly MS. 'nabor'), but F. is too abstract and, further, leaves the line metrically defective.

73. S.D. (after Cap.) Q. F. '*Exeunt.*'

76. S.D. (Dyce) Q. '*Enter Cress.*' as S.N. before
l. 77; F. '*Enter Pandarus and Cressid.*' (after l. 73).

79. *Ah, ah* (Q.) F. 'Ah, ha'.

85. *Prithee* (F.) Q. 'Pray thee'.

88–9. *knees I beseech you* (F.) Q. 'knees'.

102. *extremes* (Q.) F. 'extremitie'.

105. *I'll* (Q.) F. 'I will'.

107. *Tear...cheeks* Lydgate, describing the grief
of Troilus and Cressida, tells of Cressida's tears and how
she tears her golden hair and stains her rosy cheeks
(III, 412–34), but the actions are closer still in Guido,
who tells how she tore her cheeks ('dilacerabat').
Sommer cites the passage (I, p. cl), which Le Fèvre
omitted altogether. These were, of course, the stock
manifestations of grief; cf. Montaigne's essay (I, iv),
'Comme l'ame descharge ses passions sur des objects
fauls, quand les vrais luy defaillent'.

109. *I will* (Q. F.) The line is extra-metrical and
either 'I'll' (Pope) is wanted here or 'go' should be
omitted (Steev. conj.) later.

S.D. F. '*Exeunt.*' Q. omits.

4. 3

S.D. *Loc.* (Dyce after Theob.)   *Entry* (A.W.)
Q. '*Enter Paris, Troyl. Æneas, Deiphob, Anth. Diomedes.*' (F. '*...and Diomedes.*').

2. *For* (Q.) F. 'Of'.

3. *upon us* (A. W. after Pope) Q. F. 'vpon'. The
line is metrically defective in Q. F. and the construction
without Shakespearian parallel.

5. *her house* (Q. F.) Perhaps an error for 'th'house'
(with 'her' caught from earlier in the line), since the
stress falls very awkwardly on 'walk' instead of 'into'.

9. *own* (Q.) F. omits.

S.D. (after Cap.) Q. F. omit.

4. 4

S.D. *Loc.* (after Theob.) *Entry* (Q. F.; F. '...*Cressid.*').

3. *full, perfect* (Q.) F. 'full perfect'.

4. *violenteth* (Q.) F. 'no lesse'. F. looks like an attempt to extract sense from a word the collator had not managed to decipher.

6. *affection* (F.) Q. 'affections'.

9. *dross* (Q.) F. 'crosse'.

10. S.D. (Q. F.; F. after l. 9).

12. *ducks* (Q.) F. 'ducke'.

13. S.D. (Mal. after Cap.) Q. F. omit.

14. *spectacles* Then (as now)=(*a*) sights, and (*b*) aids to sight.

15. *O heart*... Seemingly an extract from a popular rhyme, though its source has not been found.

16. *O heavy* (A.W. after Pope) Q. F. 'heauy'.

19–20. *Because...speaking* 'Doubtless characteristic intimation lurks under the language' (Hudson, cited N.V.S.). The lines 'read oddly' (Dyce). Something may be wrong, but 'let us cast away nothing' suggests that there was never much sense in them.

24. *strained* (Q.) F. 'strange' (a misreading).

32. *Is it* (Rowe) Q. F. 'Is't'.

34. *jostles* (Q. 'iussles'; F. 'iustles').

36. *rejoindure* The only known instance of the word and perhaps merely a variant spelling of 'rejoinder' (cf. variations in the spelling of 'tenour'; at 2. 1. 90, Q. has 'tenor', F. 'tenure').

37. *embraces* (A.W. after Pope) Q. F. 'embrasures'. The Q. F. word could only suggest 'windows' to an Elizabethan audience and was probably due to the ending's having been assimilated to that of 'rejoindure'.

41. *one* (Q.) F. 'our'.

45. *With...to them* i.e. each separate farewell ratified with a kiss (see G. 'consign').

48. *Distasted* (Q.) F. 'Distasting'.

S.D. F. '*Enter Æneus.*' Since Æneas does not enter until l. 108, F.'s S.D. suggests either a book-keeper's jotting or a printing-house addition.

49. S.D. within (Q. F.).

50–1. *so Cries 'Come'* (F.) Q. 'Cries so'.

53. *Rain...wind* A deliberately ludicrous echo of the hackneyed use of these words for 'tears' and 'sighs'; cf. the serious use in *Lucr.* 1788–90, and similar ridicule in *A.Y.L.* 3. 5. 50.

54. *th'root* (F. 'the root') Q. 'my throate'. See p. 127.

S.D. (after Theob.) Q. F. omit.

55. *Grecians* (Q. F.) Var. 1803 'Greeks'. The Q. F. reading is metrically awkward and not convincing in view of l. 56.

57. *When* (Q.) F. '*Troy*. When'.

58. *my* (F.) Q. omits.

60. *expostulation* Not, I think, = 'speech, conversation' (Schmidt) or 'discourse' (On.), but in the usual sense, referring to Cressida's *remonstrance* 'how now! what wicked deem is this?'.

63. *throw...himself* i.e. 'challenge death himself'. A glove, the symbol of honour, was cast down by the defendant in a quarrel and taken up by the accuser (see Linthicum, p. 267).

64. *there's* (F.) Q. 'there is'.

70. *sleeve* Sleeves of men's doublets (and women's dresses) were detachable (see Linthicum, p. 198) and often given as tokens; cf. Chaucer, *Troilus*, v, 1043.

71. *glove* Like sleeves, gloves were often elaborate and similarly given as keepsakes (see Linthicum, p. 267).

73. *nightly* = at night.

77. *Their...nature* (F.+Sisson) Q. omits. Editors

usually interpret F.'s 'Their' as = 'They're', but this
impairs metrical smoothness and also, by generalizing,
loses the point that Troilus speaks as a lover and is
thinking of his inferiority in this special way. The
meaning is that the Greeks are accomplished wooers,
endowed with natural gifts and an abundance of
acquired graces in which they are expert (singing,
dancing, pleasing conversation, and games of skill are
particularized later as the accomplishments ('virtues')
which they have and he has not).

gifts (Theob. ii) F. 'guift'.

78. *And flowing* (Staunton) Q. 'And swelling'; F.
'Flawing and swelling'. Correction of Q. seems more
likely to have been intended than conflation with it.

arts and exercise i.e. acquired accomplishments and
practice in them (contrasted with 'gifts of nature').

79. *novelties* (F.) Q. 'nouelty'.

person (F.) Q. 'portion'.

80. *godly jealousy* A biblical phrase, as Theob.
noted, comparing 2 Cor. xi. 2.

82. *afeard* (Q.) F. 'affraid'.

97. *changeful potency* = very changeable power.

101. *true?* (Q.) F. 'true? *Exit.*'

103–8. *Whiles...it* i.e. Troilus is too simple to be
anything but genuine; cf. 3. 2. 89–97, 152–69.

107. *the...wit* i.e. the only precept he understands.

108. S.D. (Mal.) F. '*Enter the Greekes.*' (after
l. 106); Q. omits.

119. *usage* (Q.) F. 'visage'.

122. *zeal* (Warb. conj., Theob.) Q. F. 'seale'.
'Zeal' is better sense: 'the zeal...thee' = 'my zealous
petition to you'.

to thee (Q.) F. 'towards'.

123. *In* (Q.) F. 'I'.

126. *even...charge* i.e. since Diomedes will not listen
to entreaties, he must take orders.

130–2. *Let me...lust* i.e. it is no use Troilus' starting a quarrel while Diomedes is under diplomatic privilege, but when they meet on the battlefield he will gladly ('to my lust' = to my pleasure) take up the quarrel. On. takes 'to my lust' as = 'as I please', but Diomedes is taking up the challenge of ll. 126–9. Cf. 4. 1. 18, 'When occasion and contention meet'.

132. *you, lord* (Q.) F. 'my Lord'.

135. *I'll* (F.) Q. 'I'. For this emphatic use of 'I'll' Steev. compares *K. J.* 5. 6. 39, *H. V,* 1. 1. 1.

139. S.D.[1] (after Ritson conj.) Q. F. omit.
S.D.[2] F. '*Sound Trumpet.*'; Q. omits.

142. *to the field* (Q.) F. 'in the field'.

143. *him.* Q. F. 'him. *Exeu.*' (F. '*...Exeunt.*').

144–8. Deiphobus....*chivalry.* (F.) Q. omits.

144. S.N. Deiphobus. (Ritson conj., Mal.) F. '*Dio.*'.

148. S.D. (after Rowe) F. omits (cf. l. 143 n.).

4. 5

Material. See notes to ll. 16 S.D., 119, 121, 196, 215–16, 220, 231.

S.D. *Loc.* (Mal. after Cap.) *Entry* (Camb. after Theob.) Q. F. '*Enter Aiax armed, Achilles, Patroclus, Agam. Menelaus, Vlisses, Nester, Calcas. &c.*'

2. *Anticipating...courage* I accept (like most editors) Theob.'s pointing of this line. Q. F. have a period after 'time' and a comma after 'courage', but as the punctuation was Eld *A*'s it must be viewed with suspicion. The word 'starting' does not, I think, mean 'startling' but 'bounding', 'leaping' (as in Prol. 28) and this is why Ajax comes to be 'anticipating time' and is in the field, as Theob. observed, before the challenger.

4. *the* (Q. F.) Pope 'th''.

8–9. *thy sphered....Aquilon* On old maps the winds

were represented as heads, puffing from the appropriate
direction; in profile or three-quarter face this gave them
a 'bias' cheek.

9. *choller* (A.W.) Q. F. 'collick'. The Q. F. reading
seems extraordinarily irrelevant, for the picture is purely
visual and Schmidt's comparison with *1 H. IV*, 3. 1. 28
does not allow for the intentionally low and comic
associations of Hotspur's speech; 'choler' (anon. conj.
in Delius ii) does not help much. I take it that the
Q. F. reading is an error for 'choller' (=jaw, parallel
therefore with 'cheek'), a word of which the O.E.D.
records a single example *c.* 1000 and then no further
instance until 1785.

11. *blow'st* (Pope) Q. F. 'blowest'.
S.D. (Hanmer) Q. F. omit.

13. *yon* (Q. 'yond') F. 'yong'. The present
distinction between 'yon' (the demonstrative adj. and
pron.) and 'yond' (adv.), which is a helpful one, was
not made in Shakespeare's day, when compositors
appear to have normalized this, like other spellings,
according to their fancy. Differentiation in a modernized text removes a possible stumbling block to comprehension. The sense here is of, course, 'that (person)
over there'.

16. S.D. (Theob. after F2) Q. F. omit. Caxton
describes how Diomedes was among Breseyda's escort
when she was returned to the Greeks and declared his
love for her on the way; 'and he accompanied her unto
the tent of her father'. 'The coming of Breseyda pleased
much to all the Greeks. And they came thither and
feasted her'...and 'all the greatest that were there
promised her to keep her and hold her as dear as their
daughter. And then each man went into his own tent
and there was none of them but that gave to her a jewel'
(pp. 604–6). Lydgate does not mention Cressida's
welcome; cf. Introduction, pp. xl–xli.

18, 23, 25, 29, 33. S.Ds. (after Collier) Q. F. omit.

21. *kissed in general* Probably in immediate ironic recognition of Cressida for what she is, though the Greeks receive the proposal with alacrity.

24. *winter* i.e. coldness, with allusion (as N.V.S. explains) to Nestor's age.

29. *And...argument.* (Q.) F. omits.

29–30. *argument...theme* i.e. Helen is Menelaus' 'argument' (=reason for kissing, cf. l. 27) and this 'argument' (=quarrel) is the 'theme' (=subject) which is so disastrous for the Greeks.

30. S.D. Aside (A.W. after Keightley conj.) Q. F. omit.

37. S.N. Menelaus. (A.W. after Tyrwhitt conj.+ Kittredge) Q. F. '*Patr.*' There is no point, and some loss, in the intrusion of Patroclus again.

I'll...live Not satisfactorily explained, but if 'to live' ='to be valid' (Schmidt), the words mean simply 'I'll wager' or perhaps (according to Tyrwhitt) 'I'll wager my life'.

41. *You're* (Cap.) Q. F. 'You are'.

45. *o'th'* (F4) Q. F. 'a'th'.

head Because of the cuckold's horn, as Ulysses' comment shows.

48. *too* (A.W. after Ritson conj.) Q. F. 'then'. The line should rhyme with l. 47, and 'then' in Q. F. looks like an anticipation of 'then' in the next line. Having given Ulysses *leave* to beg, Cressida insists that the begging must be done. 'Why' (as interjection)=Then surely.

52. *Never's...you* 'I rather think that Ulysses means to slight her' (J.).

53. S.D. (after Pope ii) Q. F. omit.

54. *quick sense* Ambiguous words, but, as Nestor was not usually penetrating, he probably speaks in appreciation of Cressida's nimble mind. Ulysses puts

a more realistic interpretation on 'quick sense', recognizing her responsive sensual nature.

55. *language* (Q.) F. 'a language'.

59. *accosting* (Theob. conj.) Q. F. 'a coasting'. The use of 'coasting' as sb. (=approach, advance) has no parallel but 'accosting' in this sense appears in Florio, 1603. The latter is in accordance with Shakespeare's use of 'accost' and seems, on all counts, the more natural expression.

61. *tickling* (F.) Q. 'ticklish'. Q. has been widely approved, but it looks like a case of assimilation to 'sluttish' in the next line and 'tickling' gives perfectly good sense: Cressida's wanton spirits are fully disclosed to anyone who chooses to encourage them. The derivation of 'accost' (from Lat. *costa*=rib) explains Shakespeare's use of 'tickling'.

62. *For...opportunity* i.e. 'Corrupt wenches, of whose chastity every opportunity may make prey' (J.).

63. *game*. (Q.) F. 'game. *Exeunt.*'

S.D. (Theob.) Q. F. omit. Cf. 1. 64 S.D. n.

64. *Trojans'* Delius conj. 'Trojan's'.

S.D. (Cap.+Mal.) Q. '*Flowrish enter all of Troy.*' (after 1. 63); F. '*Enter all of Troy, Hector, Paris, Æneas, Helenus and Attendants. Florish.*' (after 1. 63).

65. *the* (Q.) F. 'you'.

What...done Steev. (1793) noted that this was a scriptural phrase='what honour shall he receive', comparing 1 Sam. xvii. 26.

69. *they* (Q.) F. omits.

73. S.N. Achilles. (A.W.) Cont. to Agamemnon (Q. F.) The reply of Æneas makes it evident that the close of this speech belongs to Achilles and, for this reason, editors follow a conjecture of Theob., transferring the whole ('Tis done like Hector...opposed') to Achilles. The generosity of the first half line seems more appropriate to Agamemnon.

74. *misprizing* (Q.) F. 'disprising'. Either is possible, but F. suggests assimilation to 'deal'.

78–9. *In...Hector* i.e. Hector excels in valour as in humility.

83. *half...blood* Cf. l. 120 and note.

87. *perceive*='understand' (O.E.D. 2) not 'see through'; cf. 1. 1. 38, n.

S.D. (Pope ii) Q. F. omit.

92. *breath* (Q.) F. 'breach'.

93. S.D. (Mal. after Cap.) Q. F. omit.

94–5. Ulysses. *They...heavy?* (F.) Q. '*Vlisses: what...heauy?* (as dialogue, continued to Agamemnon), omitting 'They...already'.

96. *knight;* (Q.) F. 'Knight; they call him *Troylus*;' Since the words are here extra-metrical and occur again in Q. and F. at l. 108, the obvious explanation is that they are a first thought, which Shakespeare at once discarded.

97. *matchless-firm* (A.W.) Q. 'matchlesse firme'; F. 'matchlesse, firme'. Editors either preserve F.'s comma or substitute a heavier stop. But it is not Troilus who is matchless for he is the 'second hope' (l. 109) of Troy. It is his 'word' that is 'matchlessly firm', as becomes a true knight, in spite of his immaturity.

98. *Speaking in* (F.) Q. 'Speaking'.

103. *impair* The meaning is disputed, but the sense 'unworthy', 'inferior' (*Lat.* 'impar') gives more point to 'dignifies' than any other sense suggested.

111. *with private soul*=as his personal opinion.

112. S.D. (Rowe) Q. F. '*Alarum*.'

119ff. *Why, then...* According to Caxton (pp. 589–90), early in the war, Hector encountered Ajax (described as the son of king Telamon and Hesione and his cousin-german, son of his aunt) in actual combat. Hector embraced him and invited him to Troy to visit his kinsfolk. Ajax refused but, taking advantage of Hector's goodwill, asked that hostilities should end for that day. Thus (according to Caxton), Hector's courtesy lost the Trojans the victory in the war, for never after were they in such an advantageous position.

120. *my father's sister's son* As N.V.S. notes, Cooper has the same error. According to classical authorities, Ajax was the son of Telamon and Periboea (or Eriboea).

121. *cousin-german* Caxton's words, but not Lydgate's (III. 2036 ff.). The latter describes Ajax as the son of Telamon and Hesione but otherwise merely as near in relationship.

132. *Of...feud* (F.) Q. omits.

133. *drop* (F.) Q. 'day'.

135. *Let...thee* There is no mention of any embrace in Lydgate.

141. *addition* See G. The specialized (heraldic) sense, of which O.E.D. cites one other example of 1753, receives some slight support from the opposites 'abatement' and 'diminution', but the meaning may be simply 'title' (as in Jack the Giant Killer).

142. *Neoptolemus* 'My opinion is, that by Neoptolemus the authour meant Achilles himself, and remembering that the son was Pyrrhus Neoptolemus, considered Neoptolemus as the *nomen gentilitium*, and thought the father was likewise Achilles Neoptolemus' (J.). Editors have generally agreed, though N.V.S. suggests the allusion was to the promise of Pyrrhus and the prophecy that Troy could not be taken without him.

143. *oyez* Q. F. '(O yes)' Delius, perhaps rightly, read 'loudest' for Q. F. 'loudst', because 'oyez' is monosyllabic, rhyming with 'joys', in *Wiv.* 5. 5. 41–2.

144. *could* (Q.) F. 'could'st' (assimilated to 'loud'st').

150. *As...chance* i.e. as the opportunity (for an invitation) is rare.

156. *To...part* i.e. 'to those of our party who are awaiting to know the issue of this meeting' (Deighton).

158. S.D. in F. '*Enter Agamemnon and the rest*' (Q. omits). Up till now communication between Trojans and Greeks has been carried on formally through Æneas and Diomedes (as marshals) and we must suppose them ranged according to parties. Agamemnon and the other Greeks now come forward and F.'s S.D. was either intended to suggest this or was due to officious interference; cf. 4. 4. 48 n.

161. *my own* (Q.) F. 'mine owne'.

163. *of arms* (F.) Q. 'all armes'. F.'s seems the more idiomatic expression (cf. 'deeds of arms', 'man of arms'). The greeting means no more, I think, than 'noble warrior'.

165–70. *But...integrity.* (F.) Q. omits.

167. *formless ruin of oblivion* Cf. 3. 2. 184–8.

169. *hollow bias-drawing*=insincerity; Agamemnon speaks from fullness and straightforwardness of heart.

173. S.D. (Rowe) Q. F. omit.

176. *The noble...* Æneas 'acts as master of the ceremonies' (Steev. 1793 on l. 201); cf. 1. 3. 224 n.

178. *that I...oath* (F.) Q. 'thy...earth'.

184. *Labouring...way* With allusion to Atropos, the Destiny who cuts the thread of life.

186. *Perseus* See note to 1. 3. 42.

187. *And...scorning* (F.) Q. 'Despising many'. Editors prefer Q. and, as compositor *B* set this F. page, the F. reading may be a typical perversion. At the same time, Q. seems to have no merits and is even somewhat trite.

188. *thy advancèd* (F.) Q. 'th'aduanced'.

190. *to some* (Q.) F. 'vnto'.

193. *hemmed* (F.) Q. 'shrupd'. I suspect Q. con-

ceals the truth and that F. is probably a makeshift, but until what Q. intended is better established it seems wiser to accept the traditional reading. Sisson reads 'shraped' (=trapped).

196–7. *thy grandsire...him* i.e. Laomedon, king of Troy. Caxton describes Nestor as having been with Hercules when he attacked Troy in revenge for Laomedon's hostility to Jason. Laomedon did 'marvels of arms' (pp. 349–50) in defending the city but was slain by Hercules. Lydgate (I. 4147–97), but not Caxton, describes a fierce encounter between Nestor and Laomedon. After the death of the latter, Troy was sacked and Hesione was given to Telamon as part of the spoils.

199. *O, (Q.)* F. omits.

206. *As...courtesy* (F.) Q. omits.

210. *I...time* Cf. Shallow in reminiscent mood: 'Jesus, the days that we have seen' (2 *H. IV*, 3. 2. 220).

215–16. *Since...embassy* The allusion is to the first embassy of Diomedes and Ulysses. According to Caxton, after the Greeks had landed at Tenedos and destroyed the castle, Agamemnon sent Ulysses and Diomedes to Troy, undertaking that the Greeks would return home if Helen was restored and reparation was made for the damage done in Greece by Paris. Ulysses then prophesied that, if Priam refused the offer, the city would be destroyed (pp. 558–60). Lydgate, but not Caxton, specifies as part of the prophecy that the walls and towers would be brought low (II. 6872–4).

220. *whose...clouds* Caxton (p. 508) describes the towers of Ilion as seeming, from a distance, to reach to heaven; 'wanton' = 'arrogant', since the point is that the pride of Troy shall be humbled. Pride and wantonness had a close association; cf. 3. 3. 137.

224. *The end...all* A well-known saying ('Finis coronat opus').

230. *Ulysses, thou* The pronoun is insulting and

intentionally so (like the preceding 'thee'). Achilles is riled by the exchange of courtesies and Ajax' stealing the limelight.

231 ff. *Now Hector...* Caxton tells how, during the truce between the fifth and sixth battles, Hector accepted Achilles' invitation to his tent where Achilles expressed his pleasure at seeing him for the first time unarmed: 'but yet', he said, 'I shall have more pleasure when the day shall come that thou shalt die of my hand. Which thing I most desire' (p. 602). Hector then challenged him to single combat; cf. 1.3. *Material.*

235. *pray thee* (Q.) F. 'prythee'.

243. *whether* = (metrically) 'wh'er' (Dyce).

249. *pleasantly* i.e. easily.

252. *an oracle* (Q.) F. 'the Oracle'.

255. *stithied* (F.) Q. 'stichied'.

263. *have* (Q.) F. omits.

272. *we* (Q.) F. 'you'.

274–5. *him. Beat...taborins* (F.) Q. 'him To taste your bounties'. See p. 126.

276. S.D. (after Rowe and Cap.) Q. F. '*Exeunt.*'

281. *upon...nor* (Q.) F. 'on heauen, nor on'.

284. *you* (Q.) F. 'thee'.

287. *As* (F.) Q. 'But'.

As gentle i.e. 'With like courtesy' (Deighton).

292. *she loved* (F.) Q. 'my Lord'.

is, and doth i.e. is loved, and doth love.

292–3. *doth...tooth* A perfect rhyme; cf. the pronunciation of 'do'.

5. 1

S.D. *Loc.* (after Rowe).

2. *Which* Refers to 'blood' (l. 1).

4. *core* (F.) Q. 'curre'.

5. *botch* (A.W. after Theob.) Q. F. 'batch'. The metaphor belongs, I think, to disease imagery (see G. 'crusty', 'botch') rather than food imagery;

'batch'='quantity of bread produced at one baking'.

6. *picture...seemest* Not, I think, as Deighton explained, 'fool in looks, fool in reality' but (as 'idol of idiot-worshippers' suggests) a picture (=image) of a man, and so a blockish thing or 'blockhead'.

9–11. For the quibbling, see G. 'fool', 'tent.'

10. *Who...now?* Deighton explained as a question of appeal, equivalent to 'You see that Achilles can no longer be taunted with keeping his tent', but I doubt if anything so oblique was intended in a conversation so patently begun in order to allow Achilles time to read his letter. It may mean simply 'who is still ('now') in Agamemnon's tent?'—for Achilles and Patroclus are waiting for the party to arrive.

12. *need these* (F.) Q. 'needs this'.

need F.'s irregular 3rd pers. sing. was common and has euphony to recommend it.

14. *boy* (F.) Q. 'box'.

15. *thought* (F.) Q. 'said' (an echo of l. 12?).

17–8. *the rotten...south* The south wind was generally thought of as dangerous, but the allusion here is (as Deighton noted) to syphilis, supposed to have originated in Naples (cf. 2. 3. 18). Greene in the Epistle to *A Disputation betweene a Hee Conny-catcher and a Shee Conny-catcher* ran through much the same catalogue of whorehouse diseases: 'sores incurable, vlcers brusting out of the ioyntes, and sault rhumes, which by the humour of that villanie, lepte from Naples into Fraunce, and from Fraunce into the bowels of Englande, which makes many crye out in their bones.'

18. *the guts-griping* (Q.) F. omits 'the'.

catarrhs (F.) Q. omits.

19. *o'* (F4) Q. F. 'a'.

i'th' (F.) Q. 'in the'.

19–22. *raw eyes...tetter* (Q.) F. 'and the like'.

I doubt whether F.'s abridgement had authority. The compositor may have been responsible for it.

23. *take and...discoveries* i.e. the plagues attendant on whoredom should doubly light on discoveries of unnatural vices.

25. *mean'st* (F.) Q. 'meanes'.

to curse i.e. by cursing; see Abbott, § 356.

28. *indistinguishable* Carrying on the sense of 'ruinous' (implying deformity); cf. Introduction, p. xliii, n. 1.

no (Q.) F. omits.

30. *sleave-silk* (Q.) F. 'Sleyd silke'. The F. variant is merely an alternative way of saying the same thing, 'sleyd' being the ppl. adj. of the vb. 'sleave' (=to divide (silk) into filaments); such silk (=floss silk) was, as Deighton notes, useless until woven.

34. *gall* See G.; but perhaps a different meaning (=the round excrescence on trees, as in 'oak-gall') suggested the 'finch-egg' of Thersites' reply.

35. *Finch-egg* The finch being one of the smallest birds.

41. *An oath* See 3. 3. 193–4 n.

46. S.D. (after Hanmer) F. '*Exit*.' Q. omits.

51. *quails* See G.

52–4. *goodly...cuckolds* With allusion (as Deighton explained) to Jupiter's metamorphosis into a bull to gain Europa, and Menelaus is likened to Jupiter (the bull) because he was 'horned' (=cuckolded). The bull is the 'oblique' reminder of cuckolds because the cuckold's horns were merely figurative.

52. *goodly* Ironical (like 'thrifty' in l. 54).

53. *brother* (F.) Q. 'be' (a misreading of the abbreviation 'br.').

54. *shoeing-horn* Regarded as an emblem of servility, and one kind of horn inevitably suggested another (the cuckold's).

55. *hanging* (F.) Q. omits.
brother's (F.) Q. 'bare' (a misreading).
56. *forced* Q. 'faced'.
57. *him to* A redundant preposition was common; see Abbott, § 407.
58. *he is* (F.) Q. 'her's' (for 'hee's').
59. *dog* (F.) Q. 'day'.
fitchew (F.) Q. 'Fichooke' (a variant of the same word).
62. *not* (F.) Q. omits.
63. *care not to be* = 'should not mind being' (Deighton); cf. Abbott, § 356.
64. *Hoy-day* (F.) Q. 'hey-day'.
spirits (F.) Q. 'sprites'.
spirits and fires i.e. the approaching lights.
S.D. (Theob.+Cap.) Q. '*Enter Agam: Vlisses, Nest: and Diomed with lights.*' F. '*Enter Hector, Aiax, Agamemnon, Vlysses, Nestor, Diomed, with Lights.*'
66. *lights* (Q.) F. 'light'.
67. S.D. (after F.) Q. omits.
69. *good night* (F.) Q. 'God night'.
73. S.D. Aside (A.W. after Staunton) Q. F. omit.
draught See G.
74. *sewer* Spelt 'sure' Q. F.
75. *at once* (F.) Q. omits.
77. S.D. Q. '*Exeunt Agam: Menelaus.*' F. omits.
83. S.D. (after Rowe) Q. F. omit.
85. S.D.[1] (after Cap.) Q. F. omit.
S.D.[2] (after Cap.) Q. F. '*Exeunt*'.
89. *Babbler* (A.W. after Baldwin conj.) Q. F. 'brabler'. As Baldwin (N.V.S.) noted, 'brabble' = 'quarrel' and what the sense requires here is 'babble', used especially of 'hounds that give tongue too loudly or without reason' (O.E.D. 4, citing Markham, 1611, as the first example of the verb in this specialized sense and 1732 for the noun).

90. *it; it* (Q. 'it, it') F. 'it, that it'.

94. *uses* Perhaps in the equivocal sense of 'occupy'
(see 2 *H. IV*, G. 'occupy').

Calchas' (Q. '*Calcas*') F. '*Chalcas* his'.

96. S.D. (after Hanmer) F. '*Exeunt.*' Q. omits.

5. 2

Material. Lydgate, but not Caxton, mentions that,
according to Guido, Cressida forsook Troilus the very
night that she left Troy (III. 4435–40). Lydgate also
reproves Guido for the many harsh conclusions he drew
about the double-dealing of women—their weeping with
one eye and laughing with the other (III. 4290–2); cf.
ll. 107–8.

S.D. *Loc.* (Cap. after Rowe)   *Entry* (Q. F. '*Enter
Diomed.*')

2, 5. S.D.'s. within (Hanmer) Q. F. omit.

3. *Where's* (Q. F.) J. 'Where is'.

your (Q.) F. 'you'.

5. S.D.² (Cap. after Rowe) F. '*Enter Troylus and
Vlisses.*'; Q. omits.

6. S.D. Q. F. '*Enter Cressid.*' (Q. after 'him',
l. 7).

8. S.D. (Rowe) Q. F. omit.

11. *sing...clef* (Q. '...Cliff') F. 'finde...life'.

14. S.N. (F2) Q. F. '*Cal.*'

17. *should* (F.) Q. 'shall'.

23. *forsworn* (Q.) F. 'a forsworne. -----'.

25. *juggling trick* The juggling lies in the paradox
of being 'secretly open', with quibbling in the latter
word; see G. 'open'.

28. *anything* (Q.) F. 'not any thing'.

35. *one* (F.) Q. 'a'.

37. *pray you* (F.) Q. 'pray'.

41. *Nay* (F.) Q. 'Now'.

42. *flow* Probably the image is of the rising tide; Deighton glosses as 'are rapidly hastening'.

distraction (F.) Q. 'distruction'. F.'s seems the apter word, as the dramatic point is not so much the danger Troilus is in as his mental turmoil, and it is 'patience' that he swears to in his reply.

43. *pray thee* (F.) Q. 'prethee'.

44. *all hell*'s (Q.) F. 'hell'.

47. *Why...lord* (F.) Q. 'How now my Lord'.

49. *adieu* (F.) Q. omits.

56. *luxury*=lechery, one of the Seven Deadly Sins.

57. *these* (F.) Q. omits.

59. *But* (F.) Q. omits.

60. *la* (Theob.) Q. F. 'lo'.

62. S.D. Q. F. '*Exit.*'

63. *sweet lord* (F.) Q. 'my Lord'.

65. S.D. Q. F. '*Enter Cress.*' (F. '*...Cressid.*').

67. S.D. (after Collier ii) Q. F. omit.

68. *where...faith* Noble compares Luke viii. 25.

69. Troilus. *I...will.* (F.) Q. omits.

70. S.N. Cressida (F.) Q. '*Troy:*'.

71. S.D. (A.W.) Q. F. omit.

73. *have't* (F.) Q. '*ha't*'.

79. *in* (F.) Q. 'on'.

82–3. *Nay...He* (cont. to Cressida, Thirlby conj., Theob.). Q. F. '*Dio:* Nay...*Cres:* He'.

83. *doth take* (Q.) F. 'rakes'.

S.D. (after Collier ii) Q. F. omit.

86. S.N. Cressida. (F.) Q. omits.

90. *one*'s (Q. 'on's') F. 'one'.

92. *By* (F.) Q. 'And by'.

Diana's waiting-women i.e. the stars.

103. S.N. Troilus. (Hanmer) Q. F. '*Ther:*' The tone of this speech suggests that the speaker is Troilus and, although Q. F. print it as prose, it sounds like

verse. If the speech belongs to Thersites, then prose it certainly should be, for Thersites' only excursion into verse is his mocking echo of Cressida's couplets at ll. 113–14.

you (Q.) F. 'me' (an error of anticipation).

105. *I shall be plagued* The sense is not, I think, 'punished' (Schmidt's gloss), but the weakened colloquial sense (=this is a curse); cf. 4. 2. 22, 'I shall have such a life'.

106. S.D. F. '*Exit.*' (after 'then') Q. omits.

112. *Minds...turpitude* Q. places the line in inverted commas; cf. 1. 2. 290 n.

113. *A proof...more* i.e. she could not proclaim a strong proof more forcibly.

114. *said* (Q.) F. 'say'.

118. *co-act* (F.) Q. 'Court'.

122. *th'attest* (Q.) F. 'that test'.

123. *had deceptious* (F.) Q. 'were deceptions'.

126. The line is defective and Steev. 1793 conj. 'It is most sure she was' is plausible.

133. *rather* The line is metrically awkward and either the syncopated form of this word is wanted (see Kökeritz, p. 322) or an inversion: 'think rather' would introduce the extra syllable in a more normal position.

134. *soil* (F.) Q. 'spoile'.

136. *'a* (Q.) F. 'he'.

137. *This she?* The speech is a difficult one because it is emotionally and not logically motivated, contravening (as anyone trained in forensic oratory would recognize) the formula for a debate of this kind.

139. *be sanctimonies* (Q.) F. 'are sanctimonie'.

142. *is* (F.) Q. 'was'.

142–6. *O madness...revolt* Because Troilus' heart (his 'esperance so obstinately strong' of l. 121) is in conflict with the evidence of his eyes and ears (see l. 122), he indicts reason ('discourse') as madness; for he paradoxically finds that his reason can rebel against the authority of his senses ('eyes and ears') without madness ('perdition'=loss of reason) and that loss of trust in the evidence of these senses can claim to be supremely reasonable. What he sees as the bifold authority of reason is, of course, nothing of the sort but the conflict of Will ('credence' and 'esperance' of the heart) and Judgement. The imagery is of civil war; cf. 2. 3. 170–4.

143. *itself* (Q.) F. 'thy selfe'.

144. *Bifold* (Q.) F. 'By foule'.

147. *conduce* The word (=conduct) was common enough, but the absolute construction is unusual, though the sense is plainly that this conflict is *going on*. The conflict is whether there is 'rule in unity'—whether one individual (Cressida) can be two ('Troilus' Cressida and Diomedes' Cressida).

152. *Ariachne's* (F.) Q. '*Ariathna's*' (uncorr.); '*Ariachna's*' (corr.). The form of the name may have been due, as has been suggested, to confusion with Ariadne, but the allusion is to the fable of Arachne (who was turned into a spider) and the metre requires four syllables.

157. *five* (F.) Q. 'finde'.

five-finger-tied (Hyphens Pope) 'A knot tied by giving her hand to Diomede' (J.).

160. *o'ereaten* Schmidt and On. explain as 'eaten or nibbled away on all sides', but the sense is, rather, '*excessively* consumed'; i.e. Cressida's promises to Troilus are done with. Cf. the food symbolism at 3. 3. 148–50.

faith (Q. F.) S. Walker conj. 'truth' or 'troth' (presuming that 'faith' was caught from l. 158).

given (Q.) F. 'bound'. Opinion has generally favoured F., but 'bound' seems to defeat the purpose of the distinction in ll. 154–7 between a 'bond', which is a sacred or legal obligation, and a mere 'knot'.

161. *but half* (A.W. after S. Walker conj.+ Deighton) Q. F. 'halfe'. Something is clearly wanted to avoid the anomaly of a trisyllabic 'Troilus'.

167. *as I* (F2) Q. F. 'I'.

do (Q. F.) Lettsom conj. in Camb. 'did'.

Cressid (Q.) F. '*Cressida*'.

169. *on* (Q.) F. 'in'. Either is possible (see G. 'in'), but conformity with Diomedes' word at l. 94 seems safer than with Thersites' at 5. 4. 4.

173. *sun* (Q.) F. 'Fenne'. F. seems clearly a misreading, like many of its errors, and is a strong argument against the common assumption that a collator would not alter a reading for the worse.

177. *tickle it* Mainly, I think, a scornful comment on the hyperboles of Troilus—the ranting on which Thersites has already poured scorn in l. 136; 'it'=the helmet.

concupy (Q. F. 'concupie') The word has not been found elsewhere and must be taken to mean either 'concubine' or 'concupiscence'.

189. S.D. Q. F. '*Exeunt Troyl. Eeneas and Vlisses.*'

191. *like a raven* Believed to be a bird of ill omen; cf. *Macb.* 1. 5. 37–9.

194. *commodious* See G.; but the O.E.D. gloss cites no further instance of this sense and the meaning may be the commoner one of 'convenient', 'handy'.

196. *a burning devil* With allusion to venereal disease. S.D. (after Q.) F. omits.

5. 3

Material. Caxton (pp. 610–12) tells how, the night before Hector's death, Andromache had a vision warning her that Hector would be killed if he fought the next day. Weeping, she implored him to remain at home, 'whereof Hector blamed his wife' saying that no trust was to be placed in dreams. In the morning, Andromache told her vision to Priam and Hecuba, and Priam ordered Hector to remain in Troy. Hector was angry and said many words in reproach to Andromache, who took her children and fell at his feet, beseeching him to unarm. Hecuba, Helen and Hector's sisters added their pleas, but Hector refused to unarm and was only prevented from leaving by Priam, who compelled him to return. But on hearing of the death of Margareton, his bastard brother, at the hands of Achilles, Hector joined in the battle without Priam's knowledge. See also note to ll. 37–8. What is most significant in Shakespeare's use of his source material in this scene is his avoidance of its sentimental possibilities.

S.D. *Loc.* (Cap. after Theob.).

4. *in* (Q.) F. 'gone' (? anticipating 'go' at the end of l. 5).

5. *all* (Q.) F. omits.

6. *to* = with regard to.
the day (Q. F.) Metrically 'th'day' is wanted.

14. S.N. (F.) Q. '*Cres.*'

20–2. *To hurt...charity* (F.) Q. omits.

21. *For...use* (Tyrwhitt conj., Mal.) F. 'For we would count giue much to as'. F.'s 'count' looks as if it had been caught from two lines earlier and 'as' may similarly have been caught from the line above; 'use' is not entirely convincing, partly because misreading of 'use' as 'as' is not likely and partly because 'as' might have been substituted for a simpler verb, like 'do'.

23. S.N. (F.) Q. omits (cont. to Andromache).

23–4. *It is...hold* An echo of a theme treated more fully in *K.J.* 3. 1. 263 ff.

27–8. *Life...life* i.e. every man holds life precious, but the honoured man (man who is held dear) holds honour far more preciously dear than life.

29. *Mean'st* (F.) Q. 'meanest'.

30. S.D. Q. F. '*Exit Cassan.*'

37–8. *a vice...man* According to Caxton, it was this vice of mercy which caused the Trojans to forfeit the victory early in the war (cf. 4. 5. 119 n.). 'Certes it is not wisdom when any man findeth his enemy in great peril and fortune to offer his power to deliver him thereof....And therefore Virgil saith non est misericordia in bello...a man should not show mercy but take the victory if he can' (pp. 589–90).

38. *better fits a lion* With allusion to the proverbial generosity of the lion.

41. *fair sword* Some editors suspect error, but the use of 'fair' is explicable as a general epithet of praise.

45. *mother* (Q.) F. 'Mothers'.

53. *fiery truncheon* See G. 'truncheon'. The stock epithet for Mars is transferred to his baton.

58. *But...ruin* (F.) Q. omits.

S.D. Q. F. '*Enter Priam and Cassandra.*'

69. *faith of valour* = 'the honour of a brave man' (Deighton).

73. *shame respect* = violate (filial) duty.

78. S.D. Q. F. '*Exit Androm.*'

79. *foolish, dreaming* (F.) Q. 'foolish dreaming'.

82. *do* (Q.) F. 'doth'.

84. *dolours* (Q.) F. 'dolour'.

85. *distraction* (F.) Q. 'destruction'.
amazement (Q. F.) A.W. conj. 'amaze'.

89. *yet* (Q.) F. 'yes'.

90. S.D. F. '*Exit.*' Q. omits.

91. *exclaims* (A.W. after Tannenbaum[2] conj.) Q. F. 'exclaime'.

93. *worth* (Q.) F. 'of'.

94. S.D. (after Mal.) Q. F. '*Alarum.*'

96. S.D. Q. F. '*Enter Pandar.*'

103. *what...another* (Q. F.) The construction is unusual and 'with' may have been omitted.

104. *o' these* (Rowe) Q. 'ath's'; F. 'o'th's'.

109. *Th'effect...way* i.e. the fact of the matter is the contrary—namely, that Cressida loves Diomedes. He has the substance and Troilus the shadow.

S.D. (Rowe) Q. F. omit.

110. *wind, to wind* i.e. empty words to the empty air.

112. *edifies* i.e. elevates, with ironic quibbling (as 'errors'='false beliefs' in l. 111 suggests) on the sense of 'moral edification'.

S.D. (after Mal.) Q. '*Exeunt.*'; see 112+note

112+　F. adds '*Pand.* Why, but heare you? | *Troy.* Hence brother lackie; ignomie and shame | Pursue thy life, and liue aye with thy name. | *A Larum. Exeunt.*' See 5. 10. 32–4, where the lines occupy the position in which Shakespeare finally intended them to stand, and cf. p. 123.

5.4

S.D. *Loc.* (after Rowe) *Entry* Alarums. (Cap.; cf. 5. 3. 112+n.) Q. '*Enter Thersites: excursions.*' F. '*Enter Thersites in excursion.*'

3. *that same* Sarcastic (as Deighton noted).

young (F.) Q. omits.

8. *of*=on.

O't'other (A.W.) Q. 'Ath'tother'; F. 'O'th'tother'; cf. 2. 1. 19 n.

9. *crafty-swearing* (Hyphen Kinnear conj.+Deighton). The hyphen makes the sense clearer.

stale (Q.) F. 'stole'.

10. *dog-fox* On. queries the gloss 'bloody-minded fellow', as well he might. The allusion is to Ulysses' cunning (=crafty fellow).

11. *proved not* (A.W. after anon. conj. in Camb.) Q. F. 'not proou'd'.

15. *begin* (Rowe iii) Q. F. 'began'.

15–16. *proclaim...opinion* i.e. announce a state of barbarism and organized government is falling into disrepute.

17. *t'other* (Q.) F. 'th'other'.

S.D. (Cap.) F. '*Enter Diomed and Troylus.*' (after 'opinion' l. 16); Q. omits.

19. *miscall retire* i.e. what Troilus has called 'flight' (cf. 'Fly not', l. 18) is what Diomedes calls 'retiring' from the crowd.

20. *advantageous care* i.e. care for his own advantage (='prudence').

24. S.D.[1] (after Rowe and Cap.) Q. F. omit.

25. *thou, Greek* (F.) Q. 'Greeke'.

29. S.D. (after Rowe) Q. F. omit.

34. *lechery eats itself* Cf. 1. 3. 121–4.

5. 5

Material. The scene combines material from Caxton's second battle, when Hector killed Patroclus (p. 580); from the fourth battle when Thoas, a cousin of Achilles, was taken prisoner and Palamedes sorely hurt by Polydamas (p. 596); from the fifth battle when Hector slew Doreus (p. 599), the brothers Epistrophus and Cedius (p. 599) and Polyxenes (p. 600), and Æneas slew Amphimacus (p. 599); as well as from the sixth battle when Hector slew Menon, a cousin of Achilles (p. 607) and Troilus lost his horse to Diomedes (p. 608). Between the fifth and sixth battles there occurred a three months' truce during which Cressida was sent to the Greeks; cf. 3. 3. 18–19 n. and see also notes to ll. 1–5, 7, 14, 20, 33–5 below.

S.D. *Loc.* (Camb.) *Entry* (Q '...*Diomed....*); F. '...*Diomed...Seruants.*'

1–5. *Go...proof* Caxton (p. 608) describes how, in the sixth battle, Diomedes unhorsed Troilus and 'took his horse and sent it to Breseyda; and did do say to her by his servant that it was Troilus' horse, her love; that he had beaten him by his prowess and prayed her from then forth on that she would hold him for her love and friend'.

5. S.N. (F.) Q. '*Man.*'

S.D.¹ (after Hanmer) Q. F. omit.

S.D.² (F.) Q. '*Enter Agamem.*' after 'proof', l. 5.

6. *Polydamas* (Pope) Q. '*Polidamas*'; F. '*Poli-damus*'.

7. *Margarelon* N.V.S. notes that the spelling else-where is 'Margareton'. I hesitate to emend because I do not know whether all sixteenth-century authorities have been consulted in relation to this error. On the face of it, it looks very much like a Q. misreading, which escaped correction in F.; cf. p. 138.

9. F. 'Calossus-wise'.

11. *Epistrophus* (Steev. 1773) Q. F. '*Epistropus*'. *Cedius* (Cap.) Q. F. '*Cedus*'.

12. *Thoas* (Pope) Q. F. '*Thous*'.

13. *Patroclus* See Heading (*Material*) and cf. Introduction, pp. xli–xlii.

14. *sagittary* According to Caxton, the centaur was brought to Troy by one of Priam's supporters. It was hairy like a horse and had eyes red as coal, and it was a marvellous archer. It caused great consternation among the Greeks (pp. 567–8); but it was not defen-sively armed and Diomedes killed it with his sword during the fifth battle (p. 600).

16. S.D.¹ (A.W.) Q. F. omit. Since Agamemnon takes no further part in this scene, I provide him with an exit and possibly Diomedes should accompany him to re-enter with Ajax after l. 42. When Agamemnon says 'haste we', it should be an indication that both leave the stage.

S.D.² (A.W.) Q. F. '*Enter Nestor.*' Someone other than Diomedes is wanted to carry out the orders of ll. 17–18.

18. S.D. (A.W.) Q. F. omit.

20. *Galathe* Described by Caxton as 'one of the most great and strongest horse of the world' (p. 577), killed under Hector in the second battle (p. 584) but

enjoying a new lease of life in the fifth, when it was captured by Achilles but shortly rescued (p. 600).

22. *scaléd* (F.) Q. 'scaling'. The 'scaléd sculls' (see G. 'sculls') are, I take it, the 'finny tribe'. I suspect Q.'s termination was due to assimilation to 'belching', and interpretation of 'scaling' as='fleeing' results in some tautology after 'fly'.

24. *strawy* (Q.) F. 'straying' (either a misreading or assimilated to 'belching').

25. *a* (Q.) F. 'the' (possibly from l. 24).

33–5. *Together...Hector* As N.V.S. notes, the Myrmidons belong to another part of the story. Long after Hector's death, Achilles allowed his Myrmidons to return to the assistance of the Greeks (see 2. 3. *Material*) and it was the damage done to them by Troilus that stung Achilles into action (see Caxton, pp. 634–7 and 5. 6. 13 n.).

34. *That noseless...chipped* An intentionally ludicrous picture of the damage inflicted by Hector, especially 'chipped' with its pantler and bread-cutting associations; cf. 2 *H. IV*, 2. 4. 235–7.

41. *luck* (F.) Q. 'lust'.

42. S.D. (F.) Q. '*Enter Aiax.*' as S.N. to l. 43.

43. S.D.¹ Q. F. '*Exit.*'
S.D.² (A.W.) Q. F. omit. Diomedes' speech suggests that he too is in pursuit.

44. *together.* (Cap.) Q. F. 'together. *Exit.*' It seems to me that Nestor should at least wait until Achilles has entered before withdrawing, though some recent editors accept the Q. F. direction. My suspicion is that the Q. F. '*Exit.*' was placed a line too late (cf. 43 S.D.² n.).

45. *show me* (A.W. after Pope) Q. F. 'shew'; anon. conj. in Camb. 'now show'. The line is metrically defective and Eld *A* fairly certainly omitted a word.

47. S.D. (Cap.) Q. F. '*Exit.*' See l. 44 n.

5. 6

Material. See note to l. 13.

S.D. *Loc.* (Cap.)   *Entry* (F.)   Q. 'Enter Aiax.' as S.N. to l. 1.

1. S.D. (F. '*Enter Diomed.*')   Q. 'Enter Diom.' as S.N. to l. 2.

7. *the* (A.W. after Cap.)   Q. F. 'thy' (from l. 6). *ow'st* (Cap.)   Q. F. 'owest'.

11. S.D.[1] (after Rowe) F. 'Exit Troylus.' Q. omits.

S.D.[2] (F.)   Q. omits.

12. S.D. (F.)   Q. 'Enter Achil:' as S.N. to l. 13.

13 ff. According to Caxton, on Hector's entry into the battle (see 5. 3 *Material*), he was assailed by Achilles, but Hector wounded him in the thigh so that Achilles was forced to retire to have his wound bound. He then took a great spear intending to slay Hector. Hector, meantime, had taken 'a much noble baron of Greece much quaintly and richly armed, and for to lead him out of the host at his ease had cast his shield behind him at his back and had left his breast discovered, and as he was in this point and took none heed of Achilles that came privily unto him and put this spear within his body. And Hector fell down dead to the ground' (p. 613). Long after this, according to Caxton (pp. 637–9), in the eighteenth battle, when Achilles heard that most of his Myrmidons were slain, he 'set behind him' his love for Polyxena and hastily armed, but he was badly wounded by Troilus. Then, after a six months' truce, before the nineteenth battle, Achilles assembled his Myrmidons and instructed them to surround Troilus and to hold him until he came. And when they had enclosed him and slain his horse and wounded him and razed his helm from his head, Achilles came and slew Troilus, though he was unarmed, and cut off his head,

and bound his body to the tail of his horse and dragged
his body through the host. Cf. Introduction, p. xxix.

13. *ha* (Q.) F. omits.

S.D. (A.W. after Rowe) Q. F. omit. A stage
direction seems to be wanted, but there is so much
parody of chronicle play style in these closing scenes
that what took place was probably farcical. There is
nothing in the dialogue to suggest that Achilles was
wounded, as in Caxton's account (see *Material*), and
Capell's '*dropping his Sword*' may be nearer the mark
in view of Achilles' excuse that he is out of practice. At
the same time, he may merely have been out of breath.

19. S.D. (after Q. F. '*Exit.*')

20. *much more a* For the word order, see Abbott,
§ 422.

21. S.D. (after Q. F., both after 'brother').

26. *thou end* (F.) Q. 'I end' (due to repetition).
S.D.[1] Q. F. '*Exit.*'
S.D.[2] (Mal.) Q. F. '*Enter one in armour.*'

30. S.D. (A.W.) Q. F. omit. The Greek must
presumably get a start of Hector.

31. S.D. Q. F. '*Exit.*' Mal. (+edd.) '*Exeunt.*'

5.7

Material. See note to 5. 6. 13ff.

S.D. *Loc.* (Camb.)

6. *arms* (Q.) F. 'arme'; Cap. 'aims'. The transitive
use of 'execute' = 'wield' (a weapon) is not exceptional
and the slight discrepancy between l. 3 ('Strike not a
stroke') and here is due to the first being a general
order not to embroil themselves in anything but the
main object of hemming in Hector.

8. S.D.[1] (after Rowe ii) Q. F. *Exit.*'
S.D.[2] (Mal. after Cap.) Q. F. '*Enter Thersi:
Mene: Paris.*' (F.'...*and Paris.*').

11. *double-horned* (Kellner conj.) Q. F. 'double
hen'd'. Menelaus is 'double-horned' because this is
a bull-baiting and Menelaus was a cuckold; cf. 5. 1.
52–4 n.

Spartan (Q.) F. 'sparrow'.

12. S.D.[1] Q. F. '*Exit Paris and Menelaus.*'
(Q. '...*Menelus.*').

S.D.[2] (Cap.) Q. F. '*Enter Bastard*'.

13. etc. S.N. Margarelon (Cap.) Q. F. '*Bast.*'
See p. 138.

17. *a bastard begot* (F.) Q. omits 'a'.

18–19. *One bear...another* Theob. compares
Juvenal, *Sat.* xv. 164 ('saevis inter se convenit
ursis'), and Anders (cited N.V.S.), *Ado*, 3. 2. 71–2.

22. S.D. (after Cap.) Q. F. omit.

23. S.D. (after Q.) F. '*Exeunt.*'

5. 8

Material: See note to 5. 6. 13ff.

S.D. *Loc.* (Cap.)

3. *good* (F.) Q. 'my'.

4. S.D.[1] (Kittredge after J.).

S.D.[2] (Q.) F. '...*and his*...'.

7. *darking* (F.) Q. 'darkning'. Either might be
right, but the sense is, in any case, 'growing dark',
'setting', and not 'eclipse' (On.).

10. S.D. (Cap.) Q. F. omit.

11. *next* (Q.) F. omits.

now (F.) Q. 'come'.

13. *and* (Q.) F. omits.

14. S.D. (Mal.) Q. F. '*Retreat:*'.

15. *retire* (Q.) F. 'retreat' (caught from l. 14 S.D.).

16. S.N. Myrmidon (Rowe) Q. '*One:*'; F. '*Gree.*'

Trojan trumpets (F.) Q. 'Troyans trumpet'.

sound (Q.) F. 'sounds'.

20. *bait* (Q.) F. 'bed'. See G. 'bait'.
S.D. (Mal. after Cap.) Q. F. omit.
22. S.D. F. '*Exeunt. Sound Retreat. Shout.*'
Q. '*Exeunt:*'.

5.9

S.D. *Loc.* (Camb.) *Entry* Shouts within (Cap.;
cf. 5. 8. 22 S.D. n.) Q. '*Enter Agam: Aiax, Mene:
Nestor, Diom: and the rest marching.*' (F. '*Diomed,...*').
1. *what...that* (F.) Q. 'what is this'.
3. S.N. and S.D. (Q. '*Sould: within.*') F. '*Sold.*'
6. *as good a man* (Q.) F. 'a man as good'.
10. S.D. (after Cap.) Q. F. '*Exeunt.*'

5.10

S.D. (Steev. 1778 after Cap.) *Entry* (F.) Q. omits
'and'.
2. *Never* (F.) Q. '*Troy.* Neuer'. I accept the
customary reading, but find it strange that Q. is unanimously rejected, for the attribution to Troilus is not
only more dramatic but, in association with ll. 17–20,
it gives more point to 'starve'—the idea being that it
is better to freeze in the field ('out') than to freeze
the blood of Troy by returning with the news of
Hector's death. See G. 'starve' for what is, as the text
stands, a difficult expression.
S.D. (F.) Q. after l. 1.
7. *smite* (A.W. after Hanmer+Deighton) Q. F.
'smile'. An easy but silly misreading: 'it seems
impossible, even if "*smile at* Troy" were used derisively,
that it should be followed by two lines invoking speedy
destruction' (Deighton). Nor is this kind of obliquity
Troilus' style.
17. *in to* (F.) Q. 'into'.
20. *Cold* (Q.) F. 'Coole'.

21–2. *But...dead* (F.) Q. omits.

23. *vile* (F.) Q. 'proud'.

24. *pight* (F.) Q. 'pitcht'.

30. Punctuated as in F.; Q. 'march, to Troy'.

31. S.D.[1] (after Steev.) Q. F. omit. Cf. l. 34
S.D. n.

33. *broker-lackey* (Hyphen Dyce) Q. F. 'broker,
lacky'. Cf. 5. 3. 112+n.

ignomy and (F.) Q. 'ignomyny'.

34. S.D. (after Cap.) F. '*Exeunt.*' Q. '*Exeunt all
but Pandarus.*'

35. *my* (Q.) F. 'mine'.

36. *world* (thrice F.) Q. (twice).

37. *traders* (A.W. after Craig conj.+Deighton)
Q. F. 'traitors'. Q. F. is nonsense, as the context
requires a word='go-between'.

39. *desired* (F.) Q. 'lou'd'. The 'love' and 'loath'
antithesis was so common that I find it difficult to
believe that F. would have substituted 'desir'd' for the
former without good reason. The sense 'solicited' is
entirely satisfactory and I suspect Q. of tampering.

43. *And* (Q. F.) Rowe 'But' (probably correctly).

49. *your* (F.) Q. 'my'.

55. S.D. (after Rowe iii); F. '*Exeunt.*' Q. '*FINIS*'.

GLOSSARY

Note. Where there is equivocation the meanings are distinguished by (*a*) and (*b*)

'A, he; 1. 2. 77, etc.

A', have; 2. 3. 24, etc.

ABRUPTION, breaking off (in speech), aposiopesis; 3. 2. 65

ACCENT, utterance, voice; 1. 3. 53

ACHIEVEMENT, attainment; 1. 2. 294; 4. 2. 69

ADAMANT, loadstone, magnet; 3. 2. 178

ADDITION, (i) distinctive title, style of address, attribute; 1. 2. 20; 2. 3. 244; 3. 2. 93; (ii) 'something added to a coat of arms, as a mark of honour' (O.E.D. 5); 4. 5. 141 (see note)

ADDRESS, prepare; 4. 4. 146; 5. 10. 14

ADVANCÉD, uplifted, raised; 4. 5. 188

ADVANTAGE, favourable opportunity; 2. 2. 204; 3. 3. 2; 5. 2. 130

ADVERSITY, contrariness, (concr.) quibbler; 5. 1. 12

ADVERTISE, inform; 2. 2. 211

AFFECT, love; 2. 2. 195; 4. 5. 178

AFFECTED, loved; 2. 2. 60 (see note)

AFFECTION, feeling (as opposed to reason), passion; 2. 2. 177

AFFINED, related; 1. 3. 25

AFFRONT, front, meet; 3. 2. 165

AGAINST, in expectation of; 1. 2. 177

AIR, breath, speech; 1. 3. 66

AIRY, (*a*) lofty, (*b*) in everyone's mouth (cf. *aura popularis*); 1. 3. 144

ALARUM, call to arms (usu. by drums); 1. 1. 90 S.D., etc.

ALLOW, commend (O.E.D. 1); 3. 2. 90

ALLOWANCE, commendation, praise; 1. 3. 376; 2. 3. 136

AMAZE, bewilder, stupify; 5. 3. 91

AMAZEMENT, conternation; 2. 2. 210; 5. 3. 85

AN (conj.), if; 1. 1. 43, etc.

ANSWER (sb.), acceptance (of a challenge); 1. 3. 332

ANSWER (vb.), (i) satisfy; 1. 3. 15; (ii) accept (a challenge); 2. 1. 126; 3. 3. 35; 4. 4. 132

ANTIC, grotesque, clown; 5. 3. 86

ANTIQUARY, ancient; 2. 3. 248

APPERTAINMENT, prerogative; 2. 3. 79

APPETITE, (i) self-indulgence; 1. 3. 120, 121; (ii) desire, inclination; 3. 3. 238; 5. 5. 27

APPLY, interpret; 1. 3. 32 (see note)

APPOINTMENT, equipment; 4. 5. 1

APPREHEND, perceive; 3. 2. 73;
3. 3. 124

APPREHENSION, grasp, (*a*) physical arrest, (*b*) mental perception; 2. 3. 114 (see
note)

APPROVE, attest; 3. 2. 173

APT, ready; 5. 2. 131

AQUILON, the north or north-
north-east wind; 4. 5. 9

ARGUMENT, (i) theme; Prol.
25; (ii) theme of contention;
1. 1. 94; 2. 3. 71, 94, 95,
96; (iii) reason; 4. 5. 26, 27;
(iv) (*a*) as in (iii), (*b*) as in
(ii); 4. 5. 29

ART, acquired skill, 4. 4. 78

ARTIST, one learned in the
liberal arts, scholar; 1. 3. 24

As (conj.), as if; 1. 1. 37; 1. 2.
7; 1. 3. 391; 3. 3. 167; 4. 5.
238

ASSINEGO (dim. of Sp. *asno*=
ass), young ass, fool; 2. 1.
43

ASSUBJUGATE, subjugate; 2. 3.
190

ASSUME, lay claim to; 5. 2. 145

ATTACH, seize, lay hold of;
(fig.) 5. 2. 161

ATTACHMENT, arrest; (fig.) 4.
2. 5

ATTAINT, blemish; 1. 2. 25

ATTEST (sb.), testimony; 5. 2.
122

ATTEST (vb.), call to witness;
2. 2. 132

ATTRIBUTE, reputation; 2. 3.
115

ATTRIBUTIVE, tributary; 2. 2.
58

AUTHENTIC, authoritative; 1.
3. 108; 3. 2. 180

AUTHOR, originator, prototype;
3. 2. 180

AVOID, (*a*) (*law*) invalidate,
(*b*) get rid of; 2. 2. 65

AXLE-TREE, axle-beam, axis of
revolution; 1. 3. 66 (see
note)

BAIT, (*a*) refreshment, snack,
(*b*) a lawyer's 'refresher'
(i.e. an extra fee paid to
counsel in prolonged or frequently adjourned cases);
5. 8. 20

BATTLE, army; 3. 2. 28

BAUBLE, toylike, insignificant;
1. 3. 35

BAY, bark; (fig.) 2. 3. 89

BEAM, spear (with allusion to
Goliath's spear, the staff of
which was like a weaver's
beam, 1. Sam. xvii. 7); 5. 5.
9

BEAR IT, behave, act; 2. 3.
215

BEAVER, face-guard of a helmet;
1. 3. 296

BEEF-WITTED, dull-brained; 2.
1. 13 (see note)

BEGUILE, defraud, rob; 4. 4.
35

BEHALF; 'in my behalf'=for
my benefit; 3. 3. 16

BELCH, spout; 5. 5. 23

BELLY, swell; 2. 2. 74

BEND, (i) arch; 1. 3. 379 (see
note); (ii) turn; 3. 3. 43; 4.
4. 139

BENDING, courteous, gracious;
1. 3. 236

BENEFIT, favour; 3. 3. 14

BENT, inclination; (of the ears)
1. 3. 252; (of the eyes) 4. 5.
282

BESEECH, entreaty; 1. 2. 294

BESTOWING, employment, use;
3. 2. 37

Bias (adj.), puffed out on one
    side (with allusion to the
    bias of a bowl); 4. 5. 8
Bias (adv.), awry; 1. 3. 15
Bias-drawing (sb.), inclina-
    tion; 4. 5. 169
Bifold, twofold; 5. 2. 144
Blank, document with spaces
    left blank to be filled up at
    the pleasure of the recipient,
    carte blanche; 3. 3. 231
Bless, guard, keep; 2. 3. 28
Blood, (i) the supposed seat of
    emotions, passions, 'hu-
    mours', etc.; Prol. 2; 2. 2.
    169; 2. 3. 29, 210; 5. 1. 47,
    49; (ii) noble descent; 3. 3.
    26; 5. 4. 26; (iii) kinship,
    stock; 4. 2. 98; 4. 5. 83
Blow up, swell; 1. 3. 317
    (see note)
Bob, (i) (a) bamboozle, (b)
    (perh. of diff. etymol.)
    buffet; 2. 1. 68; (ii) cheat;
    3. 1. 69
Bodement, foreboding; 5. 3. 80
Bolting, sifting; 1. 1. 19, 21
Book, 'without book'=by
    heart; 2. 1. 18
Boot, something given in
    addition; (i) 'to boot'=into
    the bargain; 1. 2. 240; (ii)
    premium, odds; 4. 5. 40
Boreas, the north wind; 1. 3. 38
Borrow, be indebted for,
    derive; 4. 5. 133
Botch, ulcer; 5. 1. 5
Botchy, ulcerous; 2. 1. 6
Bourn, boundary; 2. 3. 246
Bowels, considered as the seat
    of the tender emotions,
    (hence) compassion, mercy;
    2. 1. 48; 2. 2. 11
Boy-queller, boy-killer; 5. 5.
    45.

Bratch, bitch hound; (fig.) 2.
    1. 113
Brave (adj.), splendid; Prol.
    15; 1. 2. 186
Brave (sb.), bravado, defiance;
    4. 4. 137
Bravely, excellently, famously;
    1. 2. 183; 3. 3. 213
Brawn, muscle (esp. the
    fleshy muscles of the arm
    and leg); 1. 3. 297
Breath, (i) speech (with
    quibble on the lit. sense);
    2. 2. 74; (ii) breathing-
    space, pause; 2. 3. 111;
    4. 5. 92
Breese, gadfly; 1. 3. 48
Briareus, in Gk. myth. a
    monster with a hundred
    arms; 1. 2. 28
Bring, (i) 'to bring'; 1. 2. 280
    (see With); (ii) 'bring off'=
    preserve, rescue; 1. 3. 334;
    5. 6. 25; (iii) 'bring forth'=
    utter; 1. 3. 242
Broken, (a) (of music) em-
    ploying different families of
    instruments, (b) interrupted;
    3. 1. 50 (see note)
Broker-between,   Broker-
    lackey, pandar; 3. 2.
    202–3; 5. 10. 33
Brotherhood, fraternity, guild;
    1. 3. 104
Bruit, noise, report; 5. 9. 4
Brush, encounter, clash; 5. 3.
    34
Buckle in, confine; 2. 2.
    30
Burden, freight of a ship; 1. 3.
    71
Buss, kiss; 4. 5. 220
Butt, cask; 5. 1. 27
Buy, (fig.) be an equivalent for;
    3. 3. 28

CANCER, the Crab, the fourth sign of the zodiac, entered by the sun on 21 June; 2. 3. 194

CAPOCCHIA (*It.*), simpleton; 4. 3. 32

CAPTIVE, vanquished; 5. 3. 40

CARRY, (i) bear away as a prize; 5. 6. 24; (ii) 'carry it'=have the mastery; 2. 3. 2, 216

CASQUE, helmet; 5. 2. 170

CATLING, catgut, the smallest sized strings of musical instruments; 3. 3. 303

CENTRE, the earth (as the supposed centre of the universe); 1. 3. 85

CHAFE, heat, become angry; Prol. 2; 1. 2. 167; 4. 5. 260

CHALLENGE, lay claim to, contest; 5. 2. 95, 97

CHANCE (sb.), (i) fortune (good or bad); Prol. 31; (ii) misfortune; 1. 3. 33; (iii) good fortune, luck; 3. 3. 131

CHANCE (vb.), happen; 'how chance'=how chances it that; 3. 1. 138

CHANGE (sb. & vb.), exchange; 3. 3. 27; 4. 2. 91

CHAPMAN, trader; 4. 1. 77

CHARACTER, (i) graphic symbol, figure; 1. 3. 325; (ii) distinctive mark, brand; 5. 2. 164

CHARACTERLESS, leaving no mark; 3. 2. 187

CHARGE, cost; 4. 1. 59

CHERUBIN, cherub; 3. 2. 68

CHIDE, quarrel, brawl; 1. 3. 54

CHIVALRY, (i) knighthood; 1. 2. 230; (ii) prowess in war, bravery; 4. 4. 148; 5. 3. 32

CHOLLER, jowl; 4. 5. 9 (see note)

CIRCUMSTANCE, particulars (of a discourse); 3. 3. 114

CIRCUMVENTION, strategy; 2. 3. 15

CLAPPER-CLAW, maul; 5. 4. 1

CLEF, (*a*) key in music, (*b*) (etymol. a diff. word) cleft, fork of the legs; 5. 2. 12

CLOSE, (*a*) come to terms, (*b*) come close; 3. 2. 48

CLOSET, private apartment, study; 'closet-war' (nonce use)=study warfare; 1. 3. 205

CLOTH, 'painted cloth'= 'hanging for a room painted or worked with figures, mottoes or texts; tapestry' (O.E.D.); 5. 10. 45

CLOTPOLL, blockhead; 2. 1. 116

CO-ACT, act together; 5. 2. 118

COBLOAF, little loaf with a round head; 2. 1. 37

COGGING, cheating, deceitful; 5. 6. 11

COGNITION, (*a*) consciousness, (*b*) (*law*) 'the action of taking judicial or authoritative notice' (cf. O.E.D. 3); 5. 2. 64

COLDLY, chastely; 1. 3. 229

COLOSSUS-WISE, like the Colossus (a gigantic statue of Apollo, alleged to have spanned the harbour of Rhodes); 5. 5. 9

COME TO IT, reach maturity; 1. 2. 84, 85

COMFORT, encouragement (O.E.D. 1); 5. 10. 30

COMMERCE, transactions; 3. 3. 205

COMMIXTION, commixture; 4. 5. 124

COMMODIOUS, accommodating; 5. 2. 194 (see note)

COMMOTION, (*a*) public disorder, (*b*) mental perturbation; 2. 3. 173

COMPARE, comparison; 3. 2. 174

COMPASSED, 'compassed window'=semicircular bay window; 1. 2. 112

COMPLETE, perfectly endowed, accomplished; 3. 3. 181

COMPLIMENTAL, complimentary; 3. 1. 40

COMPOSED, made; 5. 2. 170

COMPOSURE, (i) combination; 2. 3. 98; (ii) temperament, disposition; 2. 3. 237

CON, learn by heart; 2. 1. 17

CONCEIT, understanding; 1. 3. 153

CONCUPY, concupiscence; 5. 2. 177 (see note)

CONDITION, (i) character; Prol. 25; (ii) ellipt.=on condition that, even if; 1. 2. 74; (iii) position, rank; 3. 3. 9

CONDUCE, (intr. for refl.) carry on, go on; 5. 2. 147 (see note)

CONDUCT, guidance; 2. 2. 62

CONFLUX, confluence; 1. 3. 7

CONFOUND, destroy (O.E.D. 1); 2. 3. 74; 3. 1. 118

CONJURE, call up (spirits); 2. 3. 6; 5. 2. 125

CONSIGNED, sealed, added as ratification; 4. 4. 45

CONSISTING, inherent; 3. 3. 116

CONSORT, keep company, join; 5. 3. 9

CONSTRINGE, compress; 5. 2. 173

CONTENTION, combat; 4. 1. 18; 4. 5. 205

CONTRIVE, devise, plan; 1. 3. 201

CONVENIENCE, favourable circumstance, advantage; 3. 3. 7

CONVINCE, convict; 2. 2. 130

CONVIVE, feast together; 4. 5. 272

COPE, (i) come to blows with; 1. 2. 33; (ii) prove a match for; 2. 3. 261

COPPER NOSE, 'a red nose caused by the disease *Acne rosacea*, by intemperance, etc.' (O.E.D.); 1. 2. 107 (see note)

CORE, (i) core of an ulcer; 2. 1. 6; 5. 1. 4; (ii) core of fruit; 5. 8. 1

CO-RIVAL, vie with; 1. 3. 44

CORRECT, chastise; 5. 6. 3

CORRECTION, punishment; 5. 6. 5

CORRESPONSIVE, corresponding; Prol. 18

COUCH, hide; 1. 1. 41

COUNSEL, 'soul of counsel'= inmost thoughts; 3. 2. 132

COUNTER, token (of metal, etc.) used instead of real coins in calculation; 2. 2. 28

COUNTERFEIT, (*a*) sham, (*b*) false coin; 2. 3. 24

COUPLE, link, conjoin; 1. 3. 276 (see note)

COURSE, (i) appointed (planetary) course; 1. 3. 87; (ii) 'complete courses of the sun'=years; 4. 1. 29

COURTESY, obeisance; 2. 3. 105

COUSIN, niece; 1. 2. 42; 3. 1. 35, 84; 3. 2. 2, 7, 198; 4. 2. 24

COUSIN-GERMAN, first cousin; 4. 5. 121

CRAMMED, fatted (for the table); 2. 2. 49

CREST, comb, mane (symbolic of pride); 1. 3. 379

CRITIC, detractor; 5. 2. 131

CROWNET, by-form of 'coronet'; Prol. 6

CRUSTY, scabby; 5. 1. 5

CRY, public acclamation; 3. 3. 184

CRY ON, exclaim against; 5. 5. 35

CUNNING, dexterity, skill; 5. 5. 41

CURIOUS, minutely scanned, minute; 3. 2. 65 (see note)

DAINTY, (i) 'dainty of'= fastidious about; 1. 3. 145; (ii) delightful; 5. 2. 81

DAPHNE, nymph pursued by Apollo; 1. 1. 100

DARDAN, Trojan; Prol. 13

DARKING, darkening; 5. 8. 7 (see note)

DATE, duration, season; 1. 2. 258 (see note)

DAYS, (i) 'by days'=day by day; 4. 1. 10; (ii) in the day (old genitive of time=time when); 4. 5. 12

DEAR, heartfelt, earnest; 5. 3. 9

DEARLY, richly; 3. 3. 96

DEATH-TOKEN, plague-spot betokening approaching death; 2. 3. 175

DEBONAIR, gentle, meek; 1. 3. 235

DECEPTIOUS, deceptive; 5. 2. 123

DECLINE, (i) (a) inflect, (b) refuse; 2. 3. 52 (see note); (ii) fall, descend; 4. 5. 189

DECLINED, fallen, vanquished; 4. 5. 189

DEEM, thought; 4. 4. 59

DEGREE, (i) rank, esp. high rank; 1. 3. 83; (ii) established order of precedence; 1. 3. 108, 125, 127; (iii) (a) as in (ii) with allusion to (b) astronomy; 1. 3. 86; the rung of a ladder; 1. 3. 101; academic rank; 1. 3. 104; music; 1. 3. 109

DEJECT (ppl. a.), dejected, downcast; 2. 2. 50

DEJECT (vb.), depress, lessen; 2. 2. 121

DENY, (i) refuse; 2. 2. 24; 3. 3. 22; (ii) disclaim knowledge of; 4. 2. 49

DEPEND UPON, (a) rely upon, (b) be servant to; 3. 1. 4, 5, 6

DEPENDENT, impending; 2. 3. 19

DEPRAVATION, detraction; 5. 2. 132

DEPUTATION, deputed office; 1. 3. 152

DERACINATE, uproot; 1. 3. 99

DERIVE, show the derivation of, explain; 2. 3. 60

DESIRE, (i) request; 3. 3. 21, 235; (ii) invite; 4. 5. 150

DESPITEFUL, hateful; 4. 1. 34

DETERMINATION, (judicial) decision; 2. 2. 170

DEVICE, contrivance; 1. 3. 374

DEXTER, (heraldic term) right; 4. 5. 128

DIANA, goddess of the moon and chastity, the moon; 5. 2. 92

DIE, (hyperb. and ellipt.) die of laughing; 1. 3. 176

DIGNITY, worthiness; 2. 2. 54

DILATED, extensive; 2. 3. 247

DIMINUTIVE, midget; 5. 1. 33

DIRECTIVE, subject to direction; 1. 3. 356

DISCIPLINE (sb.), instruction (O.E.D. 1); 2. 3. 29

DISCIPLINE (vb.), instruct, train (O.E.D. 1); 2. 3. 241

DISCOMFORT, dishearten; 5. 10. 10

DISCOURSE, (i) 'discourse of reason' = process of reasoning; 2. 2. 116; (ii) reasoning, thought; 5. 2. 142

DISCOVER, reveal; 1. 3. 138; 5. 2. 6

DISCOVERY, revelation, disclosure; 5. 1. 23

DISCRETION, judgement; 1. 2. 23, 252

DISME, dime, a tenth part, 'tithe'; 2. 2. 19

DISORBED, removed from its sphere; 2. 2. 46

DISPOSE, disposition; 2. 3. 162

DISPOSER, manager, mistress; 3. 1. 87 (see note), 89, 92

DISSOLVE, loosen, untie; 5. 2. 156

DISTAIN, sully, dishonour; 1. 3. 241

DISTASTE, (i) dislike; 2. 2. 66; (ii) make distasteful; 2. 2. 123; 4. 4. 48

DISTEMPERED, disordered; 2. 2. 169

DISTINCT, separate; 4. 4. 45

DISTINCTION, discrimination; 1. 3. 27; 3. 2. 27

DISTRACTION, alienation from one's senses; (i) unconsciousness; 3. 2. 23; (ii) madness, frenzy; 5. 2. 42; 5. 3. 85

DIVIDABLE, 'that divides' (On.); 1. 3. 105 (see note)

DIVULGE, proclaim, make known; 5. 2. 163

DIZZY, make dizzy; 5. 2. 174

DO, (i) (imper.) go on, continue; 2. 1. 25, 41, 52, 53; (ii) copulate; 4. 2. 26 (see note)

DOUBT, suspect, fear; 1. 2. 277

DRAUGHT, cesspool, sewer; 5. 1. 73

DRAW, cause to assemble; 2. 3. 72

DRESSED, prepared; 1. 3. 166

DRIFT, intention, aim; 3. 3. 113

DROWSY, sluggish; 2. 2. 210; 5. 5. 32

DRY, barren, sterile; 1. 3. 329 (see note); 2. 3. 221

DULL, inactive; 2. 2. 209

EDIFY, elevate; 5. 3. 112 (see note)

EFFECT, fact, reality; 5. 3. 109

ELD, old age; 2. 2. 104

EMPALE, hem in; 5. 7. 5

EMULATION, jealous rivalry; 1. 3. 134; 2. 2. 212; 3. 3. 156; 4. 5. 123

EMULOUS, (i) envious; 2. 3. 72, 228; 3. 3. 189; (ii) ambitious; 4. 1. 30

ENCOUNTERER, forward person; 4. 5. 58

ENFREED, released; 4. 1. 40

ENGAGE, (i) bind by a pledge; 2. 2. 124; 5. 3. 68; (ii) (a) as in (i), (b) embroil; 5. 5. 39

ENGINE, machine of war; 1. 3. 208; 2. 3. 133

ENGINER, (a) contriver, strategist, (b) maker of military 'engines'; 2. 3. 8

ENLARD, fatten; 2. 3. 193

ENRAPT, carried away, inspired; 5. 3. 65

ENTERTAIN, receive; 1. 3. 354

ENTREAT, treat (O E.D. 1);
4. 4. 113

ERRANT, deviating; 1. 3. 9

ESPERANCE, hope; 5. 2. 121

ESTIMATE, esteem, value; 2. 2.
54

ESTIMATION, (abstr. for concr.)
thing valued; 2. 2. 91

EVENT, consequence; 2. 2. 120

EXAMPLED, provided with an
example; 1. 3. 132

EXCITEMENT, encouragement;
1. 3. 182

EXCLAIM, outcry; 5. 3. 91

EXECUTE, bring (a weapon)
into play, wield; 5. 7. 6

EXECUTION, operation, action;
1. 3. 210

EXPECT, expectation; 1. 3. 70

EXPECTANCE, expectancy; 4. 5.
146

EXPECTER, person waiting; 4.
5. 156

EXPOSURE, unprotected condition, vulnerability; 1. 3.
195

EXPRESSURE, expression; 3. 3.
204

EXTANT, existing, present; 4.
5. 168

FACTION, (i) factious party,
association; 2. 1. 118; 2. 3.
98; (ii) factious strife; 3. 3.
190

FAINT, lose heart; 2. 2. 142

FAIR (adj.), (i) courteous; 1. 3.
219, 223; 3. 1. 44; 4. 4.
113; (ii) a complimentary
style of address; 1. 3. 304;
4. 1. 77; (iii) distinguished;
(as sb.) 1. 3. 265; (iv) sound,
wholesome; 2. 3. 119; (v)
auspicious; 3. 1. 45

FAIR, FAIRLY (adv.), (i) hon-
ourably; 1. 3. 84, 259; 3. 3.
33; 4. 4. 113; (ii) success-
fully; 1. 3. 371; (iii) 'fair
be to you'=good fortune
befall you; 3. 1. 44; (iv)
auspiciously; 3. 1. 45; 4. 5.
109; (v) quietly, still; 4. 5.
235

FAITH, ellipt. for 'in faith'=
truly; 3. 1. 10; 4. 1. 53; 5.
2. 86; 5. 3. 31

FALCON, female hawk trained
for hawking; 3. 2. 51

FALL, let fall, lower; 1. 3. 378

FALLING IN, reconciliation;
3. 1. 103

FALSE (sb.), faithless one; 3. 2.
189

FALSEHOOD, faithlessness; 3. 2.
190, 194

FAMILIAR, plain, easily understood; 3. 3. 113

FAN, (i) winnowing fan; 1. 3.
27; (ii) fanning, motion (as
of a fan); 5. 3. 41

FANCY (sb.), love; 4. 4. 25

FANCY (vb.), love; 5. 2. 165

FASHION, shape; 'fashion in'
=introduce; 4. 4. 65

FATHOMLESS, immeasurable; 2.
2. 30

FAVOUR, face, countenance;
1. 2. 94; 4. 5. 213

FEE-FARM, (law) tenure in
fee-simple (q.v.) subject to
a perpetual fixed rent ('fee'.
=absolute possession, 'farm'
=lease); (fig.) 3. 2. 49–50

FEE-SIMPLE, (law) estate held
in absolute possession; (fig.)
5. 1. 22

FEEZE, do for, settle; 2. 3. 203

FELL, cruel; 4. 5. 269; 5. 7. 6

FIELD, battlefield; 1. 1. 5, etc.

FILL, shaft of a cart; 3. 2. 45

FINE, exquisite, pure; 3. 2. 23; 4. 4. 3

FINENESS, (i) purity (of metals); 1. 3. 22; (ii) subtlety; 1. 3. 209

FIRSTLING, first product, first-fruits (cf. Gen. iv. 4); Prol. 27

FIT, (a) spasm, (b) strain of music, a stave; 3. 1. 58 (see note)

FITCHEW, polecat; 5. 1. 59

FITNESS, suitable occasion; 1. 3. 202

FIXURE, fixed position; 1. 3. 101

FLAT, (of drink) stale; 4. 1. 64

FLOOD, sea; 1. 1. 104

FLOURISH, fanfare (of trumpets, etc.) for entry or exit in state; 3. 3. S.D., etc.

FOH, exclamation of disgust; 5. 2. 23

FOIL, overthrow, defeat; 1. 3. 371

FOLD, folding, embrace; 3. 3. 223

FOLLY, wantonness; 5. 2. 19

FOND, foolish; 1. 1. 10

FOOL, (a) idiot, (b) a kind of custard; 5. 1. 9

FOOTING, step, tread; 1. 3. 156

FOR (conj.), because; 5. 3. 21

FOR (prep.), (i) against; 1. 2. 269; (ii) denoting the amount staked; 3. 2. 52; (iii) for the sake of; 5. 2. 129

FORCE, stuff, cram; 1. 2. 23; 2. 3. 220; 5. 1. 56

FORCELESS, effortless; 5. 5. 40

FOREHAND, holding the front position; 1. 3. 143

FORESTALL, obstruct, hinder; 1. 3. 199 (see note)

FORFEIT, forfeiture (of life); 4. 5. 187

FORKED, divided like two horns (alluding to cuckoldry); 1. 2. 165

FORM (sb.), (i) regularity, good order; 1. 3. 87; (ii) manner; 3. 3. 51

FORM (vb.), put into shape, frame; 2. 2. 120; 3. 3. 119

FORTH, out (to battle); 1. 2. 221

FORTHRIGHT, straight path; 3. 3. 158

FRACTION, (i) dissension; 2. 3. 97; (ii) fragment; 5. 2. 158

FRANKLY, without restraint, lavishly; 5. 8. 19

FRAUGHTAGE, freight; Prol. 13

FRAY, frighten; 3. 2. 32

FREE, (i) innocent, harmless; 1. 3. 235; (ii) unbiased; 2. 2. 170; (iii) generous; 4. 5. 100, 139

FRIEND, befriend, assist; 1. 2. 78

FRUSH, smash, batter; 5. 6. 29

FULFILLING, tightly fitting; Prol. 18 (see note)

FULL, (i) satisfaction; 3. 3. 241; (ii) 'in the full'=in full company; 4. 5. 272

FUMBLE UP, wrap up clumsily, huddle together; 4. 4. 46

FURNISH, equip; 3. 3. 33

GAGE, bind by formal promise; 5. 1. 40

GAINSAY, forbid; 4. 5. 132

GALL, (i) bitterness, rancour; 1. 3. 193, 237; 2. 2. 144; 4. 5. 30; (ii) applied abusively to a person; 5. 1. 34

GALLANTRY, gallants (collectively); 3. 1. 137

GALLED, (*a*) affected with 'galls' (=venereal sores), (*b*) chafed, offended; 5. 10. 53

GAME, amorous sport; 4. 5. 63

GAWD, toy, gewgaw; 3. 3. 176

GEAR, (i) business; 1. 1. 6; (ii) equipment, necessaries; 3. 2. 210

GENERAL (sb.), (i) that which is common to all; 1. 3. 180; (ii) the whole, the multitude; 1. 3. 342

GENERALLY, everywhere; 2. 1. 3

GENERATION, (i) procreation; 3. 1. 132; (ii) progeny; 3. 1. 134

GENEROUS, high-born, noble; 2. 2. 155

GENIUS, 'the tutelary god or attendant spirit allotted to every person at his birth to govern his fortunes and... finally to conduct him out of the world' (O.E.D. 1); 4. 4. 50

GENTLE (adj.), noble; 4. 1. 34

GENTLE (adv.), courteously; 4. 5. 287

GET, beget; 2. 3. 238; 3. 2. 103

GLIMPSE, flash, (fig.) trace; 1. 2. 24

GLOZE, make glosses, comment; 2. 2. 165

GO TO, exclam. of remonstrance; (i) 1. 1. 44; 1. 2. 128; 2. 1. 93; 3. 1. 67; (ii) of encouragement; 3. 2. 52, 196

GOD-A-MERCY, God reward you (an expression of thanks from an inferior); 5. 4. 30

GOD BU'Y YOU, goodbye (a contraction of 'God be with you'); 3. 3. 292

GOOD NOW (interj.), please; 3. 1. 113 (see note)

GOOSE OF WINCHESTER, one affected by a venereal disease known as 'Winchester goose' (with allusion to the Southwark stews formerly under the direction of the Bishop of Winchester); 5. 10. 53

GORGET, piece of armour for the throat; 1. 3. 174

GRACIOUS, righteous, godly; 2. 2. 125

GREAT, full; 'great morning' =broad day; 4. 3. 1

GREEK, 'merry Greek'= wanton; 1. 2. 110

GREEN, (i) (*a*) the colour, (*b*) immature; 1. 2. 153; (ii) (*a*) youthful, (*b*) immature, foolish; 2. 3. 251

GROSSNESS, bulk, size in full; 1. 3. 325

HAIR, (i) 'against the hair' =against the grain; 1. 2. 26–7; (ii) 'to a hair'=to a nicety; 3. 1. 145

HANDSOMENESS, good manners; 2. 1. 15 (see note)

HANG THE LIP, be downcast; 3. 1. 140

HARDIMENT, boldness; 4. 5. 28

HARNESS, armour; 5. 3. 31

HARNESSED, armed; 1. 2. 8

HASTE, urge on, hurry; 4. 3. 5

HATCHED, engraved; 1. 3. 65 (see note)

HAVE, (i) 'have with you' (a stock reply)=coming, I am ready; 5. 2. 185; (ii) 'have at you' (a stock warning of intended attack); 5. 4. 22; 5. 6. 11, 13

Having, possessions, endowments; 3. 3. 97

Hazard, 'on hazard'=at stake; Prol. 22

Heap, great company; on heaps'=in a mass; 3. 2. 28

Heavy, sad; 4. 5. 95

Hedge; (i) 'hedge out'=exclude, fob off; 3. 1. 61 (see note); (ii) 'hedge aside'=shrink away; 3. 3. 158 (see note)

Heel, dance (cf. Lavolt); 4. 4. 86

Heigh-ho, exclam. of dejection, etc.; 3. 1. 127

Height, 'to the height'=to the utmost; 5. 1. 3

Helm, helmet; 1. 2. 234; 4. 5. 255; 5. 2. 94, 169; 5. 4. 4

Hem, interjection to attract attention; 1. 2. 229

His, (i) its (see Abbott, § 228); 1. 3. 75, 207, 210, 241; 2. 2. 54; 3. 3. 123; 5. 2. 175; (ii) 's (see Abbott, § 217); 2. 1. 52; 4. 5. 177, 255; 5. 2. 164

Hold-door, pandering (cf. Per. G. 'door-keeper', 'hatch'); 5. 10. 50

Honest, decent; 5. 1. 50

Honesty, reputation for chastity; 1. 2. 263 (see note)

Horn, cuckold's horn; 1. 1. 114; 4. 5. 31, 46; 5. 7. 12

Hostess, landlady of an inn; 3. 3. 252

Hot, (i) violent; 2. 2. 6; (ii) excited, passionate; 2. 2. 116, 169; 2. 3. 171; 3. 1. 130, 131, 132, 133; 5. 3. 16; (iii) eager, keen; 4. 5. 186

How, at what price; 4. 2. 23

How now, exclam. of expostulation, surprise, welcome; 1. 1. 71, etc.

Hoy-day, exclam. of surprise; 5. 1. 64

Hulk, large ship of burden; 2. 3. 263

Humanity, human nature; 2. 2. 175

Humorous, pertaining to the 'humours' (q.v.); 2. 3. 128

Humour, the relative proportions of the four chief fluids of the body, which (acc. to mediev. and Eliz. physiology) determined temperament; 1. 2. 22; 2. 3. 210

Hurricano, waterspout; 5. 2. 172

Husbandry, a husbandman's care of business; 1. 2. 7

Hyperion, the god of the sun, the sun; 2. 3. 195

Idle, trifling; 5. 1. 30

Ignomy, ignominy; 5. 10. 33

Ilion, Ilium, Priam's palace; 1. 1. 103 (see note), etc.

Ill-disposed, indisposed; 2. 3. 76

Image, mental picture, idea; 2. 2. 60

Imbecility, weakness; 1. 3. 114

Immaterial, insubstantial, flimsy; 5. 1. 30

Imminence, that which is imminent, impending peril; 5. 10. 13

Immure, enclosing wall; Prol. 8

Impair, inferior; 4. 5. 103 (see note)

Imperious, imperial; 4. 5. 172

Import, be of importance to; 4. 2. 50

IMPORTLESS, unimportant; 1.
3. 71

IMPOSITION, task imposed; 3. 2.
78

IMPOSTUME, abscess; 5. 1. 21

IMPRESS, (*a*) conscription, (*b*)
impression made by striking;
2. 1. 97

IMPRESSURE, impression, mark;
4. 5. 131

IMPUDENT, shameless; 3. 3. 217

IMPUTATION, reputation; 1. 3.
339

IN (I'), on; 4. 2. 34; 5. 4. 4

INCH, 'to his inches'=(fig.)
intimately; 4. 5. 111

INCLUDE, embody; 1. 3. 119
(see note)

INDEX, forefinger, pointer,
(hence) prefatory table of
contents, prologue; 1. 3. 343

INDIFFERENT, tolerably; 1. 2.
224

INDISTINGUISHABLE, of inde-
terminate shape, deformed;
5. 1. 28

INDRENCHED, immersed; 1. 1.
53

INFECT (vb.), affect injuriously,
impair; 1. 3. 8

INFECT (ppl.), infected; 1. 3.
187

INFINITE (sb.), infinity; 2. 2.
29

INFLUENCE, 'the supposed
flowing from the stars or
heavens of an etherial fluid
acting upon the character and
destiny of men, and affecting
sublunary things generally'
(O.E.D. 2); 1. 3. 92

INSISTURE, steady continuance;
1. 3. 87 (see note)

INSTANCE, (i) cause; 1. 3. 77;
(ii) proof, evidence; 5. 2

153, 155; (iii) example; 5.
10. 40

INSTANT, now present; 3. 3.
153

INTELLIGENCE, news; 5. 2. 192

INTERCHANGEABLY, reciprocally
('formerly freq. in the
wording of legal compacts',
O.E.D.); 3. 2. 57

IRIS, goddess who, as messenger
of the gods, appeared as a
rainbow, the rainbow; 1. 3.
379

IRON, weapon; 2. 3. 16

ITCH, 'fingers itch'=have a
burning desire (*sc.* to strike);
2. 1. 25

JADE, ill-tempered horse; (as
a term of abuse) 2. 1. 19

JAR, discord; 1. 3. 117

JERKIN, short coat, usually
sleeved, leather jerkins being
reversible (see Linthicum,
pp. 202-3, 240); 3. 3. 264

JUDGEMENT, person of judgement; 1. 2. 192

JUSTNESS, justice, rightfulness;
2. 2. 119

KEEP, (i) keep in, remain in;
1. 3. 190; 2. 3 256; 5. 1.
10; (ii) stay, dwell; 4. 5
278

KEN, recognize; 4. 5. 14

KIN, akin; 1. 3. 25; 3. 3. 175

KIND, manner; 2. 3. 127

KINGDOMED, (*a*) having a
kingdom, (*b*) as a kingdom
in himself; 2. 3. 173

KISS, (of bowls) touch one
another (cf. MISTRESS); 3.
2. 49

KNOT, hard mass (of muscle),
muscle; 5. 3. 33

KNOW, (a) be acquainted with, (b) have sexual intercourse with; 1. 2. 64

LA, exclamation to emphasize a statement; 3. 1. 75; 5. 2. 60

LARDED, interlarded, enriched; 5. 1. 56

LARGE, 'at large'=full sized; 1. 3. 346

LAVOLT, lavolta, 'a lively dance for two persons, consisting a good deal in high and active bounds' (Nares, cited O.E.D.); 4. 4. 86

LEAVE, neglect, omit; 3. 3. 133; 5. 1. 93

LETHARGY, 'a drowsy and forgetful sickness rising of impostumation of cold phlegm putrified, especially in the hinder part of the brain, whereby memory and reason almost utterly perish' (Cooper); 5. 1. 19

LID, eyelid; 'by God's lid', a petty oath; 1. 2. 211

LIEF, dear; 'had as lief'=would as soon; 1. 2. 105

LIFTER, (a) usu. sense, (b) thief; 1. 2. 118 (see note)

LIGHT (adv.), swiftly (O.E.D. 10); 1. 2. 8

LIKE (vb. impers.), please; 5. 2. 103

LIMEKILN, (fig.) burning; 5. 1. 21

LINE, rule, 'principle' (Schmidt); 1. 3. 88

LINGER ON, prolong; 5. 10. 9

LISTS, space enclosed by palisades for tilting, etc.; 4. 5. S.D., 93 S.D.

LIVE, remain; 'live to come' =are to come; 3. 3. 16

LIVER, the supposed seat of the passions, here of courage; 2. 2. 50

'LOO, a cry to incite a dog to the chase; 5. 7. 10, 11

LOOK UPON, be an onlooker; 5. 6. 10

LOOSE, casual, 3. 3. 41; 4. 4. 46

LOVER, well-wisher, friend; 3. 3. 214

LUBBER, (pred.) loutish; 3. 3. 139

LUNES, mad freaks; 2. 3. 129 (see note)

LUST, pleasure; 'to my lust' =with pleasure; 4. 4. 132 (see note)

LUSTIHOOD, bodily vigour; 2. 2. 50

LUXURIOUS, lecherous; 5. 4. 8

LUXURY, lechery; 5. 2. 56

MACULATION, stain of impurity; 4. 4. 64

MAGNANIMOUS, noble, valiant; 2. 2. 200; 3. 3. 275

MAIDEN (adj.), innocent, bloodless; 4. 5. 87

MAIDEN (sb.), a man who has abstained from sexual intercourse; 3. 2. 209

MAIL, piece of mail-armour; 3. 3. 152

MAIN (adj.), general; 1. 3. 372

MAIN (sb.), full might; 2. 3. 259

MAINLY, strongly, very much; 4. 4. 85

MAKE, have to do with (a person or thing); 1. 1. 14, 85

MANAGE, management; 3. 3. 25

MAPPERY (nonce word, contemptuous), map-making; 1. 3. 205

MARK, target; 5. 6. 27

MARRY (a light asseveration, orig. the name of the Virgin Mary), indeed, to be sure; 2. 1. 120; 3. 1. 64

MASS, solid bulk; 1. 3. 29

MASTIC, gummy; 1. 3. 73 (see note)

MATCH, bargain; 4. 5. 37, 270

MATTER, (a) pus, (b) substance, sense; 2. 1. 8

MAY, 'you may'=go on; 3. 1. 109

MEALY, resembling meal, powdery, fragile; 3. 3. 79

MEAT, solid food; 1. 2. 243

MENDS, remedy; 1. 1. 70

MERCURY, Roman god identified with Hermes, the messenger of the gods, whose sandals were fitted with wings and whose staff of office was wreathed with serpents; 2. 2. 45; 2. 3. 11

MERE, absolute; 1. 3. 111, 287

MILO (or MILON), a famous athlete of Crotona of the 6th cent. B.C., said to have carried a bull on his shoulders; 2. 3. 244

MINCED, (a) subdivided minutely, (b) with allusion to 'minced-pie'; 1. 2. 257 (see note)

MINISTER, agent; Prol. 4

MIRABLE, marvellous; 4. 5. 142

MISPRIZE, scorn; 4. 5. 74

MISSION, sending of help (On.); 3. 3. 189

MISTRESS, (a) usu. sense, (b) small bowl, the jack; 3. 2. 49

MODEST, moderate, befitting; 2. 2. 15

MODESTLY, without exaggeration; 4. 5. 222

MOIETY, portion; 2. 2. 107

MONSTRUOSITY (old form of 'monstrosity'), marvel; 3. 2. 80

MONUMENTAL, like a monument; 3. 3. 153

MOTIVE, moving limb or organ; 4. 5. 57

MOUTH, 'spend his mouth', see SPEND; 5. 1. 88–9

MOVE, (i) exhort; 3. 3. 216; (ii) anger; 4. 4. 129

MUCH (adv.), very; 2. 3. 106

MULTIPOTENT, very powerful; 4. 5. 129

MURRAIN, plague; 'a murrain of' (or 'on'), an imprecation; 2. 1. 19

MUTINY, strife, contention; 1. 3. 96

MYRMIDON; 'the great Myrmidon'=Achilles (see next entry); 1. 3. 377

MYRMIDONS, warriors from Thessaly brought to Troy by Achilles; 5. 5. 33, etc.

NATURE, human nature; 2. 2. 173, 185; 3. 3. 175

NEAPOLITAN, 'Neapolitan bone-ache'=syphilis (supposedly originating in Naples); 2. 3. 18

NEED (vb.); 'what need'=what need is there for; 5. 1. 12 (see note)

NEGLECTION, neglect; 1. 3. 127

NEGOTIATION, business affair; 3. 3. 24

NEPTUNE, god of the sea, the sea; 1. 3. 45; 5. 2. 174

NERVE, sinew, tendon; (fig.) 1. 3. 55

Nice, precise; 4. 5. 250

Nightly, at night; 4. 4. 73

Niobe, in Gk. myth. woman turned into a stone column while weeping for her children; her tears continued to flow from the column; 5. 10. 19

Nod, (a) sign of recognition, (b) (etymol. a diff. word) noddy, fool; 1. 2. 196 (see note)

Noise, report, rumour; 1. 2. 12

Note, (i) (law) 'abstract of essential particulars relating to transfer of land by process of Fine, which was engrossed and placed on record' (O.E.D. sb.², 12), (b) observation; 2. 3. 124; (ii) notice, knowledge; 4. 1. 45

Noted, (a) set to music, (b) notorious; 5. 2. 12

Numbers, metre, poetry; 3. 2. 182

Object, spectacle, sight; 2. 2. 41; 3. 3. 180; 4. 5. 106

Obligation, bond, tie; 4. 5. 122

Observance (of), reverence (for); 1. 3. 31; 2. 3. 163

Observant, attentive; 1. 3. 203

Observing, attentive, deferential; 2. 3. 127

Odd, (i) (a) strange, (b) single, without a partner; 4. 5. 41, 42, 44; (ii) at variance; 4. 5. 265

Oddly, unequally, incongruously; 1. 3. 339

Odds, superiority (in numbers); 5. 4. 21

O'ergalléd, fretted away, worn out; 5. 3. 55

O'ereaten, eaten prodigally 5. 2. 160 (see note)

O'erwrested (cf. Wrest), strained, exaggerated; 1. 3. 157

Old, (a) in years, (b) in experience; 1. 2. 118

Olympian, Olympic; 4. 5. 194

Open, (a) frank, (b) accessible to all; 5. 2. 25

Opinion, (i) public opinion; 1. 3. 142, 186; (ii) reputation; 1. 3. 336, 353, 372; 3. 3. 263; 4. 4. 103; 5. 4. 16

Opposed, facing one another; 3. 3. 107; 4. 5. 94

Oppress, overwhelm; 4. 5. 241

Oppugnancy, conflict; 1. 3. 111

Orchard, garden (not necess. with fruit trees); 3. 2. S.D., 16

Order, (i) plan, arrangement; 1. 3. 181; (ii) mode of procedure, regulation; 4. 5. 70, 90

Orgulous, proud; Prol. 2

Orifex. The common but erroneous form of 'orifice'; 5. 2. 151

Orts (usu. in pl.), scraps of food left over; 5. 2. 158

Out, (a) not in, (b) expired; 1. 2. 258

Out, interjection expressing abhorrence; 5. 1. 34

Overbulk, surpass in size, overgrow; 1. 3. 320

Overhold, over-estimate; 2. 3. 132

Overshine, outshine, surpass; 3. 1. 159

Owe, own; 3. 3. 99

Oyez, the public cryer's call (Fr. oyez=hear) to command

silence and attention; 4. 5.
143 (see note)

PAGEANT (sb.), theatrical show,
spectacle; 3. 2. 74; 3. 3. 271

PAGEANT (vb.), mimic; 1. 3.
151

PAINTED, 'painted cloth', see
CLOTH; 5. 10. 45

PALATE, perceive (by taste);
4. 1. 61

PALE, paling, fence; 2. 3. 246

PALSY (adj.), palsied, shaky;
1. 3. 174

PALSY (sb.), paralysis; 'cold
palsies'=paralysis induced
by cold phlegm (see LETH-
ARGY); 5. 1. 19

PALTER, play fast and loose;
2. 3. 230; 5. 2. 49

PARADOX, 'make paradoxes'
=turn into absurdities; 1. 3.
184

PARD, leopard, panther; 3. 2.
193

PART (sb.), (i) portion, share;
1. 3. 352; (ii) inherent gifts,
talents; 2. 3. 239; 3. 3. 117;
4. 4. 79; (iii) parts of the
body; 2. 3. 247; (iv) party,
side; 4. 5. 156; 5. 8. 15

PARTED, gifted, talented; 3. 3.
96

PARTIAL, personal; 2. 2. 178
(see note)

PARTICULAR (adj.), individual,
personal; 1. 2. 20; 1. 3. 341;
2. 2. 53; 4. 5. 20

PARTICULAR (sb.), (i) item; 1.
2. 115; (ii) personal concern; 2. 2. 9

PASH, bash, batter; 2. 3. 201;
5. 5. 10

PASS, (i) 'it passed'=passed
description, beat everything;

1. 2. 168; (ii) experience,
undergo; 2. 2. 139

PASSAGE, course, progress; 2.
3. 130

PAST-PROPORTION, immensity;
2. 2. 29

PATCHERY, trickery, roguery;
2. 3. 70

PAVEMENT, paved thorough-
fare (for all traffic); 3. 3.
162

PAVILION, tent (usu. of a
stately kind); Prol. 15

PECULIAR, belonging to one-
self, individual; 2. 3. 164

PEEVISH, senseless; 5. 3. 16

PELTING, paltry; 4. 5. 267

PER SE, by himself, unique;
1. 2. 15

PERFECTION, performance,
achievement; 3. 2. 85, 91

PERSISTIVE, steadfast; 1. 3. 21

PERSON, personal appearance;
1. 2. 193; 4. 4. 79

PERSUADE, plead, expostulate;
5. 3. 30

PERTLY, boldly; 4. 5. 219

PETTISH, petulant, ill-
humoured; 2. 3. 129

PHOEBUS, the sun god, the sun;
1. 3. 230

PHRYGIAN, of Phrygia (the part
of Asia Minor in which
Troy was situated), Trojan;
4. 5. 186, 223; 5. 10. 24

PHYSIC, dose with medicine,
(esp.) purge; 1. 3. 377

PIA MATER, (transf.) brain;
2. 1. 70

PIECE, (a) cask of wine or
brandy, (b) contemptuous
term for a woman; 4. 1.
64

PIECE OUT, mend; 3. 1. 52

PIGHT, pitched; 5. 10. 24

PIN, type of something trifling; 5. 2. 23

PLACKET, (fig. contemptuously) woman; 2. 3. 20

PLANTAGE, plants; 3. 2. 176 (see note)

PLEASANT, merry, playful; 3. 1. 63

PLEASURE, (i) (*a*) wish, command, (*b*) enjoyment; 3. 1. 24; (ii) 'you speak your fair pleasure'=you are too kind (Schmidt); 3. 1. 49

PLIGHT, pledge; 3. 2. 160

PLUTO, god of Hades; 3. 3. 197 (see note); 4. 4. 127; 5. 2 103

POINT, summit; 'at ample point'=to the full; 3. 3. 89

POISE (sb.), weight; 1. 3. 207

POISE (vb.), weigh, balance; 1. 3. 339

POLICY, (i) conduct of affairs; 1. 3. 197; (ii) cunning, strategy; 4. 1. 20; 5. 4. 9, 12; (iii) established system of government; 5. 4. 16

PORPENTINE, porcupine; 2. 1. 25

PORRIDGE, soup, broth; 1. 2. 243

PORT, gate (usu. of a walled town); 4. 4. 111, 136

PORTLY, imposing (O.E.D. 1); 4. 5. 162

POSITION, general proposition (O.E.D. 1); 3. 3. 112

POSITIVE, absolute; 2. 3. 64

POSSESS, inform; 4. 4. 112

POSSESSED, controlled by a demon or spirit, crazy; 2. 3. 168

POST, travel with the utmost speed; 1. 3. 93

POTATO-FINGER, finger exciting lust (the Spanish or sweet potato being reputed an aphrodisiac); 5. 2. 57

POWER, armed force; 1. 3. 139; 2. 3. 259

PREGNANT, apt; 4. 4. 88

PRENOMINATE, name beforehand; 4. 5. 250

PREPOSTEROUS, unnatural; 5. 1. 23

PRESENCE, demeanour; 3. 3. 269

PRESENTLY, immediately; 2. 3. 138; 4. 3. 6

PRETTY, ingenious; 1. 2. 156

PREVENTION, precaution; 1. 3. 181

PRICK, mere point, particle; 1. 3. 343

PRIMITIVE, earliest, original; 5. 1. 53

PRIMOGENITIVE, right of primogeniture; 1. 3. 106 (see note)

PRIZE, (*a*) thing of value, (*b*) booty; 2. 2. 86

PROCESS, course, tenor; 4. 1. 9

PROFESS, make a business of; 3. 3. 268

PROMPT, ready, disposed; 4. 4. 88

PROMPTED, eager; 5. 2. 175

PROOF, (i) test, trial; 1. 2. 130; 1. 3. 34; (ii) fulfilment; 5. 5. 5, 29

PROPEND, incline; 2. 2. 190

PROPENSION, inclination; 2. 2. 133

PROPER, (i) handsome; 1. 2. 193; (ii) one's own; 2. 2. 89

PROPORTION, (i) due relationship; 1. 3. 87; (ii) see also PAST-PROPORTION; 2. 2. 29

PROPOSE, set before one's mind, expect, look for; 2. 2. 146

PROPOSED, intended; 3. 2. 13

PROPOSITION, project; 1. 3. 3

PROPUGNATION, defence; 2. 2. 136

PROTEST, protestation (O.E.D. 1); 3. 2. 174

PROTRACTIVE, protracted; 1. 3. 20

PROVIDE, prepare, make ready; 3. 2. 210

PUBLICATION, announcement; 1. 3. 326

PUBLISH, proclaim; 5. 2. 113, 119

PUN, early var. of 'pound'; 2. 1. 38

PURPOSE, import intent; 1. 3. 264

PURSUE, (i) follow with hostility, continue the fight; 4. 5. 69; (ii) follow as a suppliant, entreat; 5. 3. 10

PURSUIT, endeavour; 2. 2. 142; 4. 1. 20

PUSH, attack, onset; 2. 2. 137

PUT BACK, thrust back; 4. 4. 34

PUTTOCK, bird of prey akin to the kite; 5. 1. 60

QUAIL, (transf.) loose woman; 5. 1. 51

QUALIFY, moderate; 2. 2. 118; 4. 4. 9

QUALITY, (i) nature, cause; 4. 1. 46; (ii) natural gifts; 4. 4. 76

QUESTION, conversation; 4. 1. 13

QUOTE, (orig. to mark a book with numbers, as of chapters, etc.) mark, scrutinize; 4. 5. 233

RANK (adj.), (i) gross, foul; 1. 3. 73; (ii) luxuriant in growth; (fig.) 1. 3. 318; (iii) intemperate; 4. 5. 132

RANK (adv.), excessively; 1. 3. 196

RANSACK, carry off as plunder; Prol. 8; 2. 2. 150

RAPE, seizure by force; 2. 2. 148

RAPTURE, transport, delirium; 2. 2. 122; 3. 2. 129

RASH, urgent; 4. 2. 60

RATE, chide, exclaim against; 2. 2. 89

REACH, scope; 4. 4. 108

RECORDATION, reminder; 5. 2. 116

RECOURSE, repeated flowing; 5. 3. 55

RECREANT, villain; 1. 3. 287

RED, applied to various diseases marked by evacuation of blood or cutaneous eruptions; 2. 1. 19 (see note)

REDEEM, (a) (law) free (mortgaged property), recover (a pledge), (b) liberate; 5. 5. 39

REFUSE, renounce; 4. 5. 267

REGARD, (i) glance, look; 3. 3. 41, 254; (ii) estimation; 3. 3. 128

REIN, 'in such a rein'=(fig.) in the same way; 1. 3. 189

REJOINDURE, reunion; 4. 4. 36

RELATION, report; 3. 3. 201

REPINING, grudging; 1. 3. 243

REPROOF, refutation; 1. 3. 33

REPURÉD, 'thrice repuréd'= purified thrice over; 3. 2. 22

RESPECT, reflection; 2. 2. 49

RESTY, restive; 1. 3. 263

RETIRE (sb.), retreat; 5. 3. 53; 5. 4. 19; 5. 8. 15

RETIRE (vb.), return; 1. 3. 281

Retort, throw back, reflect;
3. 3. 101

Retreat, signal (usu. by
drums) for cessation of
hostilities; 1. 2. 177 S.D.
etc.

Reversion, (a) (*law*) 'the return of an estate to the
donor or grantor, or his
heirs, after the expiry of the
grant' (O.E.D. 1), (b) expectation; 3. 2. 91

Rheum, mucous discharge;
5. 3. 104 (cf. note to 5. 1.
17–18)

Rivelled, wrinkled; 5. 1. 22

Roisting, roistering, up-
roarious; 2. 2. 208

Rounded in, encompassed; 1.
3. 196

Roundly, straightforwardly;
3. 2. 153

Rub, (i) 'rub the vein of him'
=encourage his humour; 2.
3. 198; (ii) 'rub on', a cry
encouraging a bowl on its
course past a 'rub' (=ob-
stacle); (fig.) 3. 2. 49

Rude, (i) harsh, discordant;
1. 1. 91; (ii) brutal; 1. 3.
115; (iii) unskilled, in-
experienced; 3. 1. 57; 3. 2.
25

Rudely, roughly; 4. 4. 35

Rudeness, violence; 1. 3. 207

Rule, (i) (a) carpenter's rule,
(b) line of conduct; 5. 2. 133;
(ii) law, principle; 5. 2. 141

Run, (a) exude pus, (b) run
away; 2. 1. 5, 6

Ruthful, lamentable; 5. 3.
48

Sacred, (an epithet of royalty)
revered; 4. 5. 134

Sagittary, centaur; 5. 5. 14
(see note)

Salt, (fig.) stinging, bitter;
1. 3. 370

Sanctimony, (i) sacred thing;
5. 2. 139; (ii) sanctity; 5. 2.
140

Sarsenet, fine, soft silk fabric,
originally made by the
Saracens (see Linthicum,
pp. 121–2), here contemp-
tuously used for slightness;
5. 1. 30

Saucy, presumptuous; 1. 3. 42

Savage, uncivil (Schmidt); 2.
3. 125

Scab, (a) usu. sense, (b)
(transf.) scurvy fellow; 2. 1.
28

Scaffoldage, platform, stage;
1. 3. 156

Scalèd, with fish scales; 5. 5.
22 (see note)

Scant, stint; 4. 4. 47

Scantling, sample; 1. 3. 341

Scape, escape; 1. 3. 371

Scar, cut, incision (O.E.D.
sb.³); 1. 1. 113

School, university; 1. 3. 104

Screech-owl, barn owl, supposed a bird of ill omen;
5. 10. 16

Scruple, (i) hesitation, objection; 4. 1. 58; (ii) (of diff.
etymol.) the third part of
a drachm; 4. 1. 72

Scull, old form of 'school' (of
fish); 5. 5. 22

Scurril, scurrilous; 1. 3. 148

Seam, fat; 2. 3. 183

Seat, seat of office, throne,
(fig.) position of authority;
1. 3. 31

Second; 'in second voice'
=by proxy; 2. 3. 139

SECURE, over-confident; 2. 2. 15

SECURELY, over-confidently; 4. 5. 73

SEE, meet one another; 4. 4. 57

SEEDED, run to seed; 1. 3. 316

SEETHE, boil; (fig.) 3. 1. 41

SEIZURE, grasp; 1. 1. 59

SELD, seldom; 4. 5. 150

SELF-ADMISSION, self-approbation; 2. 3. 164

SELF-AFFECTED, self-loving, vain; 2. 3. 236

SELF-ASSUMPTION, presumption; 2. 3. 123

SENNET, trumpet or cornet fanfare for ceremonial entries and exits; 1. 3. S.D.

SENSE, (i) physical feeling; 2. 1. 21; (ii) emotional feeling; 4. 4. 4; (iii) mental perception; 4. 5. 54 (see note)

SEQUESTER, separate; 3. 3. 8

SERPIGO, creeping skin disease, esp. ringworm; 2. 3. 73

SET, (i) stake; Prol. 22; (ii) 'set...to'=pit...against; 2. 1. 85

SEVERAL (adj.), separate, individual; 2. 2. 124, 193

SEVERAL (sb.), individual quality; 1. 3. 180

SEVERALLY, separately; 4. 5. 274; 5. 3. 94 S.D.

'SFOOT (an oath), God's foot; 2. 3. 5

SHAME, (i) disgrace; 1. 3. 19; (ii) shyness, modesty (O.E.D. 1); 3. 2. 41

SHARE, (i) cut off, cleave; 1. 3. 366; (ii) participate in (quibbling on (i)); 1. 3. 367

SHARP, fierce; 5. 9. 10

SHE (sb.), woman; 1. 2. 289, 291

SHED, disperse, scatter; 1. 3. 319

SHIVER, fragment; 2. 1. 38

SHOEING-HORN, (fig.) (a) person used as a tool, (b) cuckold; 5. 1. 54

SHOULD, (i) could; 1. 2. 31; (ii) would; 1. 2. 102; 1. 3. 112, 114, 116, 118; 2. 2. 48

SHREWDLY, severely, grievously; 3. 3. 228

SHRILL FORTH, utter shrilly; 5. 3. 84

SIEVE, basket, receptacle for fragments; 2. 2. 71 (see note)

SINEW, (fig.) strength; 1. 3. 136, 143

SINISTER, (heraldic term) left; 4. 5. 128

SIRRAH, term of address to inferiors, esp. servants; 3. 2. 6

SITH, since; 1. 3. 13; 5. 2. 120

SKILLESS, ignorant; 1. 1. 12

SKITTISH, (i) lively; Prol. 20; (ii) fickle; 3. 3. 134

SLACK, slacken; 3. 3. 24

SLEAVE-SILK, filament of silk obtained by separating ('sleaving') a thicker thread, floss silk; 5. 1. 30

SLEEVELESS, (a) without the sleeve, (b) (fig.) useless; 5. 4. 8

SLIDE, skate; 3. 3. 215

SLIGHTLY, carelessly; 3. 3. 166

SLIP, escape (with quibble on 'slip'=counterfeit coin); 2. 3. 25

SLUTTISH, immoral; 4. 5. 62

SO, SO, exclam. of approval; 5. 5. 44

SODDEN (ppl. of 'seethe'), (a) boiled, (b) with allusion to 'stew'=hot bath (cf. SWEAT, STEWED); 3. 1. 42

SODDEN-WITTED, stupid; 2. 1. 42

SOFT (exclam.), stay, stop; 5. 3. 89; 5. 4. 16

SOILURE, dishonour; 4. 1. 58

SOL, the sun; 1. 3. 89

SOLE, solely; 1. 3. 244

SOMETIME, sometimes; 1.3.151

SOOTH, truth; 'good sooth', 'in good sooth' (asseverations)=indeed; 2. 1. 108; 3. 1. 57

SOP, piece of bread, or the like, dipped or steeped in liquid; 1. 3. 113

SORT (sb.), (i) lot; 1. 3. 375; (ii) manner, way; 4. 1. 25; 5. 4. 34; 5. 10. 5

SORT (vb.), suit, fit; 1. 1. 108

SOUND, utter; 4. 2. 109

SPECIALTY, (law) 'a special contract, obligation, or bond, expressed in an instrument under seal' (O.E.D. 7); (fig.) 1. 3. 78

SPECULATION, sight, vision (O.E.D. 1); 3. 3. 109

SPEED, succeed, prosper (O.E.D. 1); 3. 1. 143

SPEND, utter; 'spend his mouth' (said of hunting dogs on finding or seeing the game, O.E.D. 9b)=give tongue; 5. 1. 88

SPERR, fasten with a bar or bolt, secure; Prol. 19

SPHERÉD, rounded; 4. 5. 8

SPLEEN, considered as the seat of the emotions; (i) laughter; 1. 3. 178; (ii) courage; 2. 2. 128; (iii) anger; 2. 2. 196

SPOTTED, polluted; 5. 3. 18

SPRIGHTLY, high-spirited; 2. 2. 190

SQUARE, take the measure of (with allusion to 'square'= instrument for testing right angles), judge; 5. 2. 132

STAIN, tinge; 1. 2. 25

STALE, make common, spoil; 2. 3. 189

START, (i) leap, bound; Prol. 28; (ii) startle; 5. 2. 102

STARTING, bounding; 4. 5. 2

STARVE OUT, endure in perishing cold (O.E.D.); 5. 10. 2 (see note)

STARVED, famished, (fig.) feeble; 1. 1. 95

STATE, (i) council of state; 1. 3. 191; 2. 3. 108, 257; 4. 2. 67; 4. 5. 65, 264; (ii) Government; 3. 3. 196, 202

STAY, wait (for); 3. 2. 3, 10

STEWED, (a) cooked by simmering, (b) with allusion to 'stew'=brothel; 3. 1. 42

STICK, stab; 3. 2. 194

STICKLER-LIKE, like an umpire; 5. 8. 18

STILL (adv.), constantly, always; 3. 3. 22, etc.

STINT, stop, check; 4. 5. 93

STITHY, forge; 4. 5. 255

STOMACH, appetite, inclination; 2. 1. 124; 3. 3. 220; 4. 5. 264

STOOL, privy; 2. 1. 41

STRAIGHT (adv.), immediately; 1. 3. 389; 3. 2. 17, 31; 3. 3. 305; 4. 4. 144

STRAIN (sb.), (i) 'make no strain but that'=take it for granted that; 1. 3. 326; (ii) (of diff. etymol.) disposition; 2. 2. 154

STRAIN AT, find difficulty in, boggle at (cf. Matth. xxiii. 24); 3. 3. 112

STRAINED, purified as by filtering; 4. 4. 24; 4. 5. 169

STRANGE, (i) aloof; 2. 3. 236; (ii) new, alien; 3. 2. 9; 3. 3. 12

STRANGELY, aloofly; 3. 3. 39, 71

STRANGENESS, aloofness; 2. 3. 125; 3. 3. 45, 51

STRAWY, like straw; 5. 5. 24

STRIKE, (i) 'strike off'=cancel; 2. 2. 7; 3. 3. 29; (ii) beat a drum, etc.; 5. 10. 30

STUBBORN, (i) stiff; 3. 1. 151; (ii) ruthless, harsh; 5. 2. 131

STYGIAN, of Styx (the river of Hades across which the dead were ferried by Charon); 5. 4. 18

SUBDUEMENT, conquest; 4. 5. 187

SUBSCRIBE, (i) assent to; 2. 3. 146; (ii) yield; 4. 5. 105

SUBTLE, difficult, intricate; 4. 4. 87; (ii) fine, delicate; 5. 2. 151

SUCCESS, upshot, result; 1. 3. 340; 2. 2. 117

SUCH ANOTHER, (contemptuously) like any other; 1. 2. 259 (see note), 272

SUDDENLY, at once; 4. 4. 33

SUFFER, allow, permit; 4. 2. 30

SUFFERANCE, endurance, submission; 1. 1. 30; 2. 1. 95

SUFFOCATE, suffocated; 1. 3. 125

SUPERFICIALLY, (a) by sight, (b) slightly; 3. 1. 10

SUPPOSE, expectation; 1. 3. 11

SURETY, (i) security, guarantee; 1. 3. 220; 5. 2. 61; (ii) sense of security; 2. 2. 14, 15

SURLY, arrogantly; 2. 3. 235

SWAGGER, bluster, rant; 5. 2. 136

SWEAT, take the sweating treatment for venereal disease; 5. 10. 54

SYMPATHISE, agree; 4. 1. 27

TABLE, writing tablet, notebook; 4. 5. 60

TABORIN, 'a kind of drum, less wide and longer than the tabor, and struck with one drumstick only, to accompany the sound of a flute which is played with the other hand' (O.E.D.); 4. 5. 275

TAKE, strike with disease; 5. 1. 23

TAINT (sb.), disgrace; 1. 3. 373

TAINT (vb.), (a) strike, (b) infect; 3. 3. 232

TAME, familiar, acquainted; 3. 3. 10

TAMÉD, broached (like a cask); 4. 1. 64

TARRE ON, incite; 1. 3. 391

TASTE (vb.), (fig.) put to the proof, test; 1. 3. 337; 3. 2. 90

TAX, (i) censure; 1. 3. 197; (ii) order, enjoin; 5. 1. 40

TEMPER, disposition; 1. 3. 57

TEMPERED, composed, disposed; 2. 3. 251; 5. 3. 1

TEMPT, make trial of, risk; 4. 4. 96; 5. 3. 34

TEND, TEND ON, wait upon; 2. 3. 125; 4. 4. 146; 5. 1. 70

TENT, lint used to probe and cleanse a wound; 2. 2. 16; (with a quibble) 5. 1. 10

TERCEL, male of the falcon (q.v.); 3. 2. 52

TETTER, skin eruption; 5. 1. 22

THERE, a cry of encouragement; 5. 5. 43

THETIS, sea-nymph, daughter of Nereus and mother of Achilles, used, by metonymy, for the sea through confusion (even in Latin times) with Tethys, wife of Oceanus; 1. 3. 39

THICK (adv.), fast; 3. 2. 36

THIEVERY, things stolen; 4. 4. 43

THRIFTY, worthy; (iron.) 5. 1. 54

THROUGH, thoroughly; 2. 3. 220

THWART, athwart; 1. 3. 15

TIDE, opportune time; 5. 1. 81

TIME, period of gestation; 1. 3. 313

TIRED, exhausted; 3. 2. 175

TISICK, consumptive cough; 5. 3. 101

TITAN, Hyperion, the sun-god, the sun; 5. 10. 25

TO, a cry of encouragement; 2. 1. 108

TOAST, piece of toast often put into liquor; 1. 3. 45

TOPLESS, supreme; 1. 3. 152

TORTIVE, distorted; 1. 3. 9

TO'T, to the point; 3. 1. 31

TOUCH (sb.), (i) feeling; 2. 2. 115; 4. 2. 97; (ii) trait; 3. 3. 175

TOUCH (vb.), land at; 2. 2. 76

TRADED, skilled, practised; 2. 2. 64

TRAIN, induce; 5. 3. 4

TRANSLATE, interpret, explain; 4. 5. 112

TRANSPORTANCE, conveyance; 3. 2. 11

TRIM, excellent, fine; (iron.) 4. 5. 33

TRUE, (a conventional epithet for a sword) trusty; 1. 3. 238; 5. 3. 56

TRUMPET, trumpeter; 1. 3. 256, 263; 2. 1. 122; 4. 5. 6

TRUNCHEON, staff carried as symbol of office, e.g. by the arbitrator in a fight to give the signal for the beginning or cessation of hostilities; 5. 3. 53

TUCKET, short fanfare on a trumpet; 1. 3. 212 S.D.

TURTLE, turtle dove; 3. 2. 177

TWAIN, parted, estranged; 3. 1. 102

TYPHON, myth. monster with a tremendous voice; 1. 3. 160

UNBODIED, incorporeal; 1. 3. 16

UNBRUISÉD, unwounded; Prol. 14

UNCOMPREHENSIVE, unfathomable; 3. 3. 198

UNDERWRITE, subscribe to, submit to; 2. 3. 127

UNJUST, false; 5. 1. 87

UNKIND, unnatural; 3. 2. 148

UNPLAUSIVE, disapproving; 3. 3. 43

UNRESPECTIVE, undiscriminating; 2. 2. 71

UNSQUARED, rough (fig. from the mason's preparation of building stone); 1. 3. 159

UNTIMBERED, frail (cf. *Oth.* G. 'timbered'); 1. 3. 43

UNTRADED, unfamiliar; 4. 5. 178

UNWHOLESOME, foul, dirty; 2. 3. 119

USE (sb.), practice, habitual exercise; 5. 6. 16

Use (vb.), (i) make a habit of, continue; 2. 1. 46; (ii) perform habitually; 5. 3. 21

Uttermost, utmost; 4. 5. 91

Vail, going down; 5. 8. 7

Vantage, advantage; 5. 8. 9

Vantbrace, defensive armour for the fore-arm; 1. 3. 297

Varlet, (i) attendant on a knight or royal personage; 1. 1. 1; (ii) rogue, rascal; 5. 1. 15, 16, 96; 5. 4. 2

Vassalage, vassals (collectively); 3. 2. 38

Vaunt, beginning; Prol. 27

Vengeance, mischief; 'vengeance on', a common imprecation; 2. 3. 17

Venomed, venòmous, deadly; 5. 3. 47

Venomous, injurious, harmful; 4. 2. 12

Villain, (a) a term of endearment, (b) a bird (esp. a hawk) of a common or inferior species; 3. 2. 33

Vindicative, the usu. form at this time of 'vindictive'; 4. 5. 107

Vinewed, mouldy; 2. 1. 14

Violent, rage; 4. 4. 4

Virtue, (i) bravery; 1. 2. 255; (ii) merit; 1. 3. 30; 3. 3. 100, 169; (iii) accomplishment; 4. 4. 87

Vizard, mask; 1. 3. 83

Voice, (i) judgement, opinion; 1. 3. 187; 4. 5. 70; (ii) acclamation, praise; 1. 3. 381

Voluntary (adv.), voluntarily; 2. 1. 94, 96

Voluntary (sb.), volunteer, free agent; 2. 1. 97

Waftage, conveyance across water; 3. 2. 10

Wanton, arrogant; 4. 5. 220

Wantonness, arrogance, insolence of triumph (O.E.D. 1 e); 3. 3. 137

Ward (sb.), defensive posture (in fencing); 1. 2. 260, 264

Ward (vb.), guard; 1. 2. 268

Ware (adj.), aware; 4. 2. 55

Ware (vb.), beware; 5. 7. 12

Warrant, (i) assure; 2. 1. 86; (ii) justify, defend; 2. 2. 96

Watch (sb.), (i) vigilant guard; 1. 2. 265; (ii) (a) as in (i), (b) devotional exercise; 1. 2. 266

Watch (vb.) (a) keep an eye on, (b) keep awake; 3. 2. 43 (see note)

Watching, guarding; 1. 2. 271

Way; 'come your ways' =come along; 3. 2. 44

Weather, the way the wind is blowing; 'keeps the weather of'=keeps to windward of, has precedence of; 5. 3. 26

Wedgèd, cleft; 1. 1. 37

Weeds, clothing; 3. 3. 239

Wenching, lecherous; 5. 4. 32

What, (i) why; 3. 2. 40; 4. 2. 19; (ii) ellipt.=what with; 5. 3. 103 (see note); (iii) used to hail or summon a person; 5. 6. 5

Whate'er, (ellipt.) whatever it be; 4. 5. 77

Where, (denoting circumstances) when; 4. 4. 33

Whoremasterly, lecherous; 5. 4. 6–7

WHORESON, son of a whore, bastard; 2. 1. 40; 2. 3. 230; 5. 1 27; (fig.) 5. 3. 101

WHOSOEVER, (ellipt.) no matter who it be; 1. 2. 192

WIDE, wide of the mark, mistaken; 3. 1. 88

WILL, arbitrary (personal) choice as opposed to judgement; 1. 3. 120; 2. 2. 53, 58, 62, 63, 65, 66, 179

WIND, (i) sighs; 4. 4. 53 (see note); (ii) speech, words; 5. 3. 110 (see note)

WIT, intelligence; 1. 1. 49, etc.

WITH, 'be with you'=(a) visit you, (b) be even with you (+'to bring'=completely); 1. 2. 279 (see note)

WITTY, wise, prudent; 3 2. 31

WORD, 'good words' = be peaceable; 2. 1. 88 (see note)

WORK, act, deed; 1. 3. 18

WORTH, dignity, excellence; 2. 2. 151

WREST, tuning-key for certain wire-stringed instruments; (fig.) 3. 3. 23